The House of the Lord

Philip M. Hudson

Copyright 2020 by Philip M. Hudson.

Published 2020.

Printed in the United States of America.

All rights reserved.

No portion of this book may be reproduced, stored in a retrieval system, or transmitted in any form or by any means - electronic, mechanical, photocopy, recording, scanning, or other - except for brief quotations in critical reviews or articles, without the prior written permission of the author.

ISBN 978-1-950647-37-8

Illustrations - Google Images.

This book may be ordered from online bookstores.

Publishing Services by BookCrafters
Parker, Colorado.
www.bookcrafters.net

Table of Contents

Acknowledgements..1
Preface..5
Introduction..13

Chapter 1   The curriculum of the temple..21
Chapter 2: Vistas of eternity..53
Chapter 3: A glimpse of heaven..81
Chapter 4: Our journey to the veil..97
Chapter 5: The temple scripts God's plan to save our souls.........117
Chapter 6: The endowment: the libretto of life's three act play...129
Chapter 7: Life's greatest questions..145

Chapter 8: Trailing clouds of glory...165
Chapter 9: And they shall be one in thine hand.............................175
Chapter 10: Temple blessings are for everyone................................195
Chapter 11: Our temple covenants...203

Chapter 12: Shattering the glass ceiling of limiting beliefs..................207
Chapter 13: The connections we make in the temple..................217
Chapter 14: An exchange of rings..................233
Chapter 15: The temple perspective on marriage..................241
Chapter 16: Temple marriage is ordained of God..................247
Chapter 17: In defense of the family..................251
Chapter 18: Sealed together for all eternity..................259
Chapter 19: Worth the wrestle..................267
Chapter 20: Eternal progression in a dynamic universe..................275
Chapter 21: In the temple, we are as one..................287
Chapter 22: The unknown possibilities of existence..................293
Chapter 23: Beyond the power of the adversary..................299

Epilogue..................305
Afterword..................309
About The Author..................315
Also By The Author..................317
What More Can I Say?..................321

Joseph Smith taught that the Saints could not complete the nurturing of their spiritual connection to God until the temple had been completed. The Lord's holy house would provide the place, far from the influences of the world, where the faithful could quietly receive the sacred ordinances and the covenants pertaining to the holy priesthood.

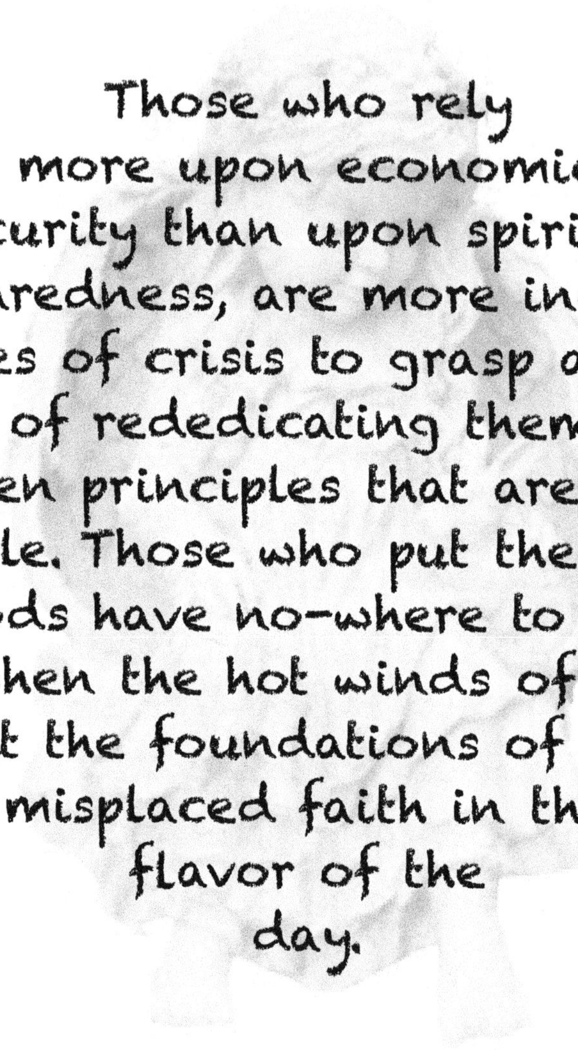

Those who rely
more upon economic
security than upon spiritual
preparedness, are more inclined
in times of crisis to grasp at straws
instead of rededicating themselves to
the proven principles that are taught in
the temple. Those who put their trust in
idea gods have no-where to look for
help when the hot winds of change
melt the foundations of their
misplaced faith in the
flavor of the
day.

Acknowledgements

In this volume, I have attributed quotations to original authors whenever possible, as well as when I have editorialized their ideas. In many cases, however, my language will naturally reflect the teachings of leaders and members of The Church of Jesus Christ of Latter-day Saints.

The list of those who have contributed to this book is endless. As I have organized my own thoughts, I have realized how heavily I have borrowed from the towering examples of those who, over the years, have been my mystical mentors, my sensible chaperones, my spiritual guides, my surrogate saviors, my compassionate critics, and everything in between.

They are my avatars, manifestations of deity in bodily forms, my na'vi, the visionaries, who communicate with God on a level to which I can only aspire,

and my tsaddik, whom I esteem as intuitive interpreters of biblical law and scripture. They are my divine teachers incarnate. They have offered listening ears, extended open arms. lifted my spirits, shown me the way, emboldened me with words of encouragement, cheered me on with wise counsel, stretched my mind, reinforced my faith, strengthened my testimony, vitalized my conversion, helped me to discover my wings, given immaterial support, provided of their means, taught me humility, been there to steady me, soothed my troubled soul, stepped in to nurture me, led me to fountains of living water, wet my parched lips with inspired counsel, and bound up my wounds.

Every family member, teacher, student, classmate, business associate, mentor, friend, priesthood brother, relief society sister, ordinance worker, and temple patron with whom I have come in contact has influenced me. Every author, poet, journalist, essayist, thespian, satirist, and lyricist, has moved me in some positive way. They have taught me to find the silk purse in every sow's ear and the silver lining in every cloud. When I have been given a lemon, they have shown me where to find the recipe for lemonade.

With their positive influence, I have learned to keep tempests in teapots where they belong, and to put them in perspective. I have tried to retain the joyful anticipation of the optimistic little boy, who, when faced with the daunting task of shoveling up an enormous pile of manure in a horse stall near his home, enthusiastically set about his task with the exclamation: "There's got to be a pony in there, somewhere!" Well did the poet teach: "No man is an island, entire of itself. Every man is a piece of the continent, a part of the main. If a clod be washed away by the sea, Europe is the less, as well as if a promontory were, as well as if a manor of thy friends or of thine own were. Any man's death diminishes me, because I am involved in mankind, and therefore never send to know for whom the bell tolls. It tolls for thee." (John Donne).

When I think of the influence of a multitude of angels thinly disguised as my family, friends, and peers, I remember the words of Sir Isaac Newton, who,

when pressed to reveal the great secret behind his accomplishments, simply replied: "I stood on the shoulders of giants." Of course, at the end of the day, I alone am responsible for the contents of this volume. But I hope my interpretation of principles and doctrine will cultivate your interest to dig deeper into the themes woven into this tapestry, by turning to the scriptures and seeking inspiration from the Spirit. My only goal is to help you to expand your insights into the telestial mile markers, the terrestrial truths, and the celestial guidelines that accompany each of us during our quest for enlightenment in the House of the Lord.

Hell is a reformatory
that has been designed to improve
the quality of our moral nature. It is
a penitentiary where faith can still convict us
of our sins. It was designed to help disobedient
spirits recognize that Christ is the Mediator of the
Covenant through His infinite and eternal Atonement.
D&C 76 teaches that the Gospel was taught to the spirits
kept in that prison. If, while there, they exercise their
agency and accept not only Christ, but also the
fullness of His Gospel, is it within the realm
of possibility that they might also inherit
celestial glory with the Saints. Surely,
this is why we build temples and,
without prejudice, perform
vicarious work for all
of our kindred
dead.

Preface

The Plan of Salvation assures us that we will be resurrected and live forever, for immortality is a free gift of God. But we have been asked to do a bit more, if we hope to inherit eternal life. "Organize yourselves," we have been instructed, and "prepare every needful thing. Establish a house, even a house of prayer, a house of fasting, a house of faith, a house of learning, a house of glory, a house of order, a house of God." (D&C 88:119).

We go to the House of the Lord to take a fix on the pole-star of the Atonement and get our bearings on eternity. The Savior promised: "Inasmuch as my people build a house unto me in the name of the Lord, and do not suffer any unclean thing to come into it, that it be not defiled, my glory shall rest upon it. Yea, and my presence shall be there, for I will come into it, and all the pure in heart that shall come into it shall (one day) see God." (D&C 97:15-16). It is in the temple

that telestial tendencies are transformed into celestial sureties in a process of generation. Without the temple, it could be argued that we cannot really be born again.

The power of the endowment and of the sealing ordinances is unlocked by the priesthood. The Lord clearly taught those who invoke the name of God: "Whatsoever thou shalt bind on earth shall be bound in heaven." (Matthew 16:19). For "Zion cannot be built up unless it is by the principles of the law of the celestial kingdom. Otherwise, I cannot receive her unto myself." (D&C 105:5). As we live in obedience to this law, we prepare ourselves to be led by the Lord in covenants of salvation, sanctification, justification, and finally exaltation. "Mine angels shall go up before you," the Lord has promised, "and also my presence." (D&C 103:20).

In vicarious acts that hint at the magnitude of the Atonement itself, Heavenly Father blesses the lives of His children through the sealing ordinances of the temple. In the Spirit World, our departed loved ones are taught the Gospel of Jesus Christ. Those who accept it there will need to have the ordinances performed in their behalf by "saviors (who) shall come up on mount Zion." (Obadiah 1:21). The Saints who perform these ordinances in the temple will "be a light unto the world, and to … the saviors of men." (D&C 103:9).

We help our ancestors by first identifying them, utilizing existing birth, marriage, or death certificates, obituaries, family bibles and histories, diaries, and journals. Relatives may be a treasure trove of information. Church and family records may reveal what ordinances have already been performed by other patrons. We make certain that those who need the ordinances actually have them completed, by performing them personally or by arranging for other temple patrons to do the work.

As we do this, there are tangential benefits, for the temple is a revelatory observatory. "When I have been weighed down by a problem or a difficulty," said Ezra Taft Benson, "I have gone to the House of the Lord with a prayer in my heart

for answers. These answers have come in clear and unmistakable ways." ("Ensign," 8/1985, p. 8). In the temple, we make regular deposits to our spiritual bank accounts, so that in times of need, when withdrawals must be made, there will be adequate reserves.

We can utilize this revelatory relationship capital when we do research aimed at identifying ancestors whose records are more difficult to find. In the temple, we extend our vision. Helen Keller wrote: "There is one tragedy in life worse than to be born without sight, and that is to be born with sight, but without vision." She also asked: "Why cannot the soul go forth from its dwelling place and, discarding the poor lenses of the body, peer thru the telescope of truth in to the infinite reaches of immortality?" Those who do family history research often have these experiences.

In the temple, we draw upon the spiritual reserves of the Master, as did the "woman which had an issue of blood twelve years, And had suffered many things of many physicians, and had spent all that she had, and was nothing bettered, but rather grew worse, When she had heard of Jesus, came in the press behind, and touched his garment. For she said, If I may touch but his clothes, I shall be whole. And straightway the fountain of her blood was dried up; and she felt in her body that she was healed of that plague. And Jesus, immediately knowing in himself that virtue had gone out of him, turned him about in the press, and said, Who touched my clothes?" (Mark 5:25-30).

The spiritually hungry came to the Savior to satisfy their yearnings. He sensed every moment when a need drew upon that source. The story of the woman in the press of the crowd gives us assurance that the Savior is sensitive to our needs, and God does hear our prayers. In conformity to the law of heaven, we can draw upon the life force that is His Spirit. When we do so, we are, in effect, touching the garment of our Redeemer.

We flee from Spiritual Babylon and go to the temple to be sanctified. There, we learn about the process by which we may be cleansed from the effects of sin. This happens when the ordinances drive "the law into (our) inward parts." (Jeremiah

31:33). We become "firmer and firmer in the faith of Christ." (Helaman 3:35). Thus spiritually renewed, we stand prepared to pass through the veil to enter the presence of the Lord. If we will sanctify ourselves, that our minds "become single

to God, the days will come that (we) shall see him (in the temple), for he will unveil his face" unto us. (D&C 88:68).

In order to be saved with our kindred dead, we may contribute family history information to the Ancestral File and involve ourselves in a number of genealogical organizations. For "the season of the world before us will be like no other in the history of mankind," declared Vaughn Featherstone in an address delivered to the Utah South Stake, in April 1987. "Satan has unleashed every evil, every scheme, and every blatant, vile perversion ever known to man in any generation. Just as this is the dispensation of the fullness of times, so it is also the dispensation of the fullness of evil. We and our wives and husbands, our children, and our members, must find safety. There is no safety in the world; wealth cannot provide it, enforcement agencies cannot assure it, and membership in this Church alone cannot bring it.

As the evil night darkens upon this generation, we must come to the temple for light and safety. In our temples we will find quiet, sacred havens where the storm cannot penetrate. There are hosts of unseen sentinels watching over and guarding our temples. Angels attend every door. As it was in the days of Elisha so it will be for us, 'Those that be with us are more than they that be against us.' Before the Savior comes, the world will darken. There will come a period of time where even the elect will lose hope if they do not come to the temples. The world will be so filled with evil that the righteous will only feel secure within these walls. The Saints will come here not only to do vicarious work, but also to find a haven of peace. They will long to bring their children here for safety's sake.

I believe we may well have living on the earth now or very soon the boy who will be the prophet of the Church when the Savior comes. Those who will sit in the

Quorum of Twelve Apostles are here. There are men in our homes and communities who will have apostolic callings. We must keep them clean, sweet, and pure in an oh-so-wicked world. There will be greater hosts of unseen beings in the temple. Prophets of old, as well as those in this dispensation, will visit the temples. Those who attend will feel their strength and feel their companionship. We will not be alone in our temples.

Our garments worn as instructed will clothe us in a manner as protective as temple walls. The covenants and ordinances will fill us with faith as a living fire. In a day of desolating sickness, scorched earth, barren wastes, sickening plagues, disease, destruction, and death, we as a people will rest in the shade of trees, and we will drink from the cooling fountains. We will abide in places of refuge from the storm; we will mount up as on eagles' wings, and we will be lifted out of an insane and evil world. We will be as fair as the sun and clear as the moon.

The Savior will come and will honor His people. Those who are spared and prepared will be a temple-loving people. They will know Him. They will cry out 'blessed be the name of He that cometh in the name of the Lord; thou art my God and I will bless thee; thou art my God and I will exalt thee.' Our children will bow down at His feet and worship Him as the Lord of Lords, and the King of Kings. They will bathe His feet with their tears and He will weep and bless them for having suffered through the greatest trials ever known to man. His bowels will be filled with compassion and His heart will swell wide as eternity, and He will love them. He will bring peace that will last a thousand years, and they will receive their reward to dwell with Him. Let us prepare, then, with the faith to surmount every trial and every condition. We will do it in these holy, sacred temples. Come, come, oh come up to the temples of the Lord and abide in His presence."

I am continually reminded of Nephi's counsel to press forward with complete dedication and steadfastness, or confidence with a firm determination in Christ, having a perfect brightness of hope, or perfect faith, and charity, or a love of God and of all men. If we do this, feasting upon the word of Christ, or receiving

strength and nourishment as we ponder the principles and doctrines of that relate to the House of the Lord, and as we endure to the end in righteousness, we shall have eternal life, which is the greatest of God's gifts. (See 2 Nephi 31:20).

It is with love, then, that I extend to you the invitation to enjoy this volume. Accept it at face value, and use its messages as a springboard to your own personal levels of discovery, as you are taught by the Spirit to move under the influence of the Holy Ghost in the direction of your dreams.

We will
not endure
for long if we
rely only upon the
light that is generated
by our casual connections
to our Heavenly Father. He will
provide an external power source
with ample energy for as long as we
manifest a desire to become members
of the Second Mile Club, which is a
select group to which we have all
been invited in consequence
of our endowment.

It is not
the point of
the endowment
to give us a second
wind in the first mile
of the race, when we have
only just begun our journey.
When we are caught up in the
trauma of temporal traps, because
we have allowed our faith to become
so flawed that we have been blinded to
the impotence of our false gods, sooner
or later, the misery that has been created
will catch up to us. Without the endowment
to give us renewed bursts of energy, those
who feel confusion, abandonment, despair,
or disillusionment, as a result of their
focus on the pleasures of the world,
will perish in Babylon.

Introduction

"The most painful state of being
is remembering the future."
(Soren Kierkegaard).

The Cryonics Society of California is an organization whose creed is: "Death, like old age, can now be regarded as a disease; a very serious disease, to be sure; indeed, generally fatal, but not necessarily incurable." To that end, a service is provided by the organization wherein the body of a deceased person is immersed in liquid nitrogen (at -320o F), and then stored, in anticipation of the day when a cure may be found for the processes that caused the death of the individual. (A less expensive alternative preserves just the head of the person!)

Contrast this desperate philosophy with the teachings of the temple relating to the immortality of the soul. Listen to the fresh perspective of the poet who wrote: "Oh,

this world has more of coming and of going than I can bear. I guess it's eternity I want, where all things are, and always will be. Where I can hold my loves a little looser. Where, finally, we realize Time is the only thing that really dies." (Carol Lynn Pearson, "Optical Illusion").

The temple binds us to eternity, and time becomes the substance of the issue. It seems to be human nature to want to hold on to it dearly, and the prospect of death is terrifying to many, as the body abruptly becomes completely inanimate, and time, at least from our perspective, grinds to a halt.

In the last scene of the last episode of "Star Trek, The Next Generation, Captain Jean Luc Picard mused: ""Someone once said that time is a predator that stalks us all our lives. I prefer to think of it as a companion that accompanies us on the journey, reminding us to cherish every moment."

Those who attend the temple are blessed with a special capacity to manage the gift of time. They have learned to budget their time as carefully as they budget their money. They use their agency to manipulate the mercurial element of time so that they can not only make the most of their gift of mortality, but also insure their happiness and continued progression in eternity, through the grace of God. Thus, they give careful attention to the frugality which they spend their time, and also the diligence with which they make time, the care with which they find time, the joy with which they give time, the wisdom with which they invest time, the pleasure with which they share time, and the discipline they exhibit in taking time. This process allows thoughtful, active temple patrons to create more time for accomplishment of the things that really matter in their already busy lives!

Only foolish people who have lost their focus on the Infinite would treat time so disdainfully that they would flagrantly waste time, steal time, or actually kill time. They recognize that the investment in time they make to attend the temple pays

immediate and lasting dividends. They realize that it is a vain attempt by desperate people to grasp at the slim chance of cheating both time and justice by playing the wild card of suspended animation in a stainless steel tank at -320 degrees F.

Turning our attention to the weightier matters of the law gives us a sense of independence, as we learn something new every day. Learning how to control our time can open our hearts and our minds to the breathtaking expansion of understanding. As we practice a learning style that embraces the Spirit, we will discover a pattern that will become our norm.

Our desire to live for eternity is instilled within us as a fire from within. This may be why Christopher Columbus intuitively recalled the driving force for his voyage of discovery by simply saying: "The Holy Spirit gave me fire for the deed." Our hearts burn within us when God blesses us with an eternal perspective "by His Holy Spirit, yea, by the unspeakable gift of the Holy Ghost." (D&C 121:26 & 28). Thus, did Jeremiah describe his feelings: "His word was in mine heart as a burning fire shut up in my bones, and I was weary with forbearing, and I could not stay." (Jeremiah 20:9). When we are enveloped in the Spirit, the Lord our God is as "a consuming fire." (Deuteronomy 4:24).

Joseph Smith was moved to declare of his revelatory experiences that clarified for all the world the hope of eternal life: "Thus saith the still small voice, which whispereth through and pierceth all things, and often times it maketh my bones to quake while it maketh manifest." (D&C 85:6).

The Spirit quickens us to work out our salvation with fear and trembling before the Lord. (Philippians 2:12). This ability to choose how we utilize our time is sometimes called "free agency." But it is never free. Agency actually carries a very high price. Some use their freedom of choice to build lean-tos, while others use the footings of true and correct principles to build temples dedicated to God and His glory, believing that we are "fellowcitizens with the Saints, and of the household of God." They are built upon the foundation of the apostles and prophets, Jesus Christ

himself being the chief cornerstone: In whom all the building fitly framed together groweth unto an holy temple in the Lord." (Ephesians 2:18-19).

Heavenly Father has blessed us with the temple as a platform of spiritual stability upon which we can become active stargazers. After the Flood, the ancients built ziggurats that were towers specifically designed to reach all the way to heaven. The Tower of Babel is a good example of these exaggerated church steeples. (See Genesis 11:4). But their architects and builders missed the point. Instead of creating physical structures, they would have more profitably spent their time if they had built upon their relationship with God.

Heavenly Father has given us the temple so that we may aim high. Its perspective allows us to discard the poor lenses of the body, with its myopic view of life, to look instead upon the vistas of eternity. "Life is a sheet of paper white where each of us may write a line or two, and then comes night. Greatly begin. If thou hast time but for a line, make that sublime. Not failure, but low aim is crime." (James Russell Lowell).

The following story illustrates the point: "A young man enrolled at Oberlin College. When the president showed him what he would have to study, the student asked: "Isn't there an easier way? Isn't there a shorter course? Can't I receive my degree in less time?" The president answered: "Oh yes. It just depends on what you want to make of yourself. When the Lord starts out to make an oak tree, he takes a hundred years, but if he wants to make a squash, he does it in six months." (LeGrand Richards, 1975 Speeches of The Year, p. 52).

The temple shows us how use our time wisely, and if we are fortunate, we can live to the life of a great oak. (See D&C 101:30, & Isaiah 65:22). But, whatever cards we are dealt in the game of life, we can be certain that, if our allotted time is well-spent, and we find the time to make our way to the temple, "whatever principle of intelligence we (have) attain(ed) unto in this life, it will rise with us in the resurrection." (D&C 130:18).

With our gifts of time, talents, agency, and spiritual gifts, our service in the temple constantly enhances the stature of our eternal selves, even as we struggle with the challenges of mortality. We do not need liquid nitrogen to hedge our bets against the specter of the void of an eternal night. Rather, we have the assurance of our Savior, Who said: "If ye are faithful, ye shall be laden with many sheaves, and crowned with honor, and glory, and immortality, and eternal life." (D&C 75:5).

Many people, not understanding why they have challenges, and feeling acutely uncomfortable in their surroundings, try to avoid the experience altogether by using mind-altering drugs, or engaging in other self-destructive behaviors. Some are so poorly disciplined that they abuse the gift of mortality to the point that life ends prematurely for them. What a tragedy that such weak-willed individuals settled for life in a "second-class hotel." While we are here, the freedom of choice that we have been given permits us to use our time constructively, as we earn our Heavenly Father's trust. He believes in us and knows we can succeed, and has provided us with an endowment of spiritual and temporal power that is enough to accomplish every needful thing.

This life, after all, is the time to prepare to meet God. In the temple, we learn the truth of Hamlet's exultation when he described what a piece of work are His creations! "How noble in reason, how infinite in faculty, in form and moving how express and admirable, in action how like an angel, in apprehension how like a god - the beauty of the world, the paragon of animals!" (Shakespeare, "Hamlet," Act 2, Scene 2).

Just as a chéf might throw a number of ingredients into a "slow cooker" and let them simmer for hours on the stove, some of the chapters in this volume only found shape and substance over time as they were nurtured in the subconscious recesses of my mind. The reduction sauce that provided flavor in other chapters was the product of the distillation of weeks, months, and even years of contemplation. And yet, now and then, a fresh thought would quickly sizzle into

existence as if the idea had been thrown into a cauldron of boiling oil.

At times, a storm did break loose in my mind, but more often than not, my experiences were more like the whispers of a gentle breeze. I do not pretend to have provided much in the way of meaning to even my little corner of the cosmos, but I have enjoyed the mental and spiritual exercise in my attempts to do so.

When, in just 24 days time, George Frideric Handel created the 259 pages of musical score that comprise "The Messiah," the notes came to him so quickly that he could barely keep up, as he furiously scratched out the oratorio on whatever paper was handy. After he had written the "Hallelujah Chorus" in a fervor of divine inspiration, he exclaimed that he had "seen all heaven before him." At the end of the manuscript, in acknowledgement of his own puny efforts, he wrote the letters "SDG" that stood for "Soli Deo Gloria" or "To God alone the glory."

On a much smaller scale, the experiences of the temple provide us with similar experiences with light and knowledge, and in its hallowed halls we are permitted, at times, to catch a glimpse of the flurry of activity that takes place just beyond the parted veil. Revelatory experiences that have been both nurturing and stimulating have, therefore, found their way into the grammar of this volume.

Too often, though, I realize how easily my thoughts and expressions can be "carefully disguised with hypocrisy and glittering words," as Einstein put it. Although I do fancy myself a wordsmith, I have tried to avoid pedestrian expressions, idle language, and lazy scholarship. I do not pretend to be an authority on the doctrine relating to the temple, and if the factual tone within the chapters is sometimes disengaging, the truth is that I typically experienced a deep personal involvement in the expression of the principles that illuminate their themes.

There are those among us who can write out pi (π) to tens of thousands of digits. In 2005, in China, Chao Lu memorized π to 67,890 digits, which was a world record. I cannot come close to that, 3.14 being the extent of my knowledge of this irrational number, but I have been blessed with an imperfect ability to grasp concepts and expand them to proportions that seem to me to be at once both timely and timeless. When you open this volume, I hope you will read it with as much enjoyment as I have experienced while creating it.

We cannot hope to find meaning in our lives if we treat the elements of the temple superficially or carelessly. A conscious appreciation of their value must be earned. If we take them for granted or if we abandon the core principles that are taught in the House of The Lord, their power to bless our lives may slip away and be lost forever.

Temple covenants
are life-generating and
life-sustaining, for just as we
are "born into the world by water,
and blood, and the spirit" and have
become of dust living souls, even so, we
"must be born again into the kingdom of
heaven, of water, and of the Spirit, and
be cleansed by blood," even the blood
of the Son of God, and receive our
endowment in the temple, that we
"might be sanctified from all sin,
and enjoy the words of eternal
life in this world, and eternal
life in the world to come,
even immortal glory."
(Moses 6:59-60).

Chapter One
The curriculum of the temple

The temple is a spiritual school, whose curriculum is sacred, not secret. If it suggests shadowy ritual to the uninitiated, it is because it is presented in a language that cannot be taught in the ivory towers of academia. Much of its liturgy is inarticulate and yet it is at the same time profoundly moving. Temple education promises direct experience with the infinite along the ill-defined terminator line between the temporal and the eternal worlds. Nothing is taught there that would be of interest to those who dance in the spotlight of a telestial stage. It is not an exclusive country club, as Neal A. Maxwell put it, situated on "a narrow ecclesiastical terrace," with membership privileges reserved only for the well connected.

Because the endowment can only be spiritually discerned, its mysteries are unfathomable to unenlightened minds, to those whose lifestyles are defined by carnal, sensual, or devilish preoccupations. Its rituals hide no formula for the unrighteous dominion that is so important to those who are focused on telestial

trivia. It permits no escape from consequences, provides no protection from poor choices, affords no justification for rationalization, and allows no tolerance for those who are mesmerized by mediocre performance. Those who only seek theological titillation cannot trespass on the sacred ground of the temple.

It teaches economic, social, behavioral, political and earth sciences, but it does so in creative ways that are alien to the understanding of Spiritual Babylon. It is where we go, as King Benjamin said, to "open (our) ears, that (we) may hear, and (our) hearts that (we) may understand, and (our) minds that the mysteries of God may be unfolded to (our) view." (Mosiah 2:9).

It is in the temple that we set our sights on the pole-star of the Atonement, and take our bearings on eternity using the sextant of the Savior. He promised: "Inasmuch as my people build a house unto me in the name of the Lord, and do not suffer any unclean thing to come into it, that it be not defiled, my glory shall rest upon it. Yea, and my presence shall be there, for I will come into it, and all the pure in heart that shall come into it shall see God." (D&C 97:15-16). It is in the temple that telestial tendencies are converted into celestial sureties. This process is not one of maturation, but of generation, for one may be "born again" in the delivery room we call The House of The Lord. (See Mosiah 5:7).

Patrons in the temple learn by personal experience that the greatest miracle is not the raising of the physically dead, but the healing of the spiritually sick. A hand picked trauma team with specialty training in advanced spiritual life support techniques attends those who come to the temple. Elder Harold B. Lee said that temple ceremonies have been "designed by a wise Heavenly Father who has revealed them to us in these last days as a guide and a protection throughout our lives, that you and I might not fail to merit exaltation in the celestial kingdom where God and Christ dwell." ("Improvement Era," 6/1967:144). It is within the walls of the temple that our Heavenly Father prepares us to receive eternal life. It is there that our eyes are opened, our vision is perfected, and our sight is lifted above the artificial horizon and limitations of mortality. It is in the temple that we are given a glimpse of eternity, where our future lies.

In the temple, we "receive an education relative to the Lord's purposes and plans in the creation and peopling of the earth, and are taught the things that must be done in order to gain exaltation in the world to come." (Bruce R. McConkie, "Mormon

Doctrine," p. 227). The temple ordinances round out our mortal experience and portray a larger view of life. The rough edges are smoothed out, as we bump and grind our way along the rocky road of experience. The endowment puts our trials and tribulations in perspective, answers the questions that trouble our spirits, but we never thought to ask, and provides us with the tools we need to comprehend the mysteries of the kingdom of God with greater clarity. The temple gathers our experiences in one, that we might establish a sure footing on the bedrock of unchanging principles that are taught without ambiguity.

The endowment that we receive in the temple illustrates our view of eternal life; it consists of receiving all those ordinances "which are necessary for us, after we have departed this life, to enable us to walk back to the presence of the Father, passing the angels who stand as sentinels, being enabled to give them the key words, the signs and tokens, pertaining to the Holy Priesthood, and gain our eternal exaltation in spite of earth and hell." (Brigham Young, J.D., 2:31). Heavenly Father wants all of His children to receive their endowment in the temple, for it consists of the spiritual and priesthood power that is necessary if we ever hope to secure safe passage through the minefields of mortality.

The erection of temples in the Last Days is one of the great evidences of the Restoration and of the divinity of the Lord's work. "Where there are temples, with the spirit of revelation resting upon those who administer therein, there the Lord's people will be found; where these are not, the Church and kingdom and the truth of heaven are not." (Bruce R. McConkie, "Mormon Doctrine," p. 781). When we correctly understand The Plan of Salvation, we see that the ordinances of the temple constitute the keystone that holds the Gospel arch firmly and securely in place.

The power of the endowment is unleashed by the priesthood that facilitates the

unification of the family by administering sealing ordinances in the temple. The endowment teaches us how to exercise priesthood power in righteousness; it instructs us in the temporal and spiritual principles of government that relate to ourselves, our families, and others. As part of that process, we covenant to consecrate our time and talents to the Church and Kingdom, and to lend our efforts to the preparation of the earth for the millennial reign of Jesus Christ.

The Lord clearly taught those who bear the priesthood: "Whatsoever thou shalt bind on earth shall be bound in heaven." (Matthew 16:19). His kingdom on earth "cannot be built up unless it is by the principles of the law of the Celestial Kingdom" that is taught in the temple and administered by the priesthood. Otherwise," said the Lord, "I cannot receive her unto myself." (D&C 105:5). As we live in obedience to these laws, we prepare ourselves through sanctification by the Spirit to be led unerringly by the Lord. We may take Him at His word when He said: "Mine angels shall go up before you, and also my presence." (D&C 103:20). With His companionship, it becomes possible to negotiate the strait and narrow path all the way to the Tree of Life, there to partake of its fruit, which is a representation of eternal life.

The most important thing we can obtain along the way is knowledge that helps us to draw closer to our Heavenly Father. If we were prevented somehow from developing a relationship with Him, the pivotal experiences of mortality, which are found in the covenants of exaltation in the temple, would be neutralized. For "this is life eternal," taught the Savior, "that they might know thee the only true God, and Jesus Christ whom thou hast sent." (John 17:3). Joseph Smith declared: "There are but a very few beings in the world who understand rightly the nature of God" and if we do not understand the character of God we do not comprehend ourselves. ("Teachings," p. 343). It is in the temple that our understanding of God expands to eternal proportion.

This is why the Lord emphasized that we should not seek "for riches, but for wisdom; and, behold, the mysteries of God shall be unfolded unto you, and then shall you be made rich. Behold, he that hath eternal life is rich." (D&C 11:7).

The mysteries of God are those truths that can be known only by revelation from the Holy Ghost. When we hunger and thirst after a comprehension of true principles, and come to the temple anticipating a spiritual feast, the doctrine of the priesthood will naturally distill upon our souls as the dews from heaven, the Holy

Ghost will be our constant companion, and by its power we may discern the truth of all things. (See D&C 121:45-46 & Moroni 10:5).

"Why gather the people of God into a Church?" rhetorically asked the Prophet Joseph Smith. He answered: "The main object was to build unto the Lord a house whereby He could reveal unto His people the ordinances of His house and the glories of His kingdom and teach the people the way of salvation." (H.C., 5:423). In chapels, after all, we organize stakes, wards, priesthood quorums, auxiliary organizations, and so on. In the temple, celestial families are organized under the direction of the priesthood to whom the sealing power has been vested.

If the worldly fail to understand the temple, it is only because the spiritual aether in which they have been enveloped by God is unable to penetrate their unprepared minds. As Paul taught: "The natural man receiveth not the things of the Spirit of God: for they are foolishness unto him: neither can he know them, because they are spiritually discerned." The Saints, on the other hand, "have the mind of Christ." (1 Corinthians 2:14 & 16).

The greater understanding of The Plan of Salvation that is revealed in the House of the Lord blesses our lives in many ways. The opportunity for dynamic change is germinated, as knowledge flows along established channels. At the same time, personal accountability, responsibility, and commitment to obedience increase. The desire to serve strengthens the bonds of brotherhood and sisterhood, and creates an interdependent community of believers that erases the artificial horizon of cultural boundaries.

Because of the temple, as our testimony of Christ swells, faith intensifies our desire to repent. Our efforts to maintain temple worthiness center our lives so that they

remain in harmony with Gospel principles. We find ourselves in a constant state of improvement leading to perfection. We are blessed to keep the law of tithing with exactness. We may be perfect in our obedience to the Word of Wisdom. We may magnify our callings to the best of our abilities. We may be unwavering in our testimony of Christ. We may unflinchingly sustain the General Authorities of the Church. As we make our way to the temple, we find that becoming Christ-like has become the ultimate, incredible journey, empowering us to become what we had heretofore scarcely dreamed was possible. It is the road less traveled, with many doctrinal detours and dead-ends, conceptual cul-de-sacs, and telestial traffic jams that threaten to lead us astray, but the rewards make perseverance and endurance worth the effort.

The way to the temple is the road less traveled but as Robert Frost mused: "I shall be telling this with a sigh somewhere ages and ages hence: Two roads diverged in a wood, and I, I took the one less traveled by, and that has made all the difference." ("The Road Not Taken").

"No form of government, no level of material well-being, will save us," wrote Abba Eban. "We will be redeemed only when towers fall, and Jerusalem triumphs over Babylon. What is at stake, finally, is not only intelligence, but also feeling. We have to change our hearts. Salvation, the prophets tell us, is preconditioned by repentance," which leads the faithful to the ordinances of the temple. "The redeeming act of God," which is consummated for us at holy altars in the House of the Lord, "waits upon our initiative." ("My People: The Story of The Jews," p. 59-60).

The temple endowment affirms the spiritual truth that we are all "children of the most High." (Psalms 82:6). It confirms that we were organized from uncreated intelligence, as spirit children of our Heavenly Father. We were "in the beginning with God." (D&C 93:29). We were "created before the world was made." (D&C 49:17). Emphatically, the Lord declared: "I was in the beginning with the Father, and am the Firstborn. Ye were also in the beginning with the Father." (D&C 93:21 & 23). As His children, we received our "first lessons in the world of spirits and

were prepared (there) to come forth in the due time of the Lord." (D&C 138:56). After mortal life, our spirit "shall return unto God who gave it" in the first place. (Ecclesiastes 12:7).

In the temple, we learn that Adam and Eve were the first of Heavenly Father's children to come to earth, and that they chose to accept Lucifer's invitation to partake of the forbidden fruit that he had plucked from the Tree of Knowledge of Good and Evil. As a result, they were separated from God's presence, suffering spiritual death. They became mortal, meaning that their physical bodies eventually died, as well. Most importantly, their transgression blessed them with the opportunity to experience mortality, during which time they would have the opportunity to make choices between right and wrong, to exercise true moral agency, and thereby to make steady progress by obedience to correct principles. In this environment, they were taught a way whereby they might overcome both spiritual and physical death.

In the temple, the endowment confirms that all who chose Heavenly Father's Plan in the pre-mortal life will burst forth out of the flood-gates that were opened by the transgression of Adam and Eve, to follow their example, and to make the same kinds of choices that had been presented to their first parents. On earth, we are free to exercise our moral agency in ways that can be duplicated nowhere else. The endowment is the highest expression of the principle that we are "free according to the flesh; and all things are given (us) which are expedient unto man. And (we) are free to choose liberty and eternal life, through the great Mediator of all men, or to choose captivity and death, according to the captivity and power of the devil." (2 Nephi 2:27).

To give us unlimited freedom to choose in an atmosphere so full of dangerous deceptions, enticing entrapments, perilous pathways, and soothing seductions entails great risk. The temple is, however, a refuge that is untainted from the blood and sins of this generation, where we may flee from Spiritual Babylon. It is a place where we may shelter our spirits, grasp the horns of sanctuary, quiet our racing

hearts, and ease the tensions that might otherwise overwhelm us, were we to allow ourselves to be caught up in the fast lanes of life. The temple is a time and a place where we can quietly reflect on the quality of our preparation to live with Heavenly Father for eternity. "For behold, this life is the time for (us) to prepare to meet

God; yea, behold the day of this life is the day for (us) to perform (our) labors," to heal the soul scars of mortality through repentance and temple attendance, and to prepare for a glorious resurrection in the Celestial Kingdom of God. (Alma 34:32).

It is natural, then, that God permits us to enter His holy house only on condition of our worthiness, for the anticipated blessings can only flow when the conduct of our lives is in harmony with His nature. In the temple, we do as the Lord commanded Moses from the burning bush on Sinai. We put off our shoes from off our feet, for the place wherein we stand is holy ground. (See Exodus 3:5).

The Lord told Joseph Smith that, according to the operation of eternal law, there are specific blessings associated with successful efforts to conform to His will. "There is a law (after all, that is) irrevocably decreed in heaven before the foundation of this world, upon which all blessings are predicated. And when we obtain any blessing from God, it is by obedience to that law upon which (the blessing) is predicated." (D&C 130:20-21).

Obedience to the commandments are always accompanied by associated blessings. These rewards are sometimes temporal, but they are always spiritual. Now and then, the world recognizes the eternal immutability of this grand law, but in general, it does not. As it comes to a greater appreciation of The Plan of Salvation, however, and of the covenants that are made before the holy altars of the temple, and as it begins to understand the nature of God through reverential worship, it will begin to see more clearly and appreciate more broadly what Joel meant when He said: "And it shall come to pass afterward," or in the Last Days, "that I will pour out my spirit upon all flesh, and your sons and your daughters shall prophesy; your old men shall dream dreams, (and) your young men shall see visions." (Joel 2:28).

When we have completely internalized the principles of the Gospel so that the conduct of our lives is in harmony with the laws of the Celestial Kingdom of God, we will all be "made free, and partakers of the heavenly gift." (4 Nephi 2-3). This path of discipleship moves us off the status quo of "being," onto the dynamic pathway of "becoming," and it leads to the temple, which "is a machine for the making of gods." (Henri Bergson). Profound obedience and recurring repentance will release us from the bondage of sin, and qualify us by worthiness to enjoy the blessings reserved for the faithful. This level of commitment will allow us to overcome the limitations of the flesh and will release the power of the Holy Ghost to mold us and shape us to reach our potential. The Spirit will break the bands of death, and will throw open for us the gates of the Celestial Kingdom. The characteristics of such a society of Saints will simply be the result of a spiritual transformation in the lives of those who live the celestial law of the Lord.

The covenants we make with God in the temple reflect His attributes. God is holy, so He gives us the Law of the Gospel, which introduces to us the acceptable standard of behavior found in His household. In consequence of the gift of His Son, Heavenly Father has given us the Law of Sacrifice, which teaches us to have empathy for the Savior, and to better comprehend His Atonement. Because He is a righteous steward, He gives us the Law of Consecration, so that we might be selfless as we handle that with which we have been entrusted. God is moral, so He puts us under the covenant of chastity, knowing that if we can control our appetites within the bounds He has set, we will be true and faithful in all other things. God has charity, so He commands us to love Him and each other, to manifest the highest expressions of brotherly kindness and benevolence. Because He is omniscient, He commands us to seek knowledge regarding The Plan of Salvation, its doctrines, principles, rites, ordinances, and covenants, so that we might be the architects of our own fate and work out our salvation with fear and trembling before Him. He is disciplined, so He fashioned the Law of Obedience, that allows us to conform our lives to eternally valid rules of conduct leading to happiness, which is the object and design of our existence, and will be the end thereof, if we are virtuous, upright, faithful, holy, and keep all the commandments of God. (See Joseph Smith, "Teachings," p. 255).

We make temple covenants with our Father in Heaven precisely because He has achieved His exaltation and we have not. Our covenants are the visa stamps on our passports to perfection. They certify that we have visited the Lord, not at vacation retreats that are designed to take our minds off our Fathers business, but in His holy house, where all things testify of His work and glory. Our signatures on our temple recommends are important, to be sure, but it is the covenants we have made with the Lord that impart to the ink on the paper an indelible quality, that is impervious to the diluting influence of the devil.

In God's omnipotence, He could give us everything He has, but what He is, we must earn on our own, as we struggle to understand ourselves, endure opposition, overcome adversity, surmount obstacles, meet challenges head-on, recognize our capabilities and gain self-mastery. Temple covenants help us to focus our efforts to become as He is. If it were not possible to become as God is, these covenants would be unnecessary.

Heavenly Father wants all of His children to reach their potential. That is why He has ordained a Plan where we may one day attain His stature and become all that He now is, but we can do this only if we incorporate into our own being and nature His image and likeness. Through that process, as we learn more about the Atonement of Christ, our corruptible bodies will become clean and pure and full of light. Thus, it is critical to the success of The Plan that the bodies we were given when we came to this earth be kept in good condition, because they are the tabernacles of our spirits. They are holy, came from God, and will eventually return to Him.

A healthy body invites spirituality, which is necessary for happiness. Happiness wrought of righteousness is equivalent to eternal life in the Celestial Kingdom of God. "For we are "spirit, the elements are eternal, and spirit and element, inseparably connected, receive a fulness of joy." (D&C 93:33). The endowment teaches that because of the Atonement of Jesus Christ, we will inherit our bodies in the resurrection. When they are reunited with our spirits, they will never again be

separated. But, the endowment promises not just immortality, but also eternal life. As we receive our endowment, the only catch is that we promise to keep our bodies as pure and as holy as are our spirits.

Long ago, Jehovah taught Israel that there is a direct relationship between physical and spiritual well-being. This is why obedience to the Word of Wisdom is a precondition for entering the temple. It is the latter-day barometer of our faith. We cannot consciously and deliberately adopt a lifestyle that is bad for our bodies without negatively influencing the expression of our spirit. In other words, "when health is absent, wisdom cannot reveal itself, culture cannot become manifest, strength cannot fight, wealth becomes useless, and intelligence cannot be applied." (Heraclitus).

Immorality stands in opposition to The Plan of Salvation for the same reasons. Even in the best of circumstances, to be left to govern our own appetites without the influence of the Holy Spirit is a recipe for disaster. Without specific guidelines, procreative power will corrupt, and absolute power will corrupt absolutely. When our hearts are set upon telestial temptations, spirituality will be weakened until the thoughts, words, and deeds that are critical to our eternal development will no longer be a conscious part of our daily lives. They will no longer direct our actions or define our character. Our internal moral compass will begin to spin wildly out of control. Those who participate in immoral behavior too easily abandon the discipline demanded by discipleship; they seek the result without accepting the responsibility. Such individuals do not think about the disastrous effects of their behavior on families, the broken hearts of spouses, the lost confidence of children, and the destruction of faith and testimony that are the inevitable consequence of their selfish acts. The situation is even worse today, inasmuch as both men and women now openly and equally flaunt lascivious behavior.

The covenant of chastity received in the temple reinforces the lesson that righteousness begins with internal attitude control and is not just an outward observance of rules of conduct. Those who receive that law by covenant have

experienced a mighty change in their hearts. Their lives will never again be governed by endocrine secretions. They are moral because they want to be, not because they are required to be. They love the Lord with all their hearts, and with all their souls, that they may live. (See Deuteronomy 30:6).

If living a moral life were simply a question of following the rules, then it would be possible to program a computer to be moral. That was precisely Lucifer's argument at the Council. But that is not the case, and it never has been. It is the desire and effort required to be moral in the face of obstacles and opposition that gives nobility to our character. That is our quest today, as much as it was in the days of Don Quixote, when he was jousting with windmills.

One of the terrible consequences of the world's fascination with Babylon and of the adoption of its lifestyle is spiritual insensitivity born of competition between individuals. Win or lose is the prevailing standard. Zero sum game is the rule of play. At best, business teaches that we don't get what we deserve, we get what we negotiate. An unenlightened Daddy Warbucks illustrated the worst in us, when he told Annie that "you don't have to be nice to those you climb over, or step on, on your way up the ladder of success, if you don't plan on coming back down again." But the Savior said: "Whosoever will be chief among you, let him be your servant." (Matthew 20:27).

Those who frequent the House of the Lord insulate themselves from such influences. In the temple, there are no distinctions by class, position, or title. All are equal in the eyes of the Lord, "and he inviteth them all to come unto him and partake of his goodness; and he denieth none that come unto him, black and white, bond and free, male and female; and he remembereth the heathen; and all are alike unto God, both Jew and Gentile." (2 Nephi 26:33).

When we read the lines of Sir Walter Scott's poem, entitled, "My Native Land," we think of the temple, and of how we are intuitively drawn to our home that is the House of the Lord. He wrote: "Breathes there the man, with soul so dead, Who never to himself hath said, This is my own, my native land! Whose heart hath ne'er within

him burn'd, as home his footsteps he hath turn'd from wandering on a foreign strand! If such there breathe, go, mark him well; for him no Minstrel raptures swell. High though his titles, proud his name, boundless his wealth as wish can claim; despite those titles, power, and pelf, the wretch, concentred all in self, living, shall forfeit fair renown, and, doubly dying, shall go down to the vile dust, from whence he sprung, unwept, unhonour'd, and unsung."

Joseph Fielding Smith, Jr. taught: "Every soul coming into this world came here with the promise that through obedience he would receive the blessings of salvation. No person was foreordained to sin, or to perform a mission of evil." ("Doctrines of Salvation," 1:61). All the Lord requires is "the hearts of the children of men." (D&C 64:22).

The endowment repetitively reinforces the principle that "the rights of the priesthood are inseparably connected to the powers of heaven, and that the powers of heaven cannot be controlled nor handled only upon the principles of righteousness." (D&C 121:36). In the temple, there is no exercise of authority through the use of violent or coercive means that are poor substitutes for leadership or power. As a matter of fact, in the temple endowment, we learn quite graphically that power and violence are mutually exclusive: where one is present the other is absent. We learn about the satanic inclination to abuse authority; we learn about those who have it, but are least prepared for positions of trust and responsibility. As the endowment unfolds, we learn the principle that God's Plan operates more by addition than by subtraction.

Isaiah foresaw the confusion of the Last Days, that was fomented by Satan's deception in the Garden, when he wrote: "Stay yourselves, and wonder; cry ye out, and cry: they are drunken, but not with wine; they stagger, but not with strong drink. For the Lord hath poured out upon you the spirit of deep sleep, and hath closed your eyes: the prophets, and your rulers, and seers hath he covered." (Isaiah 29:9-11).

"But you were always a good man of business, Jacob." said Scrooge, in Charles Dicken's "A Christmas Carol." "Business!" cried the ghost, wringing its hands again. "Mankind was my business. The common welfare was my business; charity, mercy, forbearance, and benevolence were all my business. The dealings of my trade were but a drop of water in the comprehensive ocean of my business. At this time of the rolling year," the spectre said, "I suffer most. Why did I walk through crowds of fellow-beings with my eyes turned down, and never raise them to that blessed Star which led the Wise Men to a poor abode? Were there no homes to which its light would have conducted me?"

Possibly the most significant difference that accounts for the superiority of Heavenly Father's Plan of Salvation that is revealed in the temple over any other lifestyle is the process whereby the Gospel of Jesus Christ is internalized by His disciples. This phenomenon begins with sanctification by the Spirit, and only end with covenants of exaltation. Within the walls of the House of the Lord are taught those principles that enable us to become purified so that we may be worthy to live once again in a state of holiness in the presence of our Heavenly Father. Through this process, we are cleansed from the effects of sin; our spiritual renewal prepares us to pass by angels who stand as sentinels, as we approach the veil, and prepare ourselves in a holy correspondence to enter the presence of the Lord. But first, we must submit to His will, yield our hearts to Him, and live in harmony with all of the teachings of His Gospel. We must first enter into sacred covenants before the holy altar of the temple. We do so because we trust the Lord completely when He assures us: "If ye do these things blessed are ye, for ye shall be lifted up at the last day." (3 Nephi 27:22).

When the ordinances of the temple drive the law into our inward parts, so that it is written upon our hearts, a mighty change takes place. (See Jeremiah 31:33). It is when we are born again that the desired result of all Gospel oriented teaching is achieved. As we are sanctified, holiness erases our disposition to do evil. Our "minds become single to God." (D&C 88:68).

Sanctification by the Spirit is a process, rather than a point, and during the journey those who love the Lord try to please Him in every way. For example, we honor the Sabbath Day because it is His holy day. First it was called the Holy Sabbath, then the Sabbath, then Sunday. Now, it is called the weekend. Nevertheless, the Saints should never confuse holy days with holidays. "Wherefore the Sabbath was given unto man for a day of rest; and also that man should glorify God." (J.S.T. Mark 2:26-27). The Lord has given the Sabbath to help His children to remember Him, to give them an opportunity and a setting in which to express their love and appreciation to Him. The Sabbath is inseparable from the ordinances of the Gospel that are performed on that special day; both are gifts so that we might have the Spirit more fully in our lives. Ultimately, He has blessed His children with the Sabbath so that we might be sanctified. A people who honor the Sabbath will be prepared to enjoy service in the temple. "And inasmuch as ye (keep the Sabbath day holy) with thanksgiving, with cheerful hearts and countenances ... the fulness of the earth is yours ... even peace in this world, and eternal life in the world to come." (D&C 59:15-15 & 23).

"If thou turn away ... from doing thy pleasure on my holy day, and (instead) call the Sabbath a delight, the holy of the Lord, honourable; and shalt honour him, not doing thine own ways, nor finding thine own pleasure, nor speaking thine own words, then shalt thou delight thyself in the Lord, and I will cause thee to ride upon the high places of the earth." (Isaiah 58:13-14). It is the road less traveled that climbs steadily to the mountain of the Lord's House. The temple is as a city set amidst the clouds; it is a celestial beacon nestled safely in the stratosphere of our psyche, far above the cares and beyond the comprehension of the world.

"A favorite theme of Brigham Young was that the dominion God gives to us is designed to test us and enable us to show to ourselves, our fellows, and all the heavens just how we would act if entrusted with God's power." (Hugh Nibley, "Subduing the Earth," p. 89-90). God provides the opportunity to participate in the endowment and the other ordinances of the temple, as we please. But we are not left without guidance as to what we ought to do; the commandment has been stated and reiterated: "And it shall come to pass that if you build a house unto my name,

and do not do the things that I say, I will not perform the oath which I make unto you, neither fulfil the promises which ye expect at my hands, saith the Lord. For instead of blessings, ye, by your own works, bring cursings, wrath, indignation, and judgments upon your own heads, by your follies, and by all your abominations, which you practice before me, saith the Lord." (D&C 124:47-48).

When we alienate ourselves from God's influence, we die spiritually as our eternal progression falters. "Broad is the gate," taught the Savior, "and wide the way that leadeth to the deaths; and many there are that go in thereat, because they receive me not, neither do they abide in my law." (D&C 132:25). The temple stands as a solemn witness of how we will behave when we are left on our own, after having received instruction regarding what we ought to do. The endowment asks the question: "What think ye of Jesus Christ," the Architect of the Cosmos, Whose house is one of the pillars of creation.

In fact, the world sees these "Pillars of Creation" as nothing more than elephant trunks of interstellar gas and dust in the Eagle Nebula, 7,000 light years from Earth. But, in an 1857 sermon entitled "The Condescension of Christ," London pastor Charles Spurgeon used the phrase to describe both the physical world and the force that binds it all together, stemming from the Divine. When we read his words, we think of temple worship: "Now wonder, ye angels," Spurgeon wrote of the gift of the Son of God, "the Infinite has become an infant; He, upon whose shoulders the universe doth hang, nurses at his mother's breast; He who created all things, and bears up the pillars of creation."

All that has been created is God's, and our insignificant telestial treasures are only on loan to us, after all, and we claim them as ours only for the time being. Thus, the payment of our tithes is a precondition for temple attendance, for it is a barometer of our faith and obedience. Elder Matthew Cowley gave a marvelous address that illustrates beautifully the relationship God can have with us when we are obedient to His laws. He said: "God is a wonderful partner, isn't He. I would

like to be in business with somebody like that, having my partner come up to me and say: 'Here, I'll furnish all the capital to start the business. I will furnish all the blessings. Then, you look after the business. Don't forget me. When the increase comes, you keep ninety percent, and turn over to me ten percent. You use your ninety percent any way you want to, and I'll put my ten percent right back into the business.' Wouldn't that be wonderful? That's just the kind of partner we have in this Church. We keep the ninety percent and use it any way we wish. We give him the ten percent, and here stands a temple, and there stands a tabernacle. He puts it all right back into the business, into his business. God will finance the Church, brothers and sisters, if you will obey the principles of the Gospel." ("Matthew Cowley Speaks," p. 76-77).

All we can hope for is to be taught what is best for ourselves and for the Kingdom of God, to develop a testimony that it should be, and then to work with all our capacity to make it happen, whatever the cost might be. Then, when we are so richly blessed far beyond the measure that we deserve, the price, once paid so painfully, is recalled in gladness. We receive full value. As Brigham Young said, "I never count the cost of anything. I just find out what the Lord wants me to do, and I do it."

Joseph Smith wrote: "This is good doctrine. It tastes good. I can taste the principles of eternal life, and so can you. They are given to me by the revelations of Jesus Christ; and I know that ... you believe them. I can taste the spirit of eternal life. I know it is good, and when I tell you of these things which were given me by inspiration of the Holy Spirit, you are bound to receive them as sweet, and rejoice." ("Teachings," p. 355).

We bless the lives of our extended families through the sealing ordinances of the temple. In the Spirit World, all who have died are taught the Gospel of Jesus Christ. Those who accept it there need to have the ordinances of the temple performed in their behalf by faithful members of the Lord's Church. That journey is measured in faith, not in miles, in an accounting that takes place on both sides of the veil. We "shall come up on mount Zion" (Obadiah 1:21), there "to be a light unto the world,

and ... the saviors of men," as we perform work for the dead in the temples of the Lord. (D&C 103:9). It is for this reason that Paul asked: "Else what shall they do which are baptized for the dead, if the dead rise not at all? Why are they then baptized for the dead?" (1 Corinthians 15:29).

As this work is carried out, the Lord's glory will rest upon His people. The doctrine of the priesthood will be revealed in marvelous simplicity and plainness. The Holy Ghost will purge the stain of sin from every penitent heart and will reveal all things. The faithful will leave the temple with an endowment of power. Angels will watch over them, guide them, and protect them. The kingdom will roll forth, and stakes will be organized so that the elect may be gathered. The walls of Babylon will crumble and fall. All of scattered Israel, the Lord's covenant people, will learn the truth and rejoice in the knowledge of the Savior, as the waste places are built up. Oases will spring up in the desert, and living water will slake the thirst of a people eager for its life sustaining influence. The Lord will comfort and succor the families of the Saints and all of their sick and afflicted with the bread of life and the Balm of Gilead. His kingdom will fill the earth, and will propitiously occupy the void created when the terrible and swift sword of the word of the Lord overthrows principalities, powers, and false priests who oppress. His servants will be caught up to meet Him, to dwell with Him forever.

Joseph F. Smith said: "If we would carry out that which the Lord revealed, it would only be a matter of a very short time until this people would be in the same condition as were the people of the City of Enoch." (C.R., 4/1921). That city was the City of Light, the Eternal City of Peace, and the Celestial City of God. The new city shall be "the New Jerusalem, a land of peace, a city of refuge, a place of safety for the saints of the Most High God." (D&C 45:66). It will not be long, now, before it shall once again "flourish upon the hills and rejoice upon the mountains." (D&C 49:25).

"Who shall ascend into (that) hill of the Lord?" asked the Psalmist, "or who shall stand in his holy place," before God, angels, and witnesses at the altars of His holy

House? "He that hath clean hands, and a pure heart; who hath not lifted up his soul unto vanity, nor sworn deceitfully. He shall receive the blessing from the Lord, and righteousness from the God of his salvation." (Psalms 24:3-5). If the Church takes her responsibilities relating to the temple seriously, "she shall prosper, and spread herself and become very glorious, very great, and very terrible. And the nations of the earth shall honor her, and shall say: Surely Zion is the city of our God, and surely Zion cannot fall, neither be moved out of her place, for God is there, and the hand of the Lord is there; And he hath sworn by the power of his might to be her salvation and her high tower. Therefore, verily, thus saith the Lord, let Zion rejoice." (D&C 97:18-21).

Then, every patron in the temple "shall flourish like the palm tree, (and) shall grow like a cedar in Lebanon. Those that be planted in the house of the Lord shall flourish in the courts of our God." (Psalms 92:12-13). To those unfamiliar with travel in harsh environments, palms often seem to grow in desert wastes. It is only upon closer inspection that the oases of underlying currents of life-sustaining water are noticed that bring nourishment to the roots of the thirsty trees. So, too, can the ordinances of the temple provide an underground river of sustenance to those who hunger and thirst after righteousness.

All temples stand as 'types' of the paradise lost in this world, of the place of contact between heaven and earth, and of the final temple that the earth will become when it is the habitation of the Son of God. (See 2 Chronicles 29:6). The Mountain of The Lord's House foreseen by Isaiah is both an allegorical and figurative description of the refuge for Zion in the Last Days, when it "shall be established in the tops of the mountains." (2 Nephi 12:2). Whether it is a high place of God, a place of revelation, or perhaps the temple itself, Latter-day Saints are prone to restrict the application of this phrase to one locality, that of the intermountain west, and specifically to the Valley of the Great Salt Lake. But this interpretation may be too narrow. As the Lord warned Joseph Smith: "And let them who be of Judah flee unto the mountains of the Lord's house." (D&C 133:13). Thus, commentaries likens 'the mountain of the Lord' to Jerusalem, and specifically to

Mount Zion, upon whose crown sat the temple. There is certainly ample historical precedent to do so.

We think of the ancient patriarch Zadok, who "was a spiritual man whose tired eyes

could see beyond the desert to those invisible summits of the imagination where cool air existed and where the one god, El Shaddai, lived. In later generations, people who spoke other languages would translate this old Semitic name, which actually meant 'he of the mountain' as God Almighty, for through change El Shaddai was destined to mature into that god whom much of the world would worship.

But in these fateful days, when the little group of Hebrews camped and waited for the signal to march westward, El Shaddai was the god of no one but themselves; they were not even certain that he had continued as the god of those other Hebrews who had moved on to distant areas like Egypt.

But of one thing Zadok was sure; El Shaddai personally determined the destiny of this group, for of all the peoples available to him in the teeming area between the Euphrates and the Nile, he had chosen these Hebrews as his predilected people, and they lived within his embrace, enjoying security that others did not know." (James Michener, "The Source," Chapter entitled: "An Old Man and His God" p. 177-178).

In our day, temples are being erected all over the world in order to help to establish the Zion envisioned by Zadok. Joseph F. Smith wrote of a priesthood army of endowed Saints, saying: "We entered into covenants with the Lord that we will keep ourselves pure and unspotted from the world. We have agreed before God, angels, and witnesses, in sacred places, that we will not commit adultery, will not lie, that we will not steal or bear false witness against our neighbors, or take advantage of the weak, that we will help and sustain our fellow men in the right, and take such a course as will prove most effectual in helping others to overcome their weaknesses and bring themselves into subjection to the requirements of heaven. We cannot neglect, slight, or depart from the spirit, meaning, intent, and

purpose of these covenants and agreements that we have entered into with our Father in Heaven, without shearing ourselves of our glory, strength, right and title to His blessings, and to the gifts and manifestations of His Spirit." ("Improvement Era," 8/1906).

It would be difficult to more clearly compose a statement explaining the need to establish a covenant relationship with God. It would be equally difficult to visualize a more appropriate place in which to do so than the House of The Lord. Therefore, He commanded His people: "Organize yourselves; prepare every needful thing; and establish a house, even a house of prayer, a house of fasting, a house of faith, a house of learning, a house of glory, a house of order, a house of God." (D&C 88:119, see D&C 109:8).

He gives us tools sufficient to the task. In that revelatory house, we see things as they really are, in an unpolluted atmosphere where we are able to inhale deeply of a heavenly aether as we make choices based on celestial sureties. In "the Father of lights, (there is) no variableness, neither shadow of turning." (James 1:17). We trust in Him as we trade the uncertain course adopted by the world for the bedrock of His revealed word. The Prophet Joseph Smith said: "Could we read and comprehend all that has been written from the days of Adam, on the relation of man to God and angels in a future state, we would know very little about it. Reading the experience of others, or the revelations given to them, can never give us a comprehensive view of our condition and true relation to God. Knowledge of these things can only be obtained by experience through the ordinances of God set forth for that purpose. Could you gaze into heaven five minutes, you would know more than you would by reading all that has ever been written on the subject." (H.C. 6:50). In the endowment, we glimpse eternity for an entire sacred hour and more, and then we brush up against the veil, rubbing shoulders with those on the other side. It is as we worship in the temple that we realize that "one of Joseph Smith's greatest contributions was his knowledge of what is to come after death. He did much to clarify our understanding of heaven, and to make it seem worth working for." ("My Religion and Me" Course Manual). The endowment lends rebar to our resolve to work out our salvation with fear and trembling before the Lord. (See Philippians 2:12).

Paul suggested that the Saints would be able to do so at the altars of the temple and elsewhere within its protective walls. The ordinances performed there are sacred rites that can only be appropriately conducted in the Lord's House, because they have profound spiritual meanings and effects that might too easily be compromised were it not for the protection provided by that special sanctuary. These ordinances include baptism for the dead, confirmations, bestowal of priesthood authority, washings and anointings, the endowment, and sealing ordinances.

Ordinances of exaltation are received by covenant, and are sacred agreements or mutual promises made between ourselves and God. The Lord explained that all those who desire a blessing associated with Gospel principles should first "abide the law which was appointed for that blessing, and the conditions thereof, as were instituted from before the foundation of the world." (D&C 132:5). Alma reasoned that "if there was no law given, if men sinned what could justice do, or mercy either, for they would have no claim upon the creature?" In that case, "the works of justice would be destroyed, and God would cease to be God." (Alma 42:21-22).

The ordinances "embody certain obligations on the part of the individual, such as the covenant and promise to observe the law of strict virtue and chastity, to be charitable, benevolent, tolerant and pure; to devote both talent and material means to the spread of truth and the uplifting of the race; to maintain devotion to the cause of truth; and to seek in every way to contribute to the great preparation, that the earth may be made ready to receive her King, the Lord Jesus Christ. With the taking of each covenant and the assumption of each obligation, a promised blessing is pronounced, contingent (only) upon the faithful observance of the conditions." (James E. Talmage, "The House of The Lord," p. 84).

"Born Again Christians" are those who are in a covenant relationship with the Lord. As He revealed to Joseph Smith, the "greater priesthood administereth the gospel and holdeth the key of the mysteries of the kingdom, even the key of the knowledge of God. Therefore, in the ordinances thereof, the power of godliness is

manifest. (But) without the ordinances thereof, and the authority of the priesthood, the power of godliness is not manifest unto men in the flesh" and they cannot be born again. (D&C 84:19-21). When we make covenants with God, we know what He expects of us, and we know what blessings we may expect of Him. Covenants illustrate that the Lord's Church is founded upon unchanging principles; they level the playing field and guarantee that the requirements for obtaining salvation will be the same for all His children.

It is natural, however, that the Lord would have a special relationship with His covenant people. "For thou art an holy people unto the Lord thy God, and the Lord hath chosen thee to be a peculiar people unto himself, above all the nations that are upon the earth." (Deuteronomy 14:2). "And the Lord hath avouched thee this day to be his peculiar people, as he hath promised thee, and that thou shouldest keep all his commandments." (Deuteronomy 26:18). In Hebrew, to be "peculiar" connotes a special, covenant relationship. Hence, we read about Peter's characterization of the Saints as "a chosen generation, a royal priesthood, an holy nation, (and) a peculiar people." (1 Peter 2:9).

Members of the Church of Jesus Christ of Latter-day Saints describe themselves as covenant people, and thus the temple is associated with His Church as one of its integral components. King Benjamin told his people that because of their covenant with God, they would "be called the children of Christ, his sons and his daughters." (Mosiah 5:7). Today, the term "Christian" has been demeaned and is commonly used in ways that cheapen its true meaning. True Christians have developed a testimony that "Jesus Christ (is) the Son of God, the Father of heaven and earth, the Creator of all things." (Mosiah 3:8). Those who humbly take His name upon themselves treat the temple with profound respect because it is the holy habitation of the Lord.

Just as we are known by the name of our mortal parents, so too are we called by the name of Christ in a familial way. We are His children in the sense that He has united our body and spirit through the Resurrection. "For this day He hath spiritually begotten you," explained King Benjamin. (Mosiah 5:7). There is a special family relationship reserved for the faithful, that is in addition to the reality that

we are all spirit children of our Father. (See D&C 34:3 & 121:7). Temple service fosters these relationships and, through the Spirit, nurtures our familial bond with Heavenly Father and His Son Jesus Christ.

When we enjoy the blessing of the endowment, we realize that only by making covenants with God and Christ can we break the bands of death, and are we made free. "There is no other name given whereby salvation cometh," said Benjamin; "therefore, I would that ye should take upon you the name of Christ, all you that have entered into the covenant with God." (Mosiah 5:8). Is it any wonder that The Church of Jesus Christ of Latter-day Saints builds temples, to worship within their walls? This is part of the reason why the Lord Himself proclaims that it "is the only true and living church upon the face of the whole earth, with which I, the Lord, am well pleased." (D&C 1:30). When we, as a Church, build temples, and receive our own certificates of occupancy manifest in our 'recommend,' we realize that it is not ourselves, but our Lord and Savior Who has taken up residency within its hallowed walls. It is the authority of His priesthood that drives our worship, and that binds and ratifies the covenants we make. It is His power alone that breaks the death grip of Satan, who is patiently waiting to drag our souls down to hell.

Therefore, once we have been Born Again, keeping our temple covenants is the most important thing we can do. "Can we be happy, can we be redeemed, can we be exalted without them? No. They are more than advisable or desirable, or even than necessary. More even than essential or vital. They are critical to each of us." (Boyd K. Packer, "The Holy Temple," p. 32).

Temple covenants are life-generating and life-sustaining, for just as we are "born into the world by water, and blood, and the spirit" and have become of dust living souls, even so, we "must be born again into the kingdom of heaven, of water, and of the Spirit, and be cleansed by blood," even the blood of the Son of God, and receive our endowment in the House of The Lord, that we "might be sanctified from all sin, and enjoy the words of eternal life in this world, and eternal life in the world to come, even immortal glory." (Moses 6:59-60).

Keeping our temple covenants puts us beyond the power of the adversary, for through obedience we are endowed with the priesthood and spiritual power necessary to overcome the forces of evil and obtain exaltation. The Prophet Joseph Smith said that salvation consists of our being placed beyond the power of our enemies, meaning the enemies of our progression, such as dishonesty, greediness, lying, immorality, and other vices. They are the character flaws that threaten to contaminate an then neutralize the power of temple covenants.

In contrast, we are admonished to seek higher ground and to look up to the temple for spiritual stability. As Paul said, so might we say of our own temple experiences: "Finally, brethren, whatsoever things are true, whatsoever things are honest, whatsoever things are just, whatsoever things are pure, whatsoever things are lovely, whatsoever things are of good report; if there by any virtue, and if there be any praise, think on these things." (Philippians 4:8).

By entering into covenants, the very "gates of hell shall not prevail against (us); yea, and the Lord God will disperse the powers of darkness from before (us), and cause the heavens to shake for (our) good, and His name's glory." (D&C 21:6). The gates of hell mark the entrance to the Spirit Prison of the Unjust, where disobedient spirits are allowed to go to work out their own salvation without the intercession of the Redeemer or the powerful covenants of the temple, and to personally satisfy the demands of Justice, so that they may finally be released from the iron grip of Satan's influence. (See 1 Peter 3:18, & D&C 76:73).

Although we now reside in the midst of Spiritual Babylon, keeping our covenants guarantees that we can live with confidence and high hopes for the future. We can be the happiest people on the face of the earth. In 1830, the Lord declared: "The day speedily cometh; the hour is not yet, but is nigh at hand, when peace shall be taken from the earth, and the devil shall have power over his own dominion." (D&C 1:35). "But if (we) are prepared, (we) shall not fear." (D&C 38:30).

"My peace I give unto you," promised the Savior, "not as the world giveth, give I

unto you." (John 14:27). Those who have been endowed in the temple understand the peace to which the Savior alluded. "His peace (is) not the peace of the world, of ease, of luxury, idleness, absence of turmoil, and strife, but the peace born of the righteous life, the peace that lifts the soul, that day by day brings us closer to the home of Eternal Peace, the dwelling place of our Father." (J. Reuben Clark, Jr.). The temple is our home away from home, the safe haven to which we set our course when we find ourselves on stormy seas and raked by fierce winds, during the telestial tempests that befall us.

Those who have been to the temple must therefore work tirelessly to maintain their fidelity to their covenants. "When we come to the temple and receive our endowment ... we can live ordinary lives and be ordinary souls, struggling against temptation, failing and repenting, and failing again and repenting, but always determined to keep our covenants. Then, the day will come when we will receive the benediction: 'Well done, thou good and faithful servant: thou hast been faithful over a few things, I will make thee ruler over many things; enter thou into the joy of thy lord.' (Matthew 25:21)." (Boyd K. Packer, "Let Not Your Heart be Troubled," p. 257).

Once this special covenant relationship has been established, we must not mock God by breaking our part of the bargain. There is an unalterable cause and effect relationship that is associated with the commandments. The Law of the Harvest, and the Law of Compensation, dictate results that are consistent with the quality of our efforts to keep the commandments. "For whatsoever a man soweth, that shall he also reap. For he that soweth to his flesh shall of the flesh reap corruption; but he that soweth to the Spirit shall of the Spirit reap life everlasting. And let us not be weary in well doing: for in due season we shall reap, if we faint not." (Galatians 6:7-9).

Temple experiences culminating in the endowment can have real meaning only to those who have accepted God and Christ, have entered the fold in the waters of baptism, have received the Holy Ghost, and are determined to endure to the end

in righteousness. (See D&C 20:37 & 1 Corinthians 2:14). Peter's Second Epistle, for example, was addressed to a specific, focused audience, "to them that have obtained like precious faith with us through the righteousness of God and our Saviour Jesus Christ. According as his divine power hath given unto us all things that pertain unto life and godliness, through the knowledge of him that hath called us to glory and virtue; whereby are given unto us exceeding great and precious promises: That by these ye might be partakers of the divine nature." (2 Peter 1:1, 3 & 4).

In the final analysis, "the temple is a place of beauty, it is a place of revelation, and it is a place of peace. It is the house of the Lord." (President Howard W. Hunter). It is also a place of profound symbolism. We constantly learn from the Lord through symbols. They can profoundly affect us, and although they do not convey the same message to all people, they can help us to remember important things. They can teach us abstract truths that are hard to learn in other ways. They can represent feelings, ideals, and sweeping concepts that are difficult to put into words.

The Savior frequently used symbols. He talked of lost sheep, mustard seeds, fig trees, olive branches, pearls of great price, hens, chickens, birds, flowers, and foxes, bread and water, and bitter cups. He told Moses: "All things have their likeness, and all things are created and made to bear record of me, both things which are temporal, and things which are spiritual; things which are in the heavens above, and things which are on the earth, and things which are in the earth, and things which are under the earth, both above and beneath: all things bear record of me." (Moses 6:63).

It will be difficult for individuals who have lived a telestial existence to justify their actions before God, in light of the many symbols, signs and wonders He has provided to alert them to His presence. In reality "earth is crammed with heaven, and every common bush with fire of God. But only those who see take off their shoes. The rest stand around picking blackberries." (Elizabeth Barrett Browning). Anyone who has seen the temple so beautifully constructed and carefully

maintained has "seen God moving in his majesty and power." (D&C 88:47). As Ralph Waldo Emerson wrote: "If the stars should appear one night in a thousand years, how would men believe and adore; and preserve for many generations the remembrance of the city of God which had been shown! But every night come out these envoys of beauty, and light the universe with their admonishing smile." ("Nature and Selected Essays"). In like manner do the temples of the Lord light up the landscapes of our lives.

But the Lord only reveals truth to those who are spiritually ready to understand it. Thus, we must humble ourselves as little children. (See Matthew 18:4). "Heaven lies about us in our infancy. Shades of the prison house begin to close upon the growing boy. But he beholds the light and whence it flows; he sees it in his joy. The youth, who daily farther from the east must travel, still is nature's priest. And by the vision splendid, is on his way attended. At length, the man perceives it die away, and fade into the light of common day." (William Wordsworth).

"Why speakest thou unto them in parables?" the Savior was asked. "He answered and said unto them, Because it is given unto you to know the mysteries of the kingdom of heaven, but to them it is not given. For whosoever hath, (receiveth - J.S.T.) to him shall be given, and he shall have more abundance: but whosoever hath not, (continueth not to receive - J.S.T.) from him shall be taken away even that he hath. Therefore speak I to them in parables: because they seeing see not; and hearing they hear not, neither do they understand." (Matthew 13:10-13). When truth is presented in story form, those who are spiritually prepared will better understand the meaning of the symbols that are used. Those who are not prepared, will be unable to discern the meaning. It follows that those who are spiritually unprepared cannot discern the meaning of the temple endowment, even if it has been recorded word-for-word in the Congressional Record.

The mysteries of the kingdom are the saving principles of the Gospel. When we approach a Gospel discussion with spiritual preparation, the mysteries of God may be unfolded to our view. They are referred to as mysteries since they are

unavailable to the natural man because they must be revealed by God on condition of obedience. The mysteries are designed to lead God's children, who see with the eye of faith, to eternal life. Joseph Smith described his own experience in these words: "Our minds being now enlightened, we began to have the scriptures laid open to our understandings, and the true meaning and intention of their more mysterious passages revealed unto us in a manner which we never could attain to previously, nor ever before had thought of." (After his baptism, May 15, 1829. J.S.H. 1:74).

The most sacred symbolic teachings are received in the temple. These rituals "take us on an upward journey toward eternal life, ending with a symbolic entrance into the presence of God. The characters depicted, the physical setting, the clothing worn, the signs given, and all the events covered in the temple are symbolic. When they are understood, they will help each person to recognize truth and grow spiritually." ("Temple Preparation Class Lesson Manual," p. 23).

Some of the symbols are straightforward and their meanings are readily apparent. For example, "if you have seen one of the temples at night, fully lighted, you know what an impressive sight that can be. The House of the Lord, bathed in light, standing out in the darkness, becomes symbolic of the power and the inspiration of the Gospel of Jesus Christ standing as a beacon in a world that sinks even further into spiritual darkness." (Boyd K. Packer, "The Holy Temple," p. 7).

"The baptismal font rests on the backs of twelve oxen, symbolically representing the twelve tribes of Israel. The celestial room symbolizes the exalted and reverent state that all may achieve through living the Gospel of Jesus Christ. The room represents the contentment, inner harmony, and peace" that can be attained when one's life is in conformity with God's commandments. ("Temple Open House" brochure, The Church of Jesus Christ of Latter-day Saints).

Those who serve in the temple as ordinance workers not only facilitate the experience of temple patrons, but they also represent unseen sentinels who watch over and guard the way of the righteous. In the temple, "they that be with us are

more than they that be with them." (2 Kings 6:17).

In the temple all are dressed alike in white, which is the symbol of purity. "The uniform dress symbolizes that before God our Father in heaven, all are equal. The beggar and the banker, the learned and the unlearned, the prince and the pauper sit side by side in the temple and are of equal importance, if they live righteously before the Lord God." (John A. Widtsoe, "Improvement Era," 10/1962, p. 710).

"The garment represents sacred covenants. It fosters modesty and becomes a shield and protection to the wearer. (It) is a visual and tactile reminder of (covenants made in the temple). For many Church members, the garment has formed a barrier of protection when the wearer has been faced with temptation. Among other things, it symbolizes our deep respect for the laws of God." (Boyd K. Packer, "The Holy Temple," p. 18-20).

It has been pointed out to those who are not of our faith that, unlike the priests and pastors of Christendom, and those of the Jewish faith, we wear our holy vestments on the inside, and not on the outside. But in either case, there is symbolism that can be of great comfort to those who are clothed in such raiment.

Some of the symbols are less straightforward, and the meaning is not so readily apparent. Almost every aspect of the temple ceremony is symbolic. This means that each person should prepare to be spiritually sensitive to the symbolic nature of the temple endowment. This can be accomplished through fasting, prayer, and repentance leading to faithfulness and feelings of worthiness and acceptance, that leads to an immersion in the spiritual element.

Every facet of the temple experience reminds us that we are "the nobility of heaven, a choice and a chosen generation, who have a divine destiny." (Joseph Fielding Smith, Jr.). As we learn who we really are, we will have the desire to come to the temple for light and for safety. There we will find a safe haven from the turmoil in the world.

As we mature in the Gospel, we will come to realize that our temple experiences ultimately bring us to a threshold, where we confidently stand ready to be judged by our works. When we give our report, the Lord will be eager to take us to His bosom and declare "well done, thou good and faithful servant. Thou hast been faithful over a few things. I will make thee ruler over many things. Enter thou into the joy of thy lord." (Matthew 25:21).

It will be as it was in the days of King Josiah, when he "went up into the house of the Lord, and all the men of Judah and all the inhabitants of Jerusalem with him, and the priests, and the prophets, and all the people, both small and great. And the king stood by a pillar, and (they) made a covenant before the Lord, to walk after the Lord, and to keep his commandments and his testimonies and his statutes with all their heart and all their soul, to perform the words of this covenant that were written in this book. And all the people stood to the covenant." (2 Kings 23:2-3).

Possibly, the most significant difference that accounts for the superiority of the principles of The Plan of Salvation that is revealed in the temple over other lifestyles is the process whereby the Gospel of Jesus Christ is internalized by His disciples. The wonder of our transformation begins with sanctification by the Spirit at the waters of baptism, and only end when we participate in the ordinances of exaltation that are carried out before holy altars in the House of the Lord.

Chapter Two
Vistas of eternity

"And it shall come to pass in the last days, saith God, that I will pour out my spirit upon all flesh; and your sons and your daughters shall prophesy, and your young men shall see visions, and your old men shall dream dreams." (Acts 2:27 & Joel 2:28). Today, the Holy Ghost is being poured out in rich abundance, and to the Saints in particular. Joseph Smith promised: "God shall give unto you knowledge by His Holy Spirit, yea, by the unspeakable gift of the Holy Ghost, that has not been revealed since the word was until now." Ours is a time when "nothing shall be withheld ... All thrones and dominions, principalities and powers, shall be revealed .... And also, if there be bounds set to the heavens or to the seas, or to the dry land, or to the sun, moon, or stars, (all this) shall be revealed." (D&C 121:26-31).

What are these temporal and spatial boundaries to which the Prophet referred, that are to be erased, and how will it be done? For all practical purposes, we live in a three-dimensional world and move through time in a forward direction at the rate of one day in every 24 hours. (Actually, in 23 hours, 56 minutes and 4.0916

seconds in a sidereal day. The Earth actually orbits the Sun in 365 days, 5 hours, 48 minutes and 46 seconds, in a solar day, thereby requiring a leap year every four years, but that's a story for another day).

53

We can be certain that the boundaries of the seas, land, sun, moon, and stars will continue to be mathematically defined with greater and greater precision, even as they are esoterically debated by theologians and philosophers alike. But what about heaven? We have the assurance that the relationship between finite boundaries and the metaphysical thrones, dominions, principalities and powers that relate to the eternal worlds will be revealed, as well.

In the temple, in particular, the Spirit opens the eyes of our understanding to reveal undreamed of vistas of otherwise inaccessible experience. It is there that we begin to comprehend the scope of Moroni's promise that "by the power of the Holy Ghost (we) may know the truth of all things." (Moroni 10:5).

Understanding sets us free not only from the limitations of ignorance, but also from the constraints of mortality itself. (John 8:32). In the temple, we learn to be as one with the majestic clockwork, "like a bird that, pausing in her flight a while on boughs too light, feels them give way beneath her and yet sings, knowing that she hath wings." (Victor Hugo). In the temple, the depth and breadth of our comprehension finally puts to rest the debates that have preoccupied us since the Age of Reason began. We soar to new heights as the reconciliation between science and religion harmonizes and clarifies our understanding of our place both in the universe and in the eternities.

The scriptures testify that "eye hath not seen, nor ear heard, neither have entered into the heart of man, the things which God hath prepared for them that love him," meaning that He is eager to share the knowledge of His creations with those who are prepared to receive it. (1 Corinthians 2:9). Because encounters with the Spirit defy rational explanation, "no tongue can speak, neither can there be written by any man, neither can the hearts of men conceive (the) great and marvelous things" that

God's wishes to share with us. (3 Nephi 17:7). These come only from extrasensory perceptions that have the capacity to carry us beyond the conventional boundaries of time, space, and the limitations of our five natural senses. Specialized nerve tissue puts us "in touch" with our physical surroundings, and when combined with our previous experience, creates the powerfully persuasive perceptions that form the basis of our understanding of the world around us. These also prepare us for the solemnities of eternity.

Without a temple-based perspective, our understanding of the observable universe is at risk, because it too easily sets our sights too low and calibrates our vision to focus on conceptual cul-de-sacs from which there is no retreat. Without a temple perspective, we risk sliding backward into a one-dimensional view of the world where we see things not as they really are, but only as our limited vision allows.

The inherent danger is: "Where there is no vision, the people perish." (Proverbs 29:18). The temple endows us with a multi-dimensional view of existence that provides a much more accurate matrix within which we may develop a construct of the universe in which "we live, and move, and have our being." (Acts 17:28). In this sense, "the glory of God is intelligence," which endows us with the ability to be positively influenced by both the physical and spiritual worlds around us, even the multi-dimensional world that we cannot see with our eyes. The "light and truth of intelligence" to which we are introduced in the temple provides us with a more precise representation of the Cosmos that affords us the opportunity to clarify our vision to better perceive reality. (D&C 93:36).

This experience transcends the world with which we are familiar in ways that are unfathomable to unenlightened minds. The rational approach is doomed to failure and can never hope to plumb the depths of spiritual experience because it is anchored so firmly in the temporal world, relies so heavily upon mental gymnastics and the proofs of science, and requires experimental confirmation of observable phenomena. The very logic upon which it is based is its fatal flaw and is inherently self-defeating, because it denies the existence of the only power with the capacity

to convey real understanding. Therefore, even as we make valiant efforts to focus our intellect on eternal elements, because we are bounded on all sides by a crushing present reality, if our hearts have not been softened to relate to the things of the Spirit, we cannot hope to understand God or His creations except in the most abstract, obtuse, and academic ways. As Joseph Smith declared: "We must have a change of heart to see the kingdom of God." ("Teachings," p. 328). The power of the temple is that it is a schoolmaster that mentors us by softening our hearts.

When we think rationally, we are hedged in by the very things from which we yearn to be free – our mortal perspective and perceptions, that are, sadly as it may seem, the sum and substance of our temporal experience. We intuitively seek the right answers, but are doomed to ask the wrong questions. Our efforts to construct a working definition of heaven and earth by subtraction, rather than by addition, are destined to fail when we think within the box. God's reality is infinitely richer and more satisfying than any reality the rational approach grudgingly concedes could possibly exist. His reality is more than we could ever know by relying only upon the poor lenses of the body.

For example, if we visualize something as simple as the curvature of space, and then apply Gospel principles to the concept, our understanding resonates with reason, even as it coordinates with science. It is enlarged to an unprecedented level, that sheds light on doctrine, and particularly that which relates to the temple.

Let's begin with a piece of graph paper made of a rubber sheet, and then drop a steel ball bearing onto it. As a result of the mass of the ball and its kinetic energy and inertia, the surface of the graph paper will be deformed, or puckered in spacetime. It may be thought of as a representation of two-dimensional space that has been warped by mass into a third physical dimension. By extrapolation on a larger scale, we can observe that the gravity caused by planets (bigger balls that have large mass) is a distortion in the fabric of the graph paper of three-dimensional space. By applying the laws of physics applicable to the observable universe, we can deduce that under these conditions our familiar space will be

curved and unbounded, with no edge and no center. This is about as far as we can go with the rational approach, if we refuse the further knowledge that the Lord has promised to give us regarding the subject.

In fact, He does shed light on these basic principles that have been uncovered by reason, and it is in the temple endowment that we begin our celestial schooling. "There are many kingdoms," He explained, "for there is no space in the which there is no kingdom, and there is no kingdom in which there is no space, either a greater or a lesser kingdom. And unto every kingdom is given a law; and unto every law there are certain bounds also and conditions." (D&C 88:37-38). In other words, there are many kingdoms or realities, and every one of them occupies space. But implied in the scriptural explanation (received by the Prophet Joseph Smith in 1832/33) is the suggestion that each space may be governed by certain bounds and conditions specifically tailored to its own individual and unique circumstances.

When Jehovah stood in the presence of God the Father at the time of the creation of the earth, He said to those assembled: "We will go down, for there is space there, and we will take of these materials, and we will make an earth." (Abraham 3:24, underlining mine). The three dimensional space reserved for the earth already existed; all that was necessary was for Jehovah to "go" there and establish, or set in motion, the laws, bounds and conditions by which the earth could roll into existence as a spatial entity moving through time in a forward direction. As Luke wrote, God "made the world and all things therein ... and hath determined the times ... and the bounds of their habitation." (Acts 17:24 & 26). He established both the temporal and spatial conditions and boundaries that would define life on earth.

But here is where it gets interesting, worlds without end. (See Ephesian 3:21). What if each new dimension of space builds upon the previous one. The world we perceive exists in the three-dimensions of depth, width, and height. What if it were possible to locally distort that world into a fourth physical dimension that we cannot perceive directly, in much the same way that we have demonstrated that space may

be distorted by mass? In three-dimensional space, a cube is created when we move a square five times at right angles to itself. The shadow of a cube is drawn in two dimensions as two squares with their vertices connected. In that representation of a cube, all the lines appear to be equal, but not all the angles are right angles.

The cost of losing a dimension in the geometrical reduction is that the three-dimensional object has lost its dimensional accuracy in its representation in only two dimensions.

If we carry our three-dimensional cube at right angles to itself, through a fourth physical dimension, thereby creating new bounds and conditions for the 'kingdom' thus created, in what directions could we define that fourth physical dimension? It would not be left-right, not forward-backward, not up-down, but simultaneously at right angles to every one of those directions. We cannot demonstrate what direction that is, because it is outside our experience and may not even exist in our universe. Nevertheless, in such a scenario, a four-dimensional hypercube, that is described in the literature of theoretical physics as a tesseract, is generated. It's proof lies beyond the laws, bounds, and conditions by which the earth, and for that matter our temporal and spatial universe, exists. We can only perceive the three-dimensional shadow of a tesseract resembling two nested cubes with all of the vertices connected by lines. A real tesseract, in four dimensions, would have lines of equal length at right angles to each other. The cost of losing a dimension in the geometrical reduction is that the four-dimensional object has lost its dimensional accuracy in its representation in only three dimensions. Nevertheless, it can be imagined to exist, and it can even be inferred from mathematical permutations as well as from a number of scriptures and from statements of Church leaders.

For example, Lehi declared: "It must needs be that there is an opposition in all things." (2 Nephi 2:11). In addition to the familiar applications of this basic principle, what if Lehi also meant that our world itself has an isomer? What if the world as we know it has one particular molecular formula, but the world we cannot see, that is its mirror, has a different isomeric structural formula? Could Lehi have been saying that our world itself has its opposite, one that is described as

being "without beginning of days or end of years, being prepared from eternity to all eternity, according to (God's) foreknowledge of all things?" (Alma 13:7). What if the ordinances of the endowment in the temple actually provided us with clues that reflected the isomeric structure of the universe?

It is anyone's guess if intellectual mind-games have anything to do with the presentation of the endowment, but we have been admonished to grow "in the knowledge of that which is just and true," and that out of the mouth of the Lord "cometh knowledge and understanding." (Mosiah 4:12 & Proverbs 2:6). In any event, as we sit in reverential and revelatory awe in the temple, do we ever ask ourselves these questions, or have we wondered: "Where is the center of God's universe? Is there an edge to it, and if so, what lies beyond?" Where is heaven? Where are the kingdoms of glory? Where is the spirit world? Where are the many mansions mentioned by the Savior? Where is outer darkness? How do those in one kingdom of glory move to another kingdom? What is translation? How can God immediately hear and respond to our prayers?" How can He suspend the cosmic speed limit to move instantaneously from one part of His vast kingdom to another?

These are some of the many intriguing questions relating to the Gospel that defy simple explanation, and that might be better understood within the context of higher-dimensional realities. The endowment in the temple provides us with bread crumbs of understanding, in relation to these intriguing questions. Joseph Smith once told a gathering of the Saints: "Would to God I could tell you what I know. But you would call it blasphemy." ("Joseph Smith and The Restoration," p. 522). On another occasion, he declared: "I could explain a hundred fold more than I ever have of the glories of the kingdoms manifested to me in the vision (known as Doctrine & Covenants Section 76) were I permitted, and were the people prepared to receive them." He assured the Saints "that truth, in reference to these matters, can and may be known through the revelations of God in the way of His ordinances, and in answer to prayer." (C.R., 10/9/1843, "Times and Seasons," 4:331-332).

Today, we are better prepared than ever before to explore the relationship of other-worldly dimensional realities to the Gospel Plan, and to deepen our understanding

of the innumerable powers that have been created to accomplish His mission statement. (See Moses 1:39). "For by him were all things created, that are in heaven, and that are in earth, visible and invisible, whether they be thrones, or dominions, or principalities, or powers; all things were created by him, and for him. And he is before all things, and by him all things consist." (Colossians 1:16, underlining mine). As our understanding of the physical universe expands, it could even be argued that the reconciliation between science and religion has never been more hopeful.

This much seems reasonable: If our three-dimensional universe is actually curved through a fourth physical dimension that lies outside our familiar spatial boundaries, the definitive answers to these and other equally provocative questions may lie beyond the horizon of our vision, isolated from us in that fourth dimension. Without the intervention of a higher power, these vistas might be forever inaccessible to our inquiry. The Prophet said: "The organization of the spiritual and heavenly worlds, and of spiritual and heavenly beings, was agreeable to the most perfect order and harmony (and) their limits and bounds were fixed irrevocably." (James Adams funeral sermon, "Times and Seasons," 9/15/1843, p. 331-32). Only if we subscribe to and embrace principles of eternal truth, use them as building blocks and stepping stones, turn the pieces of the puzzle over and over, examining all their permutations and combinations, and then tirelessly wrestle with eternal possibilities, will we be albe to reach satisfactory conclusions. Only then, will the more comprehensive matrix within which all mortal experience and our present reality are embedded snap into sharper focus. One of the reasons why we frequently attend the temple is so that we might experience these 'A Ha!' moments.

"The Lord's throne is in heaven," wrote the Psalmist. (Psalms 11:4). In the beginning, when God created the heaven and the earth, He made them temporally and spatially separate from each other. Their bounds and conditions were distinct. It was this stroke of genius on the part of our Father that allowed Him to manipulate the laws of physics to create a veil, as it were, so that we would forget all about our pre-mortal home in order to protect the mortal element of His Merciful Plan.

Nevertheless, we do know something about heaven, because according to the Book of Abraham's Facsimile #2, a place exists that is named Kolob, signifying the first creation, nearest to the celestial, or the residence of God. Of our relationship to that realm, William W. Phelps wrote: "No man has found pure space, nor seen the outside curtains, where nothing has a place." He clothed the matrix of the dimensional reality in which he envisioned Kolob, with these remarkable words: "There is no end to matter, space, spirit, or race, virtue, might, wisdom, or light, union, youth, priesthood, or truth, glory, love, or being." ("If You Could Hie to Kolob"). All of these things are best defined and described by bounds and conditions that are foreign to and will forever remain inaccessible to the rational mind. But the key of knowledge that would unlock our minds to expand to eternal proportion might be right before our noses, embedded within the ordinances of the temple.

Ultimately, said the Lord, "there shall be the reckoning of the time of one planet above another, until thou come nigh unto Kolob, which Kolob is after the reckoning of the Lord's time; which Kolob is set nigh unto the throne of God, to govern all those planets which belong to the same order as that upon which thou standest." (Abraham 3:9). Somehow, it is from Kolob that the order of the other creations of God is temporally and spatially governed, and from there the boundaries of heaven are established, but in such a manner that they are beyond the reach of detection by even the most sophisticated and delicately calibrated instruments utilized by terrestrial scientists. The Hubble telescope can see 13.2 billion light years into our past, almost back to the moment of creation itself at the Big Bang, but it cannot gaze into heaven for five minutes. If it could do that, we "would know more than (we) would by reading all that has ever been written on the subject." (Joseph Smith, H.C., 6:50). Especially in the case of higher temporal and spatial dimensions, of which the endowment hints, it would seem that some things need to be believed to be seen.

Isaiah confirmed that heaven and earth are spatially and temporally separate. "The heaven is my throne," the Lord revealed to him, "and the earth is my footstool."

(Isaiah 66:1). It is the Spirit, however, that has the power to carry us beyond the perceptible confines of this world to a place where boundaries become blurred, the barricade of borders disappears, and reality resonates with a clarity that is crystal-clear. As John the Revelator exclaimed when he received his apocalypse:

"Immediately I was in the spirit, and, behold, a throne was set in heaven." (Revelation 4:2). Joseph F. Smith had a similar experience, when the eyes of (his) understanding were opened, and the Spirit of the Lord rested upon (him)," and he, too, saw into the eternal world. (D&C 138:11). Normally, the veil functions as an artificial horizon that denies our senses any hint of what lies beyond. Only the Spirit generates the power to perceive what lies beyond that gossamer barrier that would otherwise isolate us from the sum and substance of reality. It is the Spirit that will answer our questions: "O God, where art thou? And where is the pavilion that covereth thy hiding place?" (D&C 121:1).

In the beginning, it was "the Gods (who) organized and formed the heavens and the earth" by defining the boundaries of the temporal universe, not to mention the eternal world. (Abraham 4:1). They did this by the power of faith. They set the conditions "by which the worlds were framed, (and) all things in heaven, on the earth, or under the earth. (These) exist by reason of faith as it existed in (the mind of the Gods). Had it not been for this principle of faith, the worlds would never have been framed, neither would man have been formed of the dust. It is this principle by which Jehovah works, and through which he exercises power over all temporal as well as eternal things." (Joseph Smith, "Lectures on Faith," #1). Perhaps this is why it is only by exercising perfect faith that we may come to an understanding of God's creations and experience His reality. (James 2:22). We call the magic of such a theophany the temple endowment. After all, it is in the House of the Lord that we are exposed to truth that "is knowledge of things as they are, and as they were, and as they are to come." (D&C 93:24).

Physics tells us that there are no privileged frames of reference. The galaxies are imbedded in time and attached to a space whose fabric is constantly expanding. If we ask where and when the creation took place, the answer is everywhere and

forever. If the universe is warped through time and space into a fourth dimension, it just might expand like a balloon, creating in every instant more space. It seems reasonable that God would utilize our everyday laws of physics to accomplish His purposes within the framework of the eternal thrones, dominions and principalities that define His higher-dimensional reality. This may explain why the Lord said to Moses: "As one earth shall pass away, and the heavens thereof, even so shall another come, and there is no end to my works." (Moses 1:38).

To understand our relationship to those who inhabit those eternal realms, it is instructive to look into a two-dimensional world that is easy to visualize because it is comfortably within our experience. We are familiar with the laws, bounds, and conditions that govern such a two-dimensional world. We visualize it as nothing more than a large, flat disk, with structures on its surface consisting of broad lines with gaps in them for entrances and exits. Trapped in the two dimensions of width and depth, inhabitants of such a world would move in only those dimensions and could perceive nothing of a third dimension (height). Without assistance, they could not move into, explain, or appreciate the perspective of the third dimension that is so familiar to us. A two-dimensional being would be at a loss for words to describe a three-dimensional experience, for there would be nothing with which to compare it. Any feeble attempts would surely be met with skepticism, disbelief, or ridicule by others. Perhaps the best that could be expected would be to declare, as did Paul, "whether in the body, or out of the body, I cannot tell." (2 Corinthians 12:3).

When we view two-dimensional space from our three-dimensional perspective, we quickly see that everything therein is open to our inspection, because there is nothing to hide 'behind.' We see every element of every object in those two-dimensions. Regardless of how many obstacles lie in the way of the beings who move about in that world, we have access to their every nook and cranny. We can even see inside two-dimensional objects, and can discern every particle therein, just as we might view every pigment on an expanse of canvas in a two-dimensional landscape portrait (which is the representation of three-dimensional objects)

hanging on a wall. In effect, we can 'enter' two-dimensional space, at will. We can pop in and out anywhere and anytime on the canvas of two-dimensional space. We can converse with beings in that two-dimensional world, and can see them as we do so, but they cannot see us. It might seem to them that our voices are coming from "above."

It is not difficult to see where this is going. By analogy, from a hyper-dimensional perspective, Heavenly Father has access to all three-dimensional space, and can view every particle of every object therein. Nothing is hidden or obscured from His view, either; for once again, from His perspective, there is nothing 'behind' which one could hide in three-dimensional space. As Jeremiah asked: "Can any hide himself in secret places that I shall not see him? Saith the Lord. Do not I fill heaven and earth?" (Jeremiah 23:24).

Because they have no 'thickness,' or depth, an infinite number of two-dimensional worlds could be 'stacked' on top of each other, like the ones and zeros of binary code on a digital video disk, but there would be absolutely no interaction between adjacent worlds. Perhaps this explains how there can be no end to the works of God. "As one earth shall pass away, and the heavens thereof, even so shall another come," in an unending succession of worlds, each oblivious to the existence of every other. (Moses 1:38).

So far, we have established basic relationships between a three-dimensional universe and the two-dimensional world layered within it. We have alluded to the possibility that our three-dimensional universe may be one of many that are nested within a four-dimensional universe. By inference, we have suggested that it might even be possible to stack an infinite number of three-dimensional worlds on top of one another within four dimensions. These would be analogous to the layers of an onion, separated by just enough space so that there could be no mutual interaction without the intervention of an omnipotent higher-dimensional power or influence. These nested universes might more accurately be described as "pluriverses," or

"multiverses." The multiverse (meta-universe, or metaverse) is the hypothetical set of multiple possible universes (including the historical universe that we experience) that together comprise everything that exists: the entirety of space, time, matter, and energy as well as the physical laws and constants that describe them. (We are reminded of those haunting lyrics of "If I Could Hie to Kolob," by William W. Phelps). The term multiverse was coined in 1895 by the American philosopher and psychologist William James. Today, we may be more familiar with the term "parallel universe" that describes a universe within a multiverse.

Think of the interaction that took place when Moses talked with Heavenly Father face to face. "The glory of God was upon Moses, therefore Moses could endure his presence" that he might better appreciate His eternal perspective. Thus prepared, he was commanded: "Look, and I will show thee the workmanship of mine hands." At the same time, however, the Lord said: "My works are without end, and also my words, for they never cease. Wherefore, no man can behold all my works, except he behold all my glory." God reminded Moses: "All things are present with me, for I know them all." (Moses 1:2-6). But to be aware of all things and to experience them as a present reality, Moses needed to receive the tangible element of the Spirit of God.

It was while he was under the influence of that spiritual element that Moses beheld "many lands, and each land was called earth, and there were inhabitants on the face thereof." We do not know if these were earths in parallel dimensions, or if they were temporal and spatial realities stacked up like so many pages in a book. We do knows that the Lord told Moses: "Worlds without number have I created ... for behold, there are many worlds that have passed away by the word of my power. And there are many that now stand, and innumerable are they unto man; but all things are numbered unto me, for they are mine, and I know them." (Moses 1:29, 33 & 35).

"When I consider the heavens," wrote David, "the work of thy fingers, the moon, and the stars, which thou hast ordained; What is man, that thou art mindful of him, and the son of man, that thou visitest him? For thou has made him a little

lower than the angels." (Psalms 8:3-5). Perhaps we are lower than the angels in a physical, as well as in a spiritual, sense. Perhaps their natural abode is within a higher dimensional reality. Perhaps the work of His fingers, even the moon and the stars, is ordained to exist in a reality that is simply beyond our comprehension. But there will come a day when "he shall reveal all things – Things which have passed, and hidden things which no man knew, things of the earth by which it was made, and the purpose and the end thereof – Things most precious, things that are above, and things that are beneath, things that are in the earth, and upon the earth, and in heaven." (D&C 101:32-34).

For now, our poor lenses are incapable of discerning what is really there. "No man hath seen God at any time in the flesh, except quickened by the Spirit of God?" (J.S.T. John 1:18). If it is true that "the light of the body is the eye," then, when the eye is single to faith, our "whole body shall be full of light." (3 Nephi 13:22). On one occasion after having received revelation, Joseph Smith confirmed the reality of that promise, and declared: "My whole body was full of light, and I could see even out at the ends of my fingers and toes." (N.B. Lundwall, "The Vision," p. 11). This may be why the angel Moroni hovered in the air during his visits to Joseph in his bedchamber, and why his hands and his feet were naked. (See J.S.H. 1:31). He could 'see' with every part of his body. Every child of God potentially possesses this gift, and the Lord has promised that it only waits to be revealed. "If your eye be single to my glory," He said, "your whole bodies shall be filled with light, and there shall be no darkness in you; and that body which is filled with light comprehendeth all things." (D&C 88:67). There will come for each of us a day when "the sun shall no more go down; neither shall (the) moon withdraw itself: for the Lord shall be (our) everlasting light." (Isaiah 60:20). Perhaps this is one of the things we need to ponder, as we are awash in the Spirit, in the House of the Lord.

Orson Pratt appreciated the ramifications of the truth that celestial beings have the ability to perceive with all parts of their bodies. "The spirit," he said, "is inherently capable of experiencing the sensations of light. I think we could then see in different directions at once. Instead of looking in one particular direction, we

could then look all around us, at the same instant." (J.D., 2:238-248).

When each of us comes face to face with eternity, as we surely will, the spiritual element in which we are immersed will transform our mortal clay. Beforehand, while we tarry on the earth, we might ask under what circumstances does that element quicken us, and how can the pure knowledge that flows out of it be vitalized? "A man's wisdom maketh his face to shine, and the boldness of his face shall be changed." (Ecclesiastes 8:1). When we are at one with God, when we have spiritually been born of Him and have internalized His divine nature, we will receive His image in our countenances. (Alma 5:14). That image and His likeness will bridge the barriers of time and space to leave indelible marks as reminders of our noble birthright. Our genetic code will be transformed as the expression of an endowment of unearthly powers.

Abinadi's "face shone with exceeding luster, even as Moses' did while on the mount of Sinai, while speaking with the Lord." (Mosiah 13:5, see Exodus 34:29). The features of Lehi and Nephi "did shine exceedingly, even as the faces of angels." (Helaman 5:36). Interestingly, to witnesses, it seemed "that they did lift their eyes to heaven; and they were in the attitude as if talking or lifting their voices to some being whom they beheld" from the unseen world. (Helaman 5:36). These observers were prompted to ask: "Who is it with whom these men do converse?" The answer could have been: "They do converse with the angels of God," who reside within the unseen world of a dimensionally superior reality. (Helaman 5:38-39).

Bathed in the glory of the Lord, Moses stood "in the presence of God, and talked with him face to face." (Moses 1:31). From that perspective, he was able to see "the inhabitants (of the earth), and there was not a soul which he beheld not; and he discerned them by the Spirit of God." (Moses 1:28). Clearly, "the Lord seeth not as man seeth; for man looketh on the outward appearance," while the Lord focuses on that inner vessel which is beyond the capacity of the five physical senses to detect. (1 Samuel 16:7). Thus, He is able to say: "I can stretch forth mine hands and hold all the creations which I have made; and mine eye can pierce them also." (Moses

7:36). We all live "under the glance of the piercing eye of the Almighty God." (Jacob 2:10). His voice "is unto all men, and there is none to escape and there is no eye that shall not see, neither ear that shall not hear, neither heart that shall not be penetrated." (D&C 1:2). As Jacob said: "He can pierce you, and with one glance of his eye he can smite you to the dust!" (Jacob 2:15). Looking at it this way clothes the endowment in new meaning and illuminates our understanding: "For the word of God is quick, and powerful, and sharper than any two-edged sword, piercing even to the dividing asunder of soul and spirit, and of the joints and marrow, and is a discerner of the thoughts and intents of the heart." (Hebrews 4:12). The Apostle John described his interaction with the heavens by writing: "I looked, and behold, a door was opened in heaven, and the first voice which I heard was, as it were, of a trumpet talking with me." (Revelation 34:1). We sometimes feel the same, as our worship in the temple comes to its climax at the veil.

Mormon said: "The day soon cometh that your mortal must put on immortality, and these bodies which are now moldering in corruption must soon become incorruptible bodies." (Mormon 6:21). This may be accomplished as our Heavenly Father carries us into the greater revelatory light of His higher dimensional, or eternal, reality in the House of the Lord. Just as an ultraviolet light is used in sterilization, (ultraviolet germicidal irradiation - UVGI), could it be that it is the physical phenomenon of the unearthly light intrinsic to God that purifies and renews our sin-stained souls? "Though your sins be as scarlet," Isaiah promised, "they shall be as white as snow; though they be red like crimson, they shall be as wool." (Isaiah 1:18).

If no unclean thing can enter the presence of God, it may be that it is the temporal and spatial transformation that takes place at the time of our resurrection that carries us from corruption to incorruption. Think of Paul's description: "There are also celestial bodies, and bodies terrestrial: but the glory of the celestial is one, and the glory of the terrestrial is another. There is one glory of the sun, and another glory of the moon, and another glory of the stars: for one star differeth from another in glory. So also is the resurrection of the dead. It is

sown in corruption; it is raised in incorruption. ... It is sown a natural body, (but) it is raised a spiritual body." (1 Corinthians 15:40-44).

Maybe nothing really ever dies, and we are simply brought into the greater light of day after the spirit leaves our mortal clay. As Mormon explained: "The day soon cometh that your mortal must put on immortality, and these bodies which are now moldering in corruption must soon become incorruptible bodies." (Mormon 6:21). Maybe from the time of the formation of the world, when the light was divided from the darkness, it was always a question of dimension, and not just of time and place. "God saw the light" when the world was created, "and that light was good." (Moses 2:4)

Perhaps we receive unanticipated and unappreciated assistance from beings existing in higher temporal and spatial dimensions, even though we may be unaware of their close proximity, ready availability, and potentially protective influence. In the Old Testament, we read that when Elisha's servant "was risen early, and (had) gone forth, behold, an host compassed the city both with horses and chariots. And his servant said unto him, Alas, my master, how shall we do? And he answered, Fear not: for they that be with us are more than they that be with them. And Elisha prayed, and said, Lord, I pray thee, open his eyes, that he may see. And the Lord opened the eyes of the young man; and he saw: and, behold, the mountain was full of horses and chariots of fire round about Elisha." (2 Kings 6:15-17). They had been there the whole time, but it was only the prophet Elisha who had been aware of their presence. It was only when the Lord touched the eyes of the young man's understanding that he, too, was able to see what had always been there. Certainly, there is more to the office of the prophet, seer, and revelator than superficially meets the eye. Joseph Smith wrote of his revelatory experiences: "The Lord touched the eyes of our understandings and they were opened, and the glory of the Lord shone round about." (D&C 76:19).

In a related incident, after an angel announced to shepherds tending their flocks by night in the fields near Bethlehem that Christ the Lord had been born,

"suddenly there was with the angel a multitude of the heavenly host praising God." (Luke 2:13). This abrupt manifestation of numerous beings from the unseen world prompted the shepherds to hurry to Bethlehem to see the things that had come to pass that the Lord had made known unto them. (See Luke 2:15).

When the Apostles were gathered together with members of the Church on the Day of Pentecost, "they were all with one accord in one place." The introduction of the Holy Ghost from the unseen world was accompanied by "a sound from heaven as of a rushing mighty wind, and it filled all the house where they were sitting." Accompanying His appearance, "there appeared unto them cloven tongues like as of fire, and it sat upon each of them." Its manifestation was so dramatic that "they were all filled ... and began to speak with other tongues as the Spirit gave them utterance." (Acts 2:1-3).

On the Mount of Transfiguration, the Apostles Peter, James, and John had an otherworldly experience. Jesus led them up "into an high mountain apart by themselves, and he was transfigured before them. And his raiment became shining, exceeding white as snow, so as no fuller on earth can white them. And there appeared unto them Elias with Moses: and they were talking with Jesus ... And there was a cloud that overshadowed them. And a voice came out of the cloud, saying, This is my beloved Son: hear him. And suddenly, when they had looked round about, they saw no man any more, save Jesus only with themselves." (Mark 9:2-8).

Perhaps, in the scriptures, we should be alert to the use of the word "suddenly," for it often seems to presage a higher-dimensional experience. (The word "suddenly" is found 48 times in the Standard Works). For example, the Lord said: "I am Jesus Christ, the Son of God; wherefore, gird up your loins and I will suddenly come to my temple." (D&C 36:8, see Malachi 3:1, Numbers 12:4, J.S.H. 1:44, & 3 Nephi 24:1). Our awakening appreciation of the epistemological reality of higher dimensions allows us to more easily understand how He could do so. "For I am the Lord thy God; I dwell in heaven; the earth is my footstool; I stretch my hand over the sea, and it obeys my voice; I cause the wind and the fire to be my chariot; I say to the mountains — Depart hence — and behold, they are taken away by a whirlwind, in an

instant, suddenly." (Abraham 2:7).

There exists a possibility regarding planes of existence, that has been raised by Carl Sagan. It is not specifically suggested by scripture, and no Church authority has strongly advocated its plausibility. And yet it is "an idea, strange, haunting, evocative, one of the most exquisite conjectures in science or religion. It is entirely undemonstrated, and it may never be proven. But it stirs the blood. There is, we are told, an infinite hierarchy of universes, so that an elementary particle, such as an electron, in our universe, would, if penetrated, reveal itself to be an entire closed universe. Within it, organized into the local equivalent of galaxies and smaller structures, are an immense number of other, much tinier elementary particles, which are themselves universes at the next level, and so on forever, an infinite downward regression, universes within universes, endlessly. And upward as well. Our familiar universe of galaxies and stars, planets and people, would be a single elementary particle in the next universe up, the first step of another infinite progression. This is the only religious idea I know that surpasses the endless number of infinitely old cycling universes in Hindu cosmology. What would those other universes be like? To enter them, we would somehow have to penetrate a fourth physical dimension ... Poised at the edge of forever, we would jump off" into life's ultimate incredible journey. ("Cosmos," p. 262-267).

Wherever, whenever, and however we fit into the cosmos, we know this: God quickens life in the sense that He provides our spirits with an animated physical world within which we freely interact; He "lends (us) breath, that (we) may live and move and do according to (our) own will, and (He supports us) from one moment to another." (Mosiah 2:21). But, at the same time, we are cautioned that our world is only a shadow of that which is to come, and without the endowment, we cannot expect to understand it at anywhere near God's level of comprehension. As Paul wrote: "For now we see through a glass, darkly; but then face to face: now I know in part; but then shall I know even as also I am known." (1 Corinthians 13:12).

"My thoughts are not your thoughts," said the Lord, "neither are your ways my ways

... For as the heavens are higher than the earth, so are my ways higher than your ways, and my thoughts than your thoughts." (Isaiah 55:8-9). His thoughts are loftier, broader, more visionary, and infinitely more expansive. His ways circumscribe the sum of our reality and encompass more than we have ever dared to dream. But, in the temple, we are treated to a glimpse of how Heavenly Father views the world in which we live. We can warm our hands before the fire of faith, and the distant glow on the eastern horizon presages our awakening spiritual comprehension.

Our own feeble attempts to describe His reality utilize abstractions, for thoughts cannot be shaped, nor words formed, nor sentences framed that could accurately capture His glory. Figures of speech are employed because we would otherwise be at a complete loss for words when grasping for even a basic explanation of these most profound metaphysical realities. To Moses, "the presence of the Lord appeared (as) a flame of fire out of the midst of a bush. And he looked, and, behold, the bush burned with fire, and the bush was not consumed." (J.S.T. Exodus 3:2). That fire on Sinai burned all the way to "the midst of heaven" itself. (Deuteronomy 4:11). Those who witnessed this manifestation thought they could see through a brilliant conduit, as it were, right into heaven itself. (See Deuteronomy 4:12).

Joseph Smith said: "Spirits can only be revealed in flaming fire and glory." (C.R., 10/9/1843, "Times & Seasons," 4:331-332). Paul wrote that God can be best described as "a consuming fire" in the sense that His hyper-dimensional Presence, His glory, is akin to fire and smoke and everlasting burnings. (Hebrews 12:29 & Deuteronomy 4:24). When He reveals Himself in our corruptible reality, or when He unveils the heavens and His glory fills the earth, the elements of our three-dimensional world will melt, mountains will flow like rivers, valleys will be exalted, and rough places will be made smooth. (See D&C 109:74).

When Elijah did nothing more than simply converse with the Lord, that experience was so overwhelming that "a great and strong wind rent the mountains, and brake in pieces the rocks before the Lord ... and after the wind an earthquake ... and after the earthquake a fire." (1 Kings 19:11-12). The Lord's Presence was manifest by these

three representations of the dramatic forces of nature. The Second Coming of The Lord will be similarly powerful insomuch that the Mount of Olives will be rent in twain, and later the whole earth will come together into one landmass, as it was in the days before Peleg (See Genesis 10:25, D&C 133:24, & the 10th Article of Faith).

When Nephi and his brother Lehi were incarcerated by their enemies, they heard a voice "as it were above the cloud of darkness" that envelops them, and they "beheld that it was not a voice of thunder, neither was it a voice of a great tumultuous noise, but behold, it was a still voice of perfect mildness, as if it had been a whisper (and yet) it did pierce even to the very soul." (Helaman 5:29-30). If this voice came from a higher dimension that envelops our world, no wonder that "notwithstanding the mildness of the voice, behold the earth shook exceedingly, and the walls of the prison trembled again, as if it were about to tumble to the earth." The natural order of their temporal and spatial reality was disrupted by the interjection of the voice of the Lord from another dimension in time and space. Evidently, God's Presence caused a rift, manifest to Nephi and Lehi as a disruption in the order of nature, so that when the voice did come, it spoke "unto them marvelous words which cannot be uttered." (Helaman 5:31 & 33).

In the Sacred Grove, Joseph Smith witnessed "a pillar of light exactly over (his) head, above the brightness of the sun, which descended gradually" until it fell upon him. (J.S.H. 1:16). Latter-day Saints are so familiar with this description of the appearance of Heavenly beings from other temporal and spatial dimensions that they characteristically overlook the unusual language Joseph Smith employed to describe the event. It was not just a light that flashed on, but it was a veritable "pillar of light," or a column with distinct borders.

Stranger still was the fact that the light "descended gradually," entering the quiet grove slowly enough that Joseph was able to gauge the rapidity of its approach until it finally reached him and enveloped him within its dazzling brilliance. It was only then that he "saw two Personages, whose brightness and glory (defied) all description." (J.S.H. 1:17). They were somehow standing in the air above him, within the encircling light. Finally, he heard a confirming voice speak peace, not only

to his ears, but to his very soul as well: "This is my Beloved Son. Hear Him!" (J.S.H. 1:17).

The New Testament tells us that when Jesus was transfigured before Peter, James, and John, "his face did shine as the sun, and his raiment was white as the light." (Matthew 17:2). In the Old Testament, we read that when Elijah was translated, "there appeared a chariot of fire, and horses of fire ... and Elijah went up by a whirlwind into heaven," there to witness unspeakable things within eternal realms. (2 Kings 2:11). We immediately think of Moroni's temporal and spatial transference, when the boy Joseph "saw, as it were, a conduit open right up into heaven, and (he saw the angel, who) ascended till he entirely disappeared." (J.S.H. 1:43). If there is a process by which mortals may move between dimensional realities, these scriptural accounts may provide our best descriptions of the mechanism by which it is accomplished.

"Who among us shall dwell with the devouring fire?" asked Isaiah. "Who among us shall dwell with everlasting burnings?" What qualifies us to experience the far journey from our present three-dimensional reality to the higher-dimensional eternal world? Isaiah answered his own question: "He that walketh righteously, and speaketh uprightly; he that despiseth the gain of oppressions, that shaketh his hands from holding of bribes, that stoppeth his ears from hearing of blood, and shutteth his eyes from seeing evil. He shall dwell on high. (His eyes) shall behold the land that is very far off" in the higher-dimensional world that is the habitation of the Gods. (Isaiah 34:14-17).

That "land unpromised and unearned is a realm of spirit." Even as we dwell upon the earth, we can still appreciate that "it is the realm of sensory delight; of fragrance, sound, and form and color. It is the realm of human associations; of gratitude, loyalty, and appreciation, of selflessness, helpfulness and forgiveness, of friendship, love and compassion. It is the realm of human growth and transcendence and of truth discovered and accepted, of beauty created and enjoyed, of goodness deepened and made manifest in life. Most of us are more at home, more at ease, in the world of things, in the world of getting and spending. So when conflicts arise between our spiritual and our material worlds,

as they inevitably do, it is usually our spiritual world that suffers," and we end up retreating into the comfort zone of our familiar temporal and spatial reality. (P.A. Christensen, "The Realm of Spirit: A Land Unpromised and Unearned," B.Y.U. Studies, 16:1).

The temple endowment promises that we may conform our lives to the character of God, to enjoy that realm of spirit as our natural environment. As we do so, we will understand that it is more vibrantly real than anything we have ever known. Our preparation for that experience includes dress rehearsals at the veil of the temple. In the meantime, we must beware, lest we strangle ourselves with illusions of reality, and with "things whose opacity obstructs our ability to see what is really there." (Gretel Erlich, "Under Wyoming's Skies," The Atlantic Magazine).

To those who are prepared, however, the Lord "will shew wonders in the heavens and in the earth, blood, and fire and pillars of smoke." (Joel 2:30). When He revealed Himself to the prophet Isaiah, presaged perhaps by three distinct knocks at the door, so powerful was the manifestation that its posts "moved at the voice of him that cried, and the house was filled with smoke. Then (Isaiah) said, Woe is me! For I am undone." (Isaiah 6:4-5). His physical frame could barely tolerate the presence of God. Even "the still small voice," wrote Joseph Smith, "whispereth through and pierceth all things, and often times it maketh my bones to quake while it maketh manifest." (D&C 85:6).

The introduction into the world of higher temporal and spatial dimensional influences is disruptive to the status quo. When Belshazzar beheld no more than the fingers of a man's hand that wrote upon the wall of the palace, his "countenance was changed, and his thoughts troubled him, so that the joints of his loins were loosed, and his knees smote one against another." (Daniel 5:5-6).

Philo Dibble was an eyewitness to the powerful influence of the Spirit upon Joseph Smith and Sydney Rigdon when they received the Vision that has been preserved in Doctrine & Covenants Section 76. He recorded in his journal: "Joseph sat firmly and calmly, all the time in the midst of a magnificent glory, but Sydney sat limp and

pale, apparently as limber as a rag. Observing which, Joseph remarked, smilingly, "Sydney is not used to it as I am." ("Juvenile Instructor," 5/1892, p. 303-304).

The Psalmist described conditions on an occasion when the Lord introduced

Himself into the everyday world: "Fire goeth before (Him), and burneth up his enemies round about. His lightnings enlightened the world: the earth saw, and trembled. The hills melted like wax at the presence of the Lord of the whole earth." (Psalms 97:3-5). As Mormon observed: "The dust of the earth moveth hither and thither, to the dividing asunder, at the command of our great and everlasting God. Yea, behold, at his voice do the hills and the mountains tremble and quake. And by the power of his voice, they are broken up, and become smooth, yea, even like unto a valley. Yea, by the power of his voice, doth the whole earth shake; Yea, by the power of his voice, do the foundations rock, even to the very center. Yea, and if he say unto the earth – Move – it is moved. Yea, if he say unto the earth – Thou shalt go back, that it lengthen out the day for many hours – it is done." (Helaman 12:8-14). In this way, the power of God is manifest. It may not be so much that He commands the earth to tremble, but rather that His influence from a higher dimensional reality causes the anatomic structure of our world to rock to the very center as it struggles to bring itself into harmony with a nature that observes laws that are superior to our own. In fact, in the day that the Lord comes as a thief in the night, "the heavens shall pass away with a great noise, and the elements shall melt with fervent heat, (and) the earth also and the works that are therein shall be burned up." (2 Peter 3:10).

In the meantime, those who have harnessed the awesome authority of the Melchizedek Priesthood, will "have power, by faith, to break mountains, to divide the seas, to dry up waters, to turn them out of their course; to put at defiance the armies of nations, to divide the earth, to break every band, to stand in the presence of God, to do all things according to his will, according to his command, subdue principalities and powers; and this by the will of the Son of God which was from before the foundation of the world. And men having this faith, coming up unto this order of God, were translated and taken up into heaven." (Genesis 14:30-32). It is

God, after all, Who "hath given a law unto all things, by which they move in their times and their seasons," and it is He Who sets the bounds and conditions of every temporal and spatial dimension. (D&C 88:42). He is the Lord Omnipotent. We can

know Him on the terms He has established, or we can know Him not at all. But let us never forget that the ordinances of the temple can be our key to theology.

Footnotes & Resources:

BYU Studies, Autumn 1975
"A Land Unpromised and Unearned"
P.A. Anderson

NOVA, 3/3/1981
"Beyond The Milky Way"

NOVA 1979
"Einstein" p. 18

"Flatland"
Edwin Abbott

"Cosmos" p. 262-267
Carl Sagan

BYU Speeches of The Year, 1974, p. 1889
"Hello in There"
Lael Woodbury

B.Y.U. Studies 20:3
"Higher Dimensional Realities"
Robert P. Burton & Bruce F. Webster

"Key to The Science of Theology"
Parley P. Pratt

1979 Devotional Speeches of The Year
"Patience"
Neal A. Maxwell

Ensign, 6/1980
"The Cheering Section"
Paul H. Dunn

Journal of Discourses 2:238-248
"The Increased Powers of Faculties of Mind in a Future State"
Orson Pratt

BYU Studies, 16:1
"The Realm of Spirit: A Land Unpromised and Unearned"
P.A. Christensen

Nibley on The Timely and Timeless, p. 263-264
"Zeal Without Knowledge"
Hugh Nibley

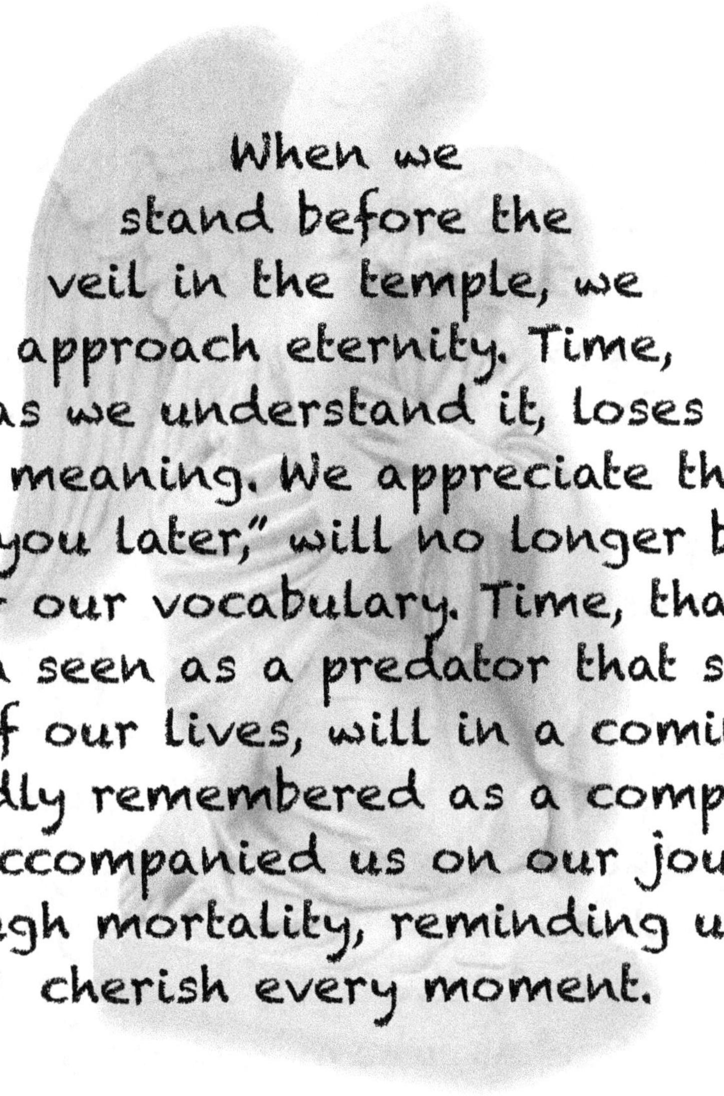

When we
stand before the
veil in the temple, we
approach eternity. Time,
as we understand it, loses
all meaning. We appreciate that
"See you later," will no longer be a
part of our vocabulary. Time, that was
so often seen as a predator that stalked
us all of our lives, will in a coming day
be fondly remembered as a companion
that accompanied us on our journey
through mortality, reminding us to
cherish every moment.

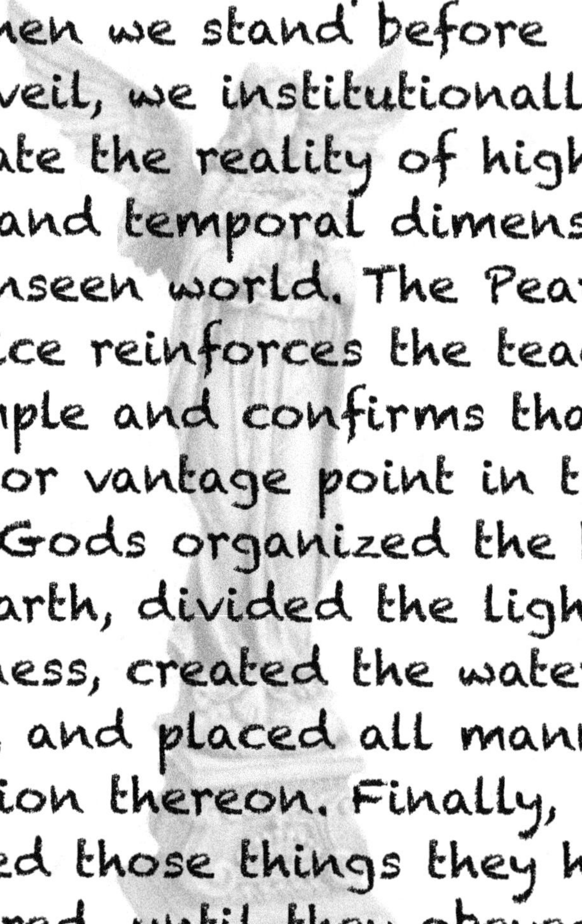

In the temple,
when we stand before
the veil, we institutionally
validate the reality of higher
spatial and temporal dimensions
in an unseen world. The Pearl of
Great Price reinforces the teachings
of the temple and confirms that from
their superior vantage point in time and
space, the Gods organized the heavens
and the earth, divided the light from
the darkness, created the waters and
the earth, and placed all manner of
vegetation thereon. Finally, they
watched those things they had
ordered, until they obeyed.
(See Abraham 4:1-18).

Chapter Three
A glimpse of heaven

During the mortal ministry of the Savior, all that could be known of His Father was His representation that was personified by His Son. Of Him, Jesus told His disciples: "Ye have neither heard his voice at any time, nor seen his shape." (John 5:37). But then He told Philip: "He that hath seen me hath seen the Father." (John 14:9). The Greeks of Paul's day were not too far from the mark when they erected an "altar with this inscription, To The Unknown God." (Acts 17:23). It is the perspective that is clarified by the temple endowment that helps us to fathom His nature.

We know by the description provided by John the Revelator that His figure is striking: "His head and his hairs were white like wool, as white as snow; and his eyes were as a flame of fire; and his feet like unto fine brass, as if they burned in a furnace; and his voice as the sound of many waters." (Revelation 1:14-15). Joseph Smith said: "Under his feet was a paved work of pure gold, in color like amber. His eyes were as a flame of fire; the hair of his head was white like the pure snow; his

countenance shone above the brightness of the sun; and his voice was as the sound of the rushing of great waters." (D&C 110:2-3).

In Sinai, the Children of Israel saw God, "and there was under his feet as it were a paved work of a sapphire stone, and as it were the body of heaven in his clearness ... And the sight of the glory of the Lord was like devouring fire on the top of the mount in the eyes of the children of Israel." (Exodus 24:9 & 17). The Three Witnesses of The Book of Mormon were also given powerful manifestations of His Presence, that it was "clear as the moon, and fair as the sun, and terrible as an army with banners." (D&C 5:12-14).

Following the destruction in Zarahemla at the time of the crucifixion, through the veil "there was a voice heard among all the inhabitants of the earth, upon all the face of this land." (3 Nephi 9:1). It was not the deafening voice of a hundred decibels, but simply a quiet sound heard by everyone regardless of their surroundings. It was a voice unlike any sound that had ever before been heard, for it came from immortal lips with an effect upon both heaven and earth that was profound.

The promise was fulfilled, that when the Lord should utter his voice, "the heavens (would) shake and the earth (would) tremble, and the trump of God (would) sound both long and loud." (D&C 43:18). To Joel, the Lord revealed that He would "roar out of Zion, and utter his voice from Jerusalem, and the heavens and the earth (would) shake, (and) the sun and the moon (would) be dark, and the stars (would) withdraw their shining, (for) the day of the Lord (would be) great and very terrible, and who (would be able to) abide it?" (Joel 3:16, 2:10 & 12).

But following the crucifixion, order throughout Zarahemla was so disjointed that "there was thick darkness upon all the face of the land, insomuch that the inhabitants thereof who had not fallen" during the destruction at the time of the crucifixion could actually "feel the vapor of darkness. And there could be no light, because of the darkness, neither candles, neither torches; neither could there be fire kindled with their fine and exceedingly dry wood, so that there could not be

any light at all. And there was not any light seen, neither fire, nor glimmer, neither the sun, nor the moon, nor the stars, for so great were the mists of darkness which were upon the face of the land. And it came to pass that it did last for the space of three days that there was no light seen." (3 Nephi 8:20-23).

There had been such a distortion in the fabric of space, that "the face of the whole earth became deformed." (3 Nephi 8:17). During the three hours of destruction following the crucifixion, "it was said by some that the time was greater," so disoriented were the people by the related temporal disturbances. (3 Nephi 8:19). The Spirit of Christ had been withdrawn, at least locally; thus, "there could not be any light at all." (2 Nephi 8:21). Truly, "the Spirit (which) giveth light to every man that cometh into the world," the Light of Christ itself, had been withheld, and its influence had been temporarily suspended. (D&C 84:46).

Zarahemla had been moved out of its place into a netherworld, as it were, to an unstable limbo, an indeterminate state somewhere outside the familiar boundaries of the land. Perhaps the Lord, who had established the laws and conditions by which the earth existed, was so intent on accomplishing the final details of the Atonement on the cross and in the tomb that His preoccupation momentarily compromised the divine concentration that would normally have held the elements cohesively together. Perhaps this had been His design from the beginning.

In any event, there was a tangible element, a palpable feeling that could only be described by those who experienced it as "a vapor of darkness." As soon as it "dispersed from off the face of the land" when the Lord again turned His attention to the earth, it "did cease to tremble, and the rocks did cease to rend, and the dreadful groanings did cease, and all the tumultuous noises did pass away, and the earth did cleave together again," as the fabric of a world that had been torn apart once again settled into order. (3 Nephi 10:9-10). Normality had been re-established, at least for the time being, although the whole face of the land had been changed. (See 3 Nephi 8:12).

Then, from no particular direction, the inhabitants of Zarahemla "heard a voice as

if it came out of heaven; and they cast their eyes round about, for they understood not the voice which they heard; and it was not a harsh voice, neither was it a loud voice; nevertheless, and notwithstanding it being a small voice it did pierce them that they did hear to the center, insomuch that there was no part of their frame that it did not cause to quake; yea, it did pierce them to the very soul, and did cause their hearts to burn." (3 Nephi 11:3).

Elijah had a similar experience, when "the Lord passed by, and a great and strong wind rent the mountains, and brake in pieces the rocks before the Lord; but the Lord was not in the wind: and after the wind an earthquake; but the Lord was not in the earthquake: And after the earthquake a fire; but the Lord was not in the fire: and after the fire a still small voice." (1 Kings 19:11).

The Psalmist wrote of those who "reel to and fro, and stagger like a drunken man, and are at their wits' end." (Psalms 107:27). Daniel described King Shalmaneser, whose "thoughts troubled him, so that the joints of his loins were loosed, and his knees smote one against another." (Daniel 5:6). When we are well-grounded in neither the physical world nor in eternity, we lose our physical, emotional, mental, and spiritual co-ordination. The neural synapses within our central nervous systems fire sporadically, and we interact with our environment erratically, inappropriately, ineffectively, and without synchronization.

From whence do these voices come? The scriptures may suggest a source that is natural to God but unfamiliar to us. Following the baptism of the Savior, Matthew recorded: "And Jesus ... went up straightway out of the water: and, lo, the heavens were opened unto him, and he saw the Spirit of God descending like a dove, and lighting upon him. And lo a voice from heaven," that all who were present could hear, "saying, This is my beloved Son, in whom I am well pleased." (Matthew 3:16-17, underlining mine).

Whether or not others that were present at His baptism experienced the manifestation is unclear. Suffice to say that the Mortal Messiah Himself had a veil experience at

the time of His baptism, to which those who participate in the temple endowment may relate. Matthew might just as easily have recorded that "Jesus saw, as it were, a conduit open right up into heaven, and the Holy Ghost descended till he entirely appeared, manifesting Himself by the sign of the dove." (See J.S.H. 2:30).

When Saul was journeying to Damascus with the intention of persecuting the Saints, "suddenly there shined round about him a light from heaven. And he fell to the earth, and heard a voice saying unto him, Saul, Saul, why persecutest thou me? ... And he trembling and astonished said, Lord, what wilt thou have me to do? ... And the men which journeyed with him stood speechless, hearing a voice, but seeing no man." (Acts 9:3-7).

Zion is also susceptible to influences from beyond the veil. Its inhabitants enjoy peace and rest from the cares of the world that greatly enhances their power to preach the Gospel, bring souls unto Christ, and build the kingdom of God. It was in this state that "Enoch beheld angels descending out of heaven, bearing testimony of the Father and Son; and the Holy Ghost fell on many, and they were caught up by the powers of heaven" through a portal that connected them to "Zion." (Moses 7:27). Enoch and the inhabitants of his city became the prototype for all who would be removed from the earth by the phenomenon of translation to another dimension. It has not been revealed where they go, how they get there, how long they stay, or if their transference is stable.

Recently, terrestrial scientists have conjectured that conventional travel from one part of our universe to another seems to be out of the question, because of the limitations established by the cosmic speed limit, that is to say, nothing can move faster than the speed of light. Alternatively, could it be that translated beings simply have a change wrought upon their bodies giving them the capability to move at will both temporally and spatially between dimensions in the physical and eternal worlds that are sandwiched on top of each other?

Perhaps only millennial man will be able to make the transition back and forth from our every-day world to dimensionally superior realms while yet in the

flesh, for they "will live in a state akin to translation." (Bruce R. McConkie, "The Millennial Messiah," p. 644). During the Millennium, the relationship between the eternal world and ours may be so well-defined and stabilized that these transitions will be much more frequently, predictably, and easily accomplished.

At the Second Coming, all the Saints will experience spatial transference when they are "caught up together ... in the clouds, to meet the Lord in the air." (1 Thessalonians 4:17). When we leave this mortal clay, "we shall all be changed, in a moment, in the twinkling of an eye" enabling us to enjoy God's reality as our natural states of being. (1 Corinthians 15:51-52).

Even now, we are occasionally privileged to see beyond our mortal horizons. We even have a name for these states of being, calling them "the depths of eternity." The promise is that we "shall inherit thrones, kingdoms, principalities, and powers, (and) dominions, (of) all heights and depths." (D&C 132:19). The question is: In what direction will these "heights and depths" take us? We have determined that we cannot reach them by going to the left, or to the right, and certainly not by going forward or backward, or up or down. Perhaps we can only reach them by going simultaneously at right angles to every one of those directions. When John looked with the eye of faith into those heights and depths, he saw a door "opened in ("into" in the J.S.T.) heaven: and the first voice which (he) heard was as it were of a trumpet talking with (him); which said, Come up hither, and I will shew thee things which must be hereafter. And immediately (he) was in the spirit: and, behold, a throne was set in heaven, and one sat on the throne. And he that sat was to look upon like a jasper ... and there was a rainbow round about the throne, in sight like unto an emerald." (Revelation 4:1-3).

John had been taken from his mortal surroundings into the presence of God, into the "depths of eternity," into the "hereafter," if you will. He was somehow, at the same, time both "here" and "after," which although vague, is about as specific as we can get when referring to eternity. Thus, John described what he both saw and heard, not only as a trumpet speaking to him, but also as "lightnings and thunderings and voices." (Revelation 4:5). To Joseph Smith, the voice of the Great Jehovah struck a

similar chord; it was "as the sound of the rushing of great waters." (D&C 110:3).

In the scriptures there have been a number of well-documented 'closed room' visitations by beings from the unseen world. For example, when the Apostles were gathered together shortly after Christ's death, the doors had been "shut where the disciples assembled for fear of the Jews. (Then) came Jesus and stood in their midst." (John 20:19). Because 'the doors were shut,' such an abrupt manifestation of His tangible presence can be explained only if He came into the room from another dimension. Another 'closed room' event occurred as the resurrected Lord walked to Emmaus. (See Luke 24:13-32). After stopping for the evening with two fellow travelers, they recognized the Savior as He blessed the meal, after which He abruptly disappeared from the closed room. "And it came to pass, while he blessed them, he was parted from them, and carried up into heaven." (Luke 24:51).

When Zacharias was alone in the temple, there suddenly "appeared unto him an angel of the Lord standing on the right side of the altar of incense. And when Zacharias saw him, he was troubled, and fear fell upon him." (Luke 1:11-12). After delivering his message, the angel explained that he was "Gabriel, that (stood) in the presence of God," and that he was sent to speak unto Zacharias, and to show him glad tidings." (Luke 1:19).

With the Sons of Mosiah, Alma the Younger witnessed the appearance of an angel who "descended as it were in a cloud; and he spake as it were with a voice of thunder, which caused the earth to shake upon which they stood." (Mosiah 27:11, underlining mine). He asked Alma: "Can ye dispute the power of God? For behold, doth not my voice shake the earth? And can ye not also behold me before you?" Lest there be any confusion regarding where he had come from, he declared: "I am sent from God." (Mosiah 27:15). "These were the last words which the angel spake unto Alma, and he departed. And now Alma and those that were with him fell again to the earth ... for with their own eyes they had beheld an angel of the Lord; and his voice was as thunder, which shook the earth; and they knew that there was nothing save the power of God that could shake the earth and cause it to tremble as

though it would part asunder." (Mosiah 27:17-18).

A little bit closer to home, three times in one night, the angel Moroni visited the boy Joseph Smith's chamber. Without reservation or apology, Joseph provided in his history perhaps the most detailed description of the appearance of a being from the unseen world: "I discovered a light appearing in my room," he wrote, "which continued to increase until the room was lighter than at noonday, when immediately a personage appeared at my bedside, standing in the air, for his feet did not touch the floor ... The room was exceedingly light, but (strangely) not so very bright as immediately around his person ... After this communication, I saw the light in the room begin to gather immediately around the person of him who had been speaking to me, and it continued to do so until the room was again left dark, except just around him; when, instantly, I saw, as it were, a conduit open right up into heaven, and he ascended till he entirely disappeared, and the room was left as it had been before this heavenly light had made its appearance." (J.S.H. 2:30, 32 & 43, underlining mine).

In that era without electricity, and long before the wonders of Industrial Light and Magic, Computer Generated Imagery (CGI), and green screens, Joseph Smith witnessed his closed chamber gradually flooding with blinding light, followed immediately by the appearance of an angel within an even brighter part of the room. That light later gathered around the angel as the rest of the room went dark. It defies logic and the laws of physics to suggest that a room would at first go dark only in the peripheries, and then gradually around some central object, until the light finally winked out! We can digitally recreate such a scenario, but we cannot duplicate it in the real world. When we flip an electric switch, the result is instantaneous and uniform. If we think of an angel coming from the glory of God in an adjacent dimensionally superior realm, however, it is easier to conceptualize how the light might have first appeared and then disappeared gradually and as described, as the angel entered and then departed a narrowly-defined portion of three-dimensional space within Joseph Smith's bed chamber.

There have also been many open area visitations by beings from eternal realms. The day following the visit of the angel Moroni in Joseph's bedchamber, he had another manifestation from the unseen world, in broad daylight. While working in the fields, he recalled: "My strength entirely failed me, and I fell helpless on the ground, and for a time was quite unconscious of anything. The first thing that I can recollect was a voice speaking unto me, calling me by name. I looked up, and beheld the same messenger standing over my head, surrounded by light, as before." (J.S.H. 1:48-49). He later asked: "Now, what do we hear? Moroni (and) the voice of Michael ... of Peter, James, and John ... and again, the voice of God ... of Gabriel, and of Raphael, and of divers angels, from Michael or Adam down to the present time." (D&C 128:19-21).

A well-documented open area visitation occurred in Book of Mormon lands, at the temple in Bountiful. The Nephites who had gathered there after the crucifixion "saw a Man descending out of heaven; and he was clothed in a white robe; and he came down and stood in the midst of them; and the eyes of the whole multitude were turned upon him, and they durst not open their mouths, even one to another, and wist not what it meant, for they thought it was an angel" from the unseen world "that had appeared unto them." (3 Nephi 11:8).

On several occasions during His mortal ministry, Jesus spatially transported Himself. When He angered the Jews by suggesting that "before Abraham was, I am," the Jews took "up stones to cast at him: but Jesus hid himself, and went out of the temple, going through the midst of them, and so passed by." (John 8:59).

Jesus was also spatially transported when the devil tempted him as He fasted in the wilderness of Judea following His baptism. Matthew recorded: "The devil taketh him up to the holy city, and setteth him on a pinnacle of the temple." (Matthew 4:5). Then, "the devil, taking him up into an high mountain, shewed him all the kingdoms of the world, in a moment of time." (Luke 4:5).

The earth has also been spatially transformed, as when Israel walked on dry

ground over the bed of the Red Sea. "And Moses stretched out his hand over the sea; and the Lord caused the sea to go back by a strong east wind all that night, and made the sea dry land, and the waters were divided. And the children of

Israel went into the midst of the sea upon the dry ground: and the waters were a wall unto them on their right hand, and on their left." (Exodus 14:21-22).

Perhaps the solar system itself experienced a temporal distortion, when "the sun stood still, and the moon stayed, until the people had avenged themselves upon their enemies. Is not this written in the book of Jasher? So the sun stood still in the midst of heaven, and hasted not to go down about a whole day." (Joshua 10:13). It is interesting that when Mormon gave his account of this manifestation, he wrote: "And thus, according to his word the earth goeth back, and it appeareth unto man that the sun standeth still; yea, and behold this is so; for surely it is the earth that moveth, and not the sun." (Helaman 12:15). As an astronomer, Mormon seems to have been well ahead of his time.

How do God and angels move around in this manner, without violating the laws of physics? Even at the speed of light, it would take at least 93 billion years to traverse the known universe, from one "end" to the other, so physically moving from one point to another within it seems unlikely. (Actually, it could never be done, because of the continuing expansion of the universe. See Quora.com). How can we reconcile that physical reality with the fact that after we have captured the Lord's attention, His intercession can be virtually instantaneous. Samuel was once moved to exclaim: "In my distress I called upon the Lord, and cried to my God: and he did hear my voice out of his temple, and my cry did enter into his ears. Then the earth shook and trembled; the foundations of heaven moved and shook," as God instantly responded to his entreaty in a powerful manifestation that disrupted to its center the fabric of his every day world. (2 Samuel 22:7-8).

James declared: "The effectual fervent prayer of a righteous man availeth much." (James 5:16). When the faithful pray to Heavenly Father, He hears His children and has the power to immediately respond to their needs. It may be a over-

simplification, but if God dwelt in an adjacent spatial dimension, without the inherent limitations of our familiar three-dimensional space, He would have the ability to hear all of His children's petitions simultaneously wherever and whenever they may be.

Prophetic insight into adjacent spatial dimensions comes from accounts of the creation of the earth. Brigham Young used very unusual language when referring to the earth as it was at the time of the Fall, and how it will be when it receives its paradisiacal glory. He said: "When the earth was framed and brought into existence and man was placed upon it, it was near the throne of our Father in Heaven. And when man fell ... the earth fell into space, and took up its abode in this planetary system, and the sun became our light. This is the glory the earth came from, and ... it will return again unto the presence of the Father, and it will dwell there." (J.D., 17:143). This description of falling into space and then leaving to return to the presence of the Father suggests an adjacent spatial dimension. As Micah prophesied: "The Lord cometh forth out of his place, and will come down, and tread upon the high places of the earth." (Micah 1:3). So, not only was Mormon an astronomer, but Brigham Young and Micah were theoretical physicists. Alma also weighed in, when he explained that in regard to the Spirit World, "there is a space between death and the resurrection of the body." (Alma 40:21, underlining mine). (So does Orson Pratt, later in this chapter!)

Looking down on all the seraphic host, not by going to the left, or to the right, and not by going forward or backward, or up or down, but by going simultaneously at right angles to every one of those directions, God is in an ideal position to bring to pass our immortality and eternal life. From His undefinable perspective, He confidently promises: "The soul shall be restored to the body, and the body to the soul; yea, and every limb and joint shall be restored to its body; yea, even a hair of the head shall not be lost; but all things shall be restored to their proper and perfect frame." Perhaps this is the mechanism of "the restoration of (those things) which has been spoken by the mouths of the prophets." (Alma 40:22-24).

There may be lateral moves, as well. As the Savior explained to the Nephites: "I have

other sheep, which are not of this land, neither of the land of Jerusalem, neither in any parts of that land round about whither I have been to minister. For they of whom I speak are they who have not as yet heard my voice; neither have I at any time manifested myself unto them." (3 Nephi 16:1-2). Those of whom the Lord spoke were the Lost Ten Tribes of Israel, whose disappearance may illustrate the experience of mortals who move between dimensions. Going to visit these "other sheep" may be a way for the Lord to describe His travel to other dimensions, in a way that is cognitively comfortable for those of us who have never had the experience.

The apocryphal writer Esdras suggested that the Ten Tribes entered another state when they were carried "over the waters, and so came they into another land. But they took this counsel among themselves, that they would leave the multitude of the heathen, and go forth unto a further country, where never mankind dwelt, that they might there keep their statutes, which they never kept in their own land. And they entered into Euphrates by the narrow passage of the river. For the most High then shewed signs for them, and held still the flood, till they were passed over. For through that country there was a great way to go, namely, of a year and a half: and the same region is called Arsareth. Then dwelt they there until the latter times; and now when they shall begin to come, the Highest shall stay the stream again, that they may go through." (Apocrypha, 2 Esdras 13:40-47).

The holy scriptures record: "They who are in the north countries shall come in remembrance before the Lord; and their prophets shall hear his voice, and shall no longer stay themselves; and they shall smite the rocks, and the ice shall flow down at their presence. And an highway shall be cast up in the midst of the great deep, like as it was in the day that (Israel) came up out of the land of Egypt." (D&C 133:26-17, see Isaiah 11:16). It may not be a literal highway, but the Lord will nevertheless prepare a way for them, that they might reach their destination. Perhaps, for the time being, He has also prepared a spatial distortion for them to remain hidden from the world until they are prepared to fulfill their millennial destiny.

Latter-day Saints are not unfamiliar with these distortions. The recognize the "spirit world" as an adjacent state-of-being. It "is a tangible sphere where disembodied spirits live in one of several conditions according to what their mortal lives have merited." (Dale Mouritsen, "The Spirit World, Our Next Home," Ensign, 1/1977). The Prophet Joseph Smith said that we should focus our study on the spirit world "day and night." He declared: "If we have any claim on our Heavenly Father for anything, it is for knowledge on this important subject." ("Teachings," p. 324). He also said: "The spirits of the just are exalted to a greater and more glorious work; hence they are blessed in their departure to the world of spirits. Enveloped in flaming fire, they are not far from us, and know and understand our thoughts, feelings, and motions, and are often pained therewith. Flesh and blood cannot go there; but flesh and bones, quickened by the Spirit of God, can." ("Teachings," p. 326).

Brigham Young asked: "When you lay down this tabernacle, where are you going? Into the spiritual world. Where is the spirit world? It is right here. Do the spirits go beyond the boundaries of this organized earth? No, they do not. They can see us, but we cannot see them, unless our eyes are opened." ("The Contributor," 10:9, quoted in N.B. Lundwall, "The Vision," p. 55-56, see D.B.Y., p. 376). This only makes sense if they are in a higher spatial dimension that may be similar to being in a room with a one-way mirror through which they can look down and witness our every-day world. But to those of us within the room, trapped in the here-and-now, trying to see what lies in the other 'direction' beyond the mirror is fruitless. Bound by the laws and conditions of our temporal and spatial reality, all we can hope to gain by observation is a confirmation of the validity of that which we already know, which frustratingly, is generally only a reflection of our own experience. Only when we have veil experiences can we begin to penetrate that curtain.

Parley P. Pratt similarly taught that the spirit world "is here on the very planet where we were born. The earth and other planets of like sphere have their inward or spiritual spheres, as well as their outward, or temporal spheres. The one is peopled by temporal tabernacles, and the other by spirits. A veil is drawn between

the one sphere and the other, whereby all the objects in the spiritual sphere are rendered invisible to those in the temporal." ("Key to Theology," p. 126-7). In today's vernacular, he might have said that temporal and spiritual worlds exist in nested dimensions that are separate and distinct realities.

Brigham Young chose another way of expressing this concept. He said that "spirits are composed of matter so refined as not to be tangible to this coarser organization." (D.B.Y., p. 379). Joseph Smith said: "There is no such thing as immaterial matter. All spirit is matter, but it is more fine or pure, and can only be discerned by purer eyes. We cannot see it, but when our bodies are purified we shall see that it is all matter." (D&C 131:7-8, see H.C. 5:392-3). (Could he have been hinting at 'dark matter' first postulated to exist in 1884?)

Perhaps it is only our experiences in the temple that will help us to achieve that state of refinement. It is there that we get a glimpse of heaven, and join the Dead Sea Covenantor who wrote: "Behold, for mine own part, I have reached the inter-vision, and through the spirit thou hast placed within me, come to know Thee, my God." (Eleventh Hymn, Quoted in Preston Robinson's "Christ's Eternal Gospel," p. 111). Perhaps the "inter-vision" is the state of consciousness that we sometimes slip into when we immerse ourselves in temple worship, that enables us to see with the eye of faith to embrace the sum of reality.

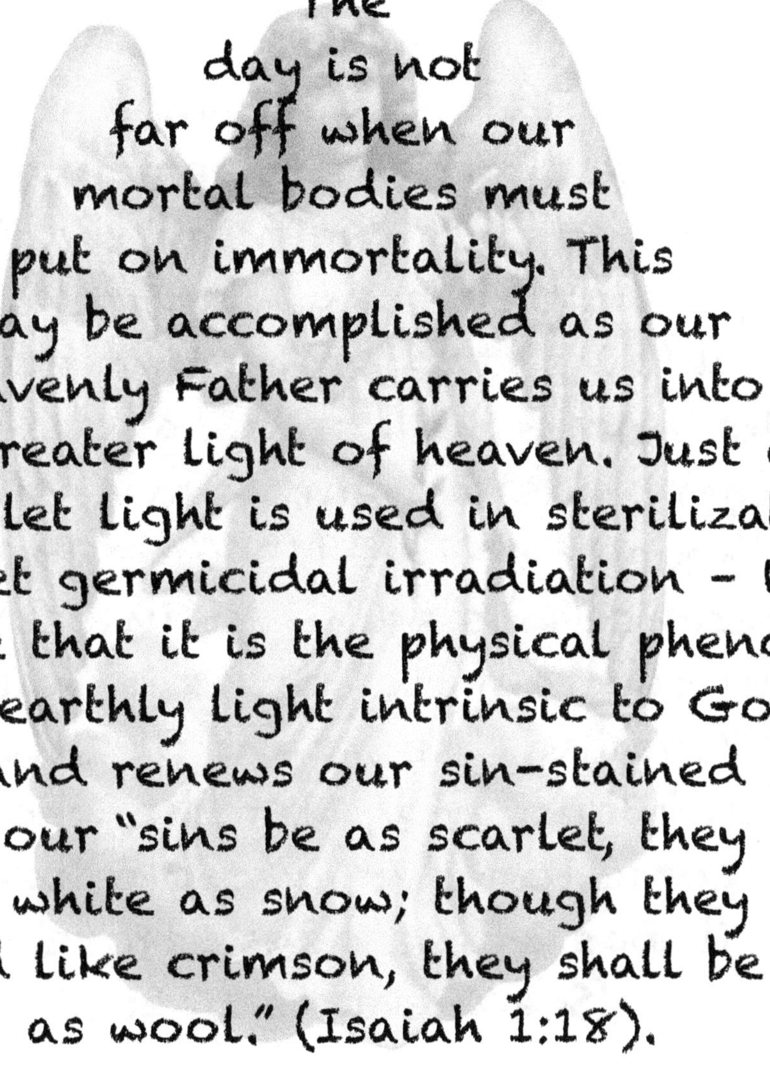

The
day is not
far off when our
mortal bodies must
put on immortality. This
may be accomplished as our
Heavenly Father carries us into
the greater light of heaven. Just as
ultraviolet light is used in sterilization,
(ultraviolet germicidal irradiation – UVGI),
could it be that it is the physical phenomenon
of the unearthly light intrinsic to God that
purifies and renews our sin-stained souls?
Though our "sins be as scarlet, they shall
be as white as snow; though they be
red like crimson, they shall be
as wool." (Isaiah 1:18).

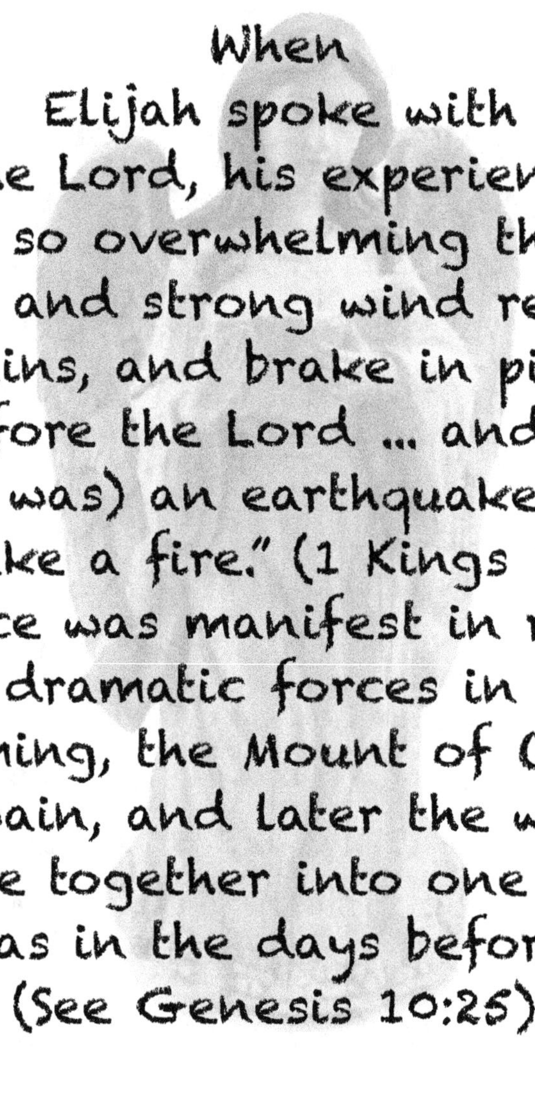

When
Elijah spoke with
the Lord, his experience
was so overwhelming that "a
great and strong wind rent the
mountains, and brake in pieces the
rocks before the Lord ... and after the
wind (there was) an earthquake ... and after
the earthquake a fire." (1 Kings 19:11-12). The
Lord's Presence was manifest in representations
of the most dramatic forces in nature. At His
Second Coming, the Mount of Olives will be
rent in twain, and later the whole earth
will come together into one landmass
as it was in the days before Peleg.
(See Genesis 10:25).

Chapter Four
Our journey to the veil

"And, behold, the
veil of the temple was
rent in twain from the top
to the bottom; and the earth
did quake, and the rocks rent;
and the graves were opened; and
many bodies of the saints which slept
arose, and came out of the graves after
his resurrection, and went into the holy
city, and appeared unto many."
(Matthew 27:51-53).

Why, we might ask ourselves, do we undertake our journey to the veil? Helen Keller gave us much needed perspective, when she wrote: "For three things I thank God

every day of my life: thanks that he has vouchsafed me knowledge of his works; deep thanks that he has set in my darkness the lamp of faith, and deepest thanks that I have another life to look forward to - a life joyous with light and flowers and heavenly song."

Her religion suggests a future state where we shall see from multiple perspectives, freed from the myopic vision that currently limits our sight to the physical and temporal present within a very narrow band of electromagnetic energy. As Albert Einstein wrote of the passing of one of his old friends: "His death signifies nothing. For us believing physicists, the distinction between past, present, and future is only an illusion, even if a stubborn one." ("Einstein," NOVA, 1979, p. 18).

Those who have had near-death experiences confirm the presence of adjacent dimensions of light, and flowers, and heavenly song. An individual teetering on the brink between this life and the next "feels himself moving rapidly through a long, dark tunnel. After this, he suddenly finds himself outside his own physical body, and sees his own body from a distance, as though he were a spectator. He notices that he still has a body, but one with very different powers from the physical body he has left behind. Soon, others come to meet and help him. He glimpses the spirits of relatives and friends who have died. At some point, he finds himself approaching a sort of barrier or border. He finds that he must go back to the earth, that the time for his death has not yet come. At this point, he resists, for by now he is taken up with his experiences in the afterlife and does not want to return. He is overwhelmed by intense feelings of joy, love, and peace. Despite his attitude, though, he somehow re-unites with his physical body.

Later, he tries to tell others, but he has trouble doing so. He can find no words adequate to describe these unearthly episodes. He also finds that others scoff, so he stops telling them. Those who have had near-death experiences describe a spiritual body that is invisible to others and lacks solidity. Travel in this state, once one gets the hang of it, is apparently exceptionally easy. Physical objects present no barrier, and movement from one place to another can be rapid, almost instantaneous.

What we learn about death may make an important difference in the way we live our lives. If experiences of this type are real, they have profound implications for what every one of us is doing with his life. For then, it would be true that we cannot fully understand this life until we catch a glimpse of what lies beyond it." (Raymond Moody, M.D., "Life after Life").

The doctrine of The Church of Jesus Christ of Latter-day Saints, and specifically the teachings of the temple, suggest that we cannot be complete or whole until we appreciate our potential as children of a God Who has sent us to earth to lead us, guide us, walk beside us, and help us find our way back home. If this is the case, then, as Joseph Smith said: "The only difference between the old and young dying is, one lives longer in heaven and eternal light and glory than the other, and is freed a little sooner from this miserable, wicked world." (H.C., 4:553-554). Clearly, he felt the afterlife would be soul-expanding with virtually unlimited options, in contrast to the limited scope of our potential for as long as we remain here on earth.

Notwithstanding the promise of this glory, we frequently lose sight of it, and mourn the loss of our departed loved ones. Stretching our minds, however, "speaks volumes of happiness, of joy and gratitude to (the) soul. Thank the Lord he has revealed these principles to us," in the temple and in the other liturgy of the Church. (Joseph Smith, "Teachings," p. 197).

A reminiscence by a friend and associate of the Prophet reflects the gossamer fabric of the veil separating the world we know from the world of spirits. "'I am getting tired and would like to go to my rest,' said Joseph. His words and tone thrilled and shocked me, and like an arrow, pierced my hopes that he would long remain with us, and I said, as with a heart full of tears: 'Oh, Joseph, what could we, as a people, do without you and what would become of the great latter-day work if you should leave us?' He saw and was touched by my emotions, and in reply he said, 'Benjamin, I would not be far away from you, and if on the other side of the veil,

I would still be working with you, and with a power greatly increased, to roll on this kingdom.'" (Benjamin F. Johnson, in N.B. Lundwall, "The Vision," p. 140-141). Did the Prophet mean that he would possess the ability to freely move between temporal and spatial dimensions? Perhaps he shared the vision of Abraham, who said of the creations of God: "They existed before, they shall have no end, they shall exist after, for they are ... eternal." (Abraham 3:18).

Wilford Woodruff related a personal experience that bears directly on the Prophet's assurance of his close proximity to us after his death. "While I was upon my knees praying," he said, "my room was filled with light. I looked, and a messenger stood by my side. I arose, and this personage told me he had come to instruct me. He presented before me a panorama. He told me he wanted me to see with my eyes and understand with my mind what was coming to pass in the earth before the coming of the Son of Man. After this passed by me, he disappeared. It made an impression upon me that has never left me from that day to this. The next day, I was a lost man. I hardly knew where I was, so enveloped was I in that which I had seen." (Wilford Woodruff, Weber Stake Conference, Ogden, Utah, 10/19/1896).

One day we will all "see the Son of man sitting on the right hand of power, and coming in the clouds of heaven." (Mark 14:62). The Savior will come "down from heaven, not to do (His) own will, but the will" of His Father. (John 6:38). Where is heaven? Jesus simply declared: "I proceeded forth and came from God." (John 8:42). We know that "every good gift and every perfect gift is from above, and cometh down from the Father of lights." God is the author, embodiment, and source of light, His presence is real, and in Him there "is no variableness, neither shadow of turning." (James 1:17). Evidently, eternity eliminates ambiguity and creates clarity in a flood of unearthly light of unimaginable intensity.

Prophetic visions also suggest the existence of a veil that separates us from higher spatial an temporal dimensions. For example: "Moses cast his eyes and beheld the earth, yea, even all of it; and there was not a particle which he did not behold, discerning it by the spirit of God. And he beheld also the inhabitants thereof, and

there was not a soul which he beheld not; and he discerned them by the Spirit of God; and their numbers were great, even numberless as the sand upon the sea shore." (Moses 1:27-29). He beheld these things as a spiritual witness that figuratively parted the veil so that he could see beyond the portal of eternity. Without such spiritual acuity, he would have been oblivious to these mysteries of the kingdom, for "no man" on his own merits "can find out the work that God maketh from the beginning to the end." (Ecclesiastes 3:11). With it, however, they "have no end, neither beginning." (D&C 29:33).

In the first chapter of Ezekiel, the prophet wrote: "Now it came to pass ... that the heavens were opened, and I saw visions of God ... And I looked, and, behold, a whirlwind came out of the north, a great cloud, and a fire infolding itself, and a brightness was about it ... Also out of the midst thereof came the likeness of four living creatures. And this was their appearance: they had the likeness of a man. And every one had four faces, and every one had four wings ... Their wings were joined one to another; they turned not when they went; they went every one straight forward ... As for the likeness of the living creatures, their appearance was like burning coals of fire, and like the appearance of lamps ... and the fire was bright, and out of the fire went forth lightning. And the living creatures ran and returned as the appearance of a flash of lightning. Now, as I beheld the living creatures ... they four had one likeness: and their appearance and their work was, as it were, a wheel in the middle of a wheel. When they went, they went upon their four sides; and they turned not when they went." (Ezekiel 1:16).

The language Ezekiel used to describe what he saw was complex, metaphorical, stylistic, symbolical, and, yes, confusing, and might well have been the result of his inability to describe the introduction into our world of higher-dimensional objects and events. In particular, his characterization of a "wheel in the middle of a wheel" could have been an attempt to describe a four-dimensional tesseract, just as a hypercube is often represented as a cube within a cube. His references to a fire infolding itself and to multiple-sided beings who went straight forward even though they were facing in multiple directions may be the best descriptions we have

of a hyper-object entering our three-dimensional space.

This may not have been Ezekiel's only higher-dimensional experience. "I beheld, and lo a likeness as the appearance of fire," he wrote, "from the appearance of his loins even downward, fire; and from his loins even upward, as the appearance of brightness, as the colour of amber. And (God) put forth the form of an hand, and took me by a lock of mine head; and the spirit lifted me up between the earth and the heaven, and brought me in the visions of God to Jerusalem, to the door of the inner gate ... And, behold, the glory of the God of Israel was there, according to the vision that I saw." (Ezekiel 8:2-4). Thus, did Ezekiel recount how the Lord had brought him through both time and space to witness events as they unfolded in the holy city.

In a related vision, Ezekiel was carried "into the land of Israel, and set ... upon a very high mountain." "Behold, with thine eyes," he was told, "and hear, with thine ears, and set thine heart upon all that I shall shew thee." (Ezekiel 30:2 & 4). The prophet was able to see and hear with his physical faculties, but with a power greatly increased because of the influence of the Spirit. It "took me up," he said, "and brought me into the inner court; and, behold, the glory of the Lord filled the (temple)." (Ezekiel 43:5). "There is no apparent limit," wrote Parley P. Pratt, "to the speed attainable by the body, when unchained and set free from the elements which now enslave it." ("Key to The Science of Theology," p. 162).

Brigham Young believed that "the brightness and glory of the next apartment" to a higher-dimensional temporal and spatial reality beyond the veil "is inexpressible." Those who reside there "move with ease and like lightning. If we want to visit Jerusalem, or this, that, or the other place, there we are. If we want to behold Jerusalem as it was in the days of the Savior, or if we want to see the Garden of Eden as it was when created, there we are. We may behold the earth as at the dawn of creation, or we may visit any city we please that exists upon its surface." (J.D., 4:231). It seems that temporal and spatial transportations were not unfamiliar concepts to the prophets, for whom the arrow of time easily moved in two directions.

Many of the higher-dimensional veil experiences of the personalities in the scriptures simply cannot be articulated. When Paul wrote of being "caught up to the third heaven," he deferred from a lengthy explanation by simply stating: "Whether in the body, I cannot tell, or whether out of the body, I cannot tell. God knoweth."

(2 Corinthians 12:2). When the Three Nephites "were caught up into heaven, (they) saw and heard unspeakable things. And it was forbidden them that they should utter; neither was it given unto them power that they could utter the things which they saw and heard." (3 Nephi 28:13-14).

Helen Keller, who was blessed with neither sight nor hearing, nevertheless very perceptively wrote about feeling; about her own journey to the veil. "Only He who made all things can gaze upon unveiled glory. We could not behold untempered splendour, and live. That is why man is permitted to look at everything only as in a glass, darkly, and gaze only upon the shadows in one small, dimly lighted chamber. Why should he speak of the mysteries of heaven so doubtingly, when really he apprehends so little of earth, and that only with veiled senses? Why cannot the soul with equal freedom go forth from its dwelling place, and discarding the poor lenses of the body, peer thru the telescope of truth into the infinite reaches of immortality?" ("My Religion," p. 77).

Adjacent dimensional realities may define the infinite reaches of immortality that lie just beyond the veil. They seem to be the focus of The Pearl of Great Price, wherein "many lands" were described, and each "was called earth, and there were inhabitants on the face thereof." (Moses 1:29). We gain additional insight by studying Abraham's similar vision, when the Lord "put his hand upon (his) eyes, and (Abraham) saw those things which his hands had made, which were many, and they multiplied before (his) eyes, and (he) could not see the end thereof." (Abraham 3:12).

If we accepted the possibility that there is a fourth spatial dimension, the next logical question is: "What about a fifth dimension, or a sixth, or a tenth? Is there any end to the creations and adjacent spatial dimensions of God? These inquiries relate to the doctrine of dominions, and of eternal progression, for as Brigham

Young declared: "How many kingdoms of glory there are, I know not; and how many degrees of glory there are in these kingdoms, I know not; but there are multitudes of them … The kingdoms that God has prepared are innumerable." (J.D.,

8:154 & 9:107). Perhaps our veil experiences in the temple are but a foretaste and a prelude to our awakening comprehension of the glories and wonders of eternity.

Doctrine & Covenants Section 76 teaches that there are three kingdoms of glory, the celestial, the terrestrial, and the telestial, and that the inhabitants of a particular kingdom cannot visit higher kingdoms but can visit lower kingdoms. For example, the inhabitants of the telestial kingdom "shall be servants of the Most High; but where God and Christ dwell they (simply) cannot come" as long as they remain in their present state of unpreparedness. (D&C 76:112). It may be that this limitation exists because each higher kingdom has at least one more spatial dimension than the next lower kingdom. In this sense, those in a lower kingdom could no more move into a higher kingdom than we could, by our own efforts, move from our three-dimensional world into a four-dimensional world. It would take the intervention of a higher power and undiscovered laws of physics for them, or for us, to do so. At the same time, however, those inhabiting a higher dimensional world could freely move from there into a lower dimensional world, just as we can, from our three-dimensional perspective, interact with two-dimensional and one-dimensional space with ease.

Eternal progression can be thought of in much the same way. Joseph Smith asked: "What did Jesus do? Why, I do the things I saw my Father do when worlds came rolling into existence. My Father worked out His kingdom with fear and trembling, and I must do the same; and when I get my kingdom, I shall present it to my Father, so that He may obtain kingdom upon kingdom, and it will exalt Him in glory. He will then take a higher exaltation, and I will take His place, and thereby become exalted myself." ("Teachings," p. 347-348). So Jesus follows in the footsteps of His Father, to claim His inheritance. This makes us think of descriptions of the coming of the Lord, when the veil will be rent in twain to allow Him and a

multitude of heavenly beings, to pass from one dimension to another.

Once we have been resurrected to glory in the Celestial Kingdom of God, our eternal progression might then involve advancement to a dimensionally higher state of being as soon as we are prepared to take that giant leap. In this case, we might eventually progress to have dominion over any number of dimensionally inferior realms similar in make-up to our previous habitations. This would allow those within the influence of our stewardship to advance to the position that we had formerly occupied. Once again, consider this insight from the Doctrine and Covenants: "All kingdoms have a law given; And there are many kingdoms; for there is no space in the which there is no kingdom; and there is no kingdom in the which there is no space, either a greater or a lesser kingdom. And unto every kingdom is given a law; and unto every law there are certain bounds also and conditions." (D&C 88:36-38). As Job said of man: "Thou hast appointed his bounds that he cannot pass." (Job 14:5). However, when its inhabitants have mastered the bounds and conditions of their particular kingdom, would they not reasonably merit advancement to dimensionally superior, or higher, kingdoms? If so, this would certainly involve veil experiences of unimaginable intensity.

Of our own earth, the Doctrine and Covenants teaches that "in its sanctified and immortal state, (it) will be made like unto crystal and will be a Urim and Thummim to the inhabitants who dwell thereon, whereby all things pertaining to an inferior kingdom, or all kingdoms of a lower order, will be made manifest to those who dwell on it." (D&C 130:9). The next verse suggests that there will be an order of kingdoms higher than the one that will exist on this earth after its sanctification. "The white stones mentioned in Revelation 2:17 will become a Urim and Thummim to each individual who receives one, whereby things pertaining to a higher order of kingdoms will be made known." (D&C 130:10). As Brigham Young stated: "When we have passed into the sphere where Joseph (Smith) is, there is still another department, and then another, and another, and so on to an eternal progression in exaltation and eternal lives." (J.D., 3:375).

The magnitude of these kingdoms is beyond our comprehension, but prophetic insight provides a degree of clarity. Joseph Smith said: "The great Jehovah contemplated the whole of the events connected with the earth, pertaining to The Plan of Salvation, before it rolled into existence, or ever 'the morning stars sang together' for joy; the past, the present, and the future were and are, with him, one eternal now." (Teachings," p. 220). The Savior exists in the past, present, and future tense; He is "the Great I AM, Alpha and Omega," that are the first and last letters of the Greek alphabet, "the beginning and the end, the same which looked upon the wide expanse of eternity, and all the seraphic hosts of heaven, before the world was made." (D&C 38:1-2). His "course is one eternal round, the same today as yesterday, and forever." (D&C 35:1). In this sense, time itself is a dimension that will one day reveal superior states of being that will allow us to see at once, or perhaps more accurately, from multiple perspectives in time, "the beginning and the end." (D&C 84:120). As Alma explained to Corianton: "All is as one day with God, and time only is measured unto men." (Alma 40:8). Einstein confirmed the truth of that principle, when he demonstrated that time is relative; hence, his hopeful observation about his recently departed friend. (See above).

It is fortunate that, for "the time being," the veil keeps us insulated from the other dimensions of reality. It solidly grounds us on the familiar bedrock of the present, buttressed by our memories of the past, and our confident anticipation of the future. For now, the arrow of time moves in only one forward direction. The stability of this handy frame of reference allows us to live in an orderly fashion through a time-line that is woven into the tapestry of three-dimensional space. It reassures us that the sun will come up tomorrow, and that there will be (roughly) 24 hours in each day. Without the veil, life would simply be too confusing for most people! When the veil that envelops us in time is no more, time itself will be no more. This gives a sense of urgency to the admonition that this life is the time for us to prepare to meet God. (See Alma 34:32). In fact, it may be the only time for us to do so.

When the Lord redeems His people, Satan will be bound and time will no longer

exist, because all things will be gathered in one. (See Revelation 20:2 & D&C 45:55). Zion will come down from above and up from below at one and the same time, the veil will be rent, and the earth will be clothed with the glory of God, who will stand revealed in the midst of the temple. (See D&C 84:100).

"Even now, time is clearly not our natural dimension," wrote Neal A. Maxwell. "Thus it is, that we are never really at home in time. Alternately, we find ourselves impatiently wishing to hasten the passage of time or to hold back the dawn. We can do neither, of course. Whereas the bird is at home in the air, we are clearly not at home in time, because we belong to eternity. Time, as much as any one thing, whispers to us that we are strangers here. If time were natural to us, why is it that we have so many clocks, and wear wristwatches?

There are poignant and frequent reminders of the veil," he continued, "adding to our sense of being close, but still outside. In our deepest prayers, when our agency encounters the omniscience of God, we sometimes sense, if only momentarily, how very provincial our petitions are. We perceive that there are more good answers than we have good questions; and we realize that we have been taught more than we can tell, for the language used is not that which the tongue can transmit.

We experience this same close separateness when a baby is born," he observed, "but also as we wait with those who are dying - for then we brush against the veil, as goodbyes and greetings are said almost within earshot of each other. In such moments, this resonance with realities on the other side of the veil is so obvious that it can be explained in only one way. No wonder the Savior said that His sheep would recognize His doctrines, that they would know His voice, and that they would follow Him. (See John 10:14).

Without the veil," he concluded, "we would lose that precious insulation so necessary for our mortal probation and maturation. Without the veil, our brief mortal walk in a darkening world would lose its meaning, for one would scarcely carry the flashlight of faith at noonday and in the presence of the Light of the world." ("Ensign," 10/1980).

In spite of the veil, those who participate in temple ordinances understand that there exists a 'second order of mind.' Our experiences in the House of the Lord repetitively reinforce the shadow of another world. We realize that the endowment cannot be exposed, for it is symbolic and is spiritually discerned. When we stand before the veil of the temple, we institutionally validate the reality of higher spatial and even temporal dimensions in an unseen world. The Pearl of Great Price reinforces the teachings of the endowment, and confirms that from the superior vantage point of the Gods, from outside the conventional boundaries of time and space, they organized the heavens and the earth, divided the light from the darkness, created the waters and the earth, and placed all manner of vegetation thereon. Finally, they "watched those things which they had ordered, until they obeyed." (Abraham 4:1-18).

We can scarcely imagine what our faculties will be when we pass through the veil and are free of the confines and limitations of our mortal bodies. Orson Pratt spoke of the ability to consider many different ideas at the same time, instead of thinking in a single channel only and of following just one course of reasoning. "Suppose God should give us a sixth sense, a seventh, an eighth, a ninth, or a fiftieth? All these different senses would convey to us new ideas, as much so as the senses of tasting, smelling, or seeing communicate different ideas from that of hearing. Do we suppose the five senses of man converse with all the elements of nature," he asked? "No."

He believed that we should pay attention to our perceptions when we stand before the veil and rehearse our interview with God, when we return and report. The time will come when "knowledge will rush in from all quarters; it will come in like the light which flows from the sun, penetrating every part, informing the Spirit, and giving understanding concerning ten thousand things at the same time; and the mind will be capable of receiving and retaining all. Not one object at a time, but a vast multitude of objects (will) rush before our vision, and will be present before our mind, filling us in a moment with the knowledge of worlds more

numerous than the sands of the seashore. Will we be able to bear it? Yes, our minds (will be) strengthened in proportion to the amount of information imparted. It is this tabernacle in its present condition that prevents us from a more enlarged understanding.

When this tabernacle is taken off," he continued, "we shall look, not in one direction, but in every direction. This will be calculated to give us new ideas concerning the immensity of the creations of God. This will give us information and knowledge we never can know as long as we dwell in this mortal tabernacle. We shall have other sources of gaining knowledge, besides these inlets called senses. We will be endowed, after we leave this tabernacle, with powers and faculties which we now have no knowledge of, by which we may learn what is round about us." ("The Increased Powers of Faculties of Mind in a Future State," Excerpted from "Temples of The Most High," p. 299-312, also J.D., 2:238-248).

Hugh Nibley has also considered the element of perspective as we make our journey to the veil. He reasoned: "As to taking a calm and deliberate look at more than one thing at a time, that is a gift denied us at present. I cannot imagine what such a view of the world would be like, but it would be more real and correct than the one we have now. Once we can see the possibilities that lie in being able to see more than one thing at a time, the universe takes on new dimensions and God takes over." We should then be as the Brother of Jared, who, when overshadowed by the Spirit, could look upon past, present, and future generations at once. "They all came before him, and there was not a soul that he did not behold." (Mormon 8:35).

Dr. Nibley continued: "Let us remember that quite peculiar to the genius of Mormonism is the doctrine of a God who could preoccupy Himself with countless numbers of things. "The heavens they are many," the scriptures teach, "and they cannot be numbered unto man; but they are numbed unto me, for they are mine." (Moses 1:36). Plainly, we are dealing with a higher order of mind. "For my thoughts are not your thoughts, neither are your ways my ways, saith the Lord. For as the heavens are higher than the earth, so are ... my thoughts than your thoughts." (Isaiah

55:8-9)." ("Zeal Without Knowledge," "Nibley on The Timely and Timeless," p. 263-264).

Brigham Young said: "I long for the time that a point of the finger, or motion of the hand, will express every idea without utterance. When we are full of the light of eternity, then the eye is not the only medium through which we see, nor the brain the only means by which we understand. When our bodies are full of the Holy Ghost, we can see behind ourselves with as much ease, without turning our heads, as we can see before us. If you have not had that experience, you ought to have. It is not the optic nerve alone that gives the knowledge of surrounding objects to the mind." (J.D., 1:70-71).

As we participate in the veil experience in the temple, time loses its significance, and we get a taste of eternity. We begin to realize that "See you later," will not exist in the vocabulary of eternal beings. Time, that we too frequently viewed as a predator that stalked us all our lives, will in a coming day be fondly remembered as a companion that accompanied us through mortality, reminding us to cherish every moment. Our journey to the veil prepares us for a much larger reality, and our perspective remains faulty only for as long as we believe it to be unique. The veil helps us to appreciate that mortality is not our natural dimension. It helps us to discover why we sometimes feel like "strangers and pilgrims on the earth." (Hebrews 11:13). Our experiences at the veil explain our innate thrust always toward the future, and always beyond the horizon. Time is the fire in which we burn, in the sense that the Spirit introduces us to God, Who Himself dwells in everlasting burnings.

The veil helps us to realize that growing "old" is nothing more than a brilliant mechanism designed by Heavenly Father that affords us an opportunity to gauge the approach of our reunion with Him in eternity. We realize that we have been living in only one dimly lighted corner of reality, with a very narrow perspective that has been frozen in time. As we journey to the veil, we appreciate that we will one day "flourish in immortal youth, unhurt amidst the war of elements, the wreck of matter, and the crash of worlds." (Joseph Addison, "Cato," Act 5, Scene 1). The veil

helps us to recognize the significance of the subtle messages that are reflected in the passage of time.

Our journey to the veil helps us to realize that time is an artificial and relative dimension in which we could never be completely comfortable, for we are eternal beings. Time is transitory by definition, and it is only our perspective that makes it seem that it is we who move through it, when it is really the other way around. In our youth, time never seemed to pass quickly enough. Perhaps we were so recently removed from the eternal world that we were impatient to return to the familiarity of that more natural and stable environment. As we approach the event horizon that separates mortality from immortality, however, our perception of the passage of time changes again, and we ask ourselves where did it go. Time really is relative, especially as we draw closer to eternity.

Could we view time dispassionately, perhaps we would realize that when we kill time, we damage our eternal selves, for as the Lord warned, "in an hour when ye think not the summer shall be past, and the harvest ended, and your souls not saved." (D&C 45:2). We might realize that with the passage of every second of every day, we are one tick of the clock closer to the higher-dimensional reality of "the undiscovered country, from whose bourne no traveler returns." (Shakespeare, "Hamlet," Act 3, Scene 1).

When we approach the veil, we find that we have come home to a more comfortable and expansive dominion, where free will takes on a new meaning that was beforehand only dimly perceived. As the poet wrote: "Oh, this world has more of coming and of going than I can bear. I guess it's eternity I want, where all things are, and always will be. Where I can hold my loves a little looser. Where, finally, we realize time is the only thing that really dies." (Carol Lynn Pearson, "Optical Illusion," "Beginnings"). In fact, it is only "in the dark recesses of memory, in unbidden suggestions, in trains of thought unwittingly pursued, in multiplied waves and currents all at once flashing and rushing, in dreams that cannot be laid to rest, in the force of instinct, in the obscure, but certain, intuitions of the spiritual

life, that we have glimpses of a great tide of life ebbing and flowing, rippling and roiling and beating about where we cannot see it." (E.S. Dallas). At the veil, with silent, lifting mind, we tread upon the high untrespassed sanctity of space, put out our hands, and touch the face of God. (See John G. Magee, Jr., "High Flight").

Without the veil, we can only indirectly appreciate the eternities. By actively seeking learning, even by study and also by faith, "we can make our lives sublime, and departing, leave behind us footprints on the sands of time." (Henry Wadsworth Longfellow, "A Psalm of Life"). Our journey to the veil makes it less likely that those footprints will be washed away by the incessant wave action of mortality that beats upon our shores. We need to make sure that the tide in our affairs is taken at the flood, that it might lead on to fortune. (See Shakespeare, "Julius Caesar," Act 4, Scene 2). Our veil experiences were prepared in the pre-earth existence, are molded in mortality, and will be established in eternity, that the heavens might smile upon us and clothe us in the glory of God.

In our journey to the veil, as we lose ourselves in temple service, we once again recall the profound wisdom of Miss Helen Keller, who taught us that "there is joy in self-forgetfulness." She tried to "make the light in others' eyes (her) sun, the music in others' ears (her) symphony, and the smile on others' lips (her) happiness."

The veil of the temple acknowledges that we are living in eternity, now. It is our sanctuary when the winds blow and the rains beat down upon an ocean of life that seems to be in turmoil. It is the source to which we look for the buoyancy we so desperately seek, and it is the fountain of living water where we may satisfy our thirst, as we pursue the answers to life's greatest questions that continually vex our spirits. It is our shelter, when we have been tossed about as flotsam and jetsam, when our doubts begin to weigh us down, and we feel that we might perish before we reach the safe harbor of steadfast faith.

Many advantages are extended to us by the eternal perspective of the veil of the temple. Not the least of these is that when we raise our sights to its proffered expansive view of life, we are up and moving on the pathway to personal re-discovery and self-actualization. We will only enter into God's Rest when we have

gained a perfect knowledge of the divinity of the work, and are liberated from fear, doubt, apprehension of danger, the religious turmoil of the world, and from the vagaries of men. When we have cast off the self-limiting conditions and self-defeating behaviors that blind us to the reality of life beyond the veil, we will enjoy a settled conviction of the truth in our minds that affords us the peace that follows obedience to celestial principles. The invitation to follow the Savior is prefaced by the action verb "to come." Our journey to the veil propels us toward an incomprehensively larger view of life.

The veil prepares us to be clothed with immortality and eternal life, to more closely resemble our Father in Heaven in both His image and likeness. It extends to us an invitation to consider that we are gods and goddesses in embryo, with a genome that was created in a heavenly laboratory. It plants within our minds the acorn of a mighty oak. C.S. Lewis observed: "It is a serious thing to live in a society of possible Gods and Goddesses - to remember that the dullest and most uninteresting person you talk to may one day be a creature which if you saw it now you would be strongly tempted to worship. It is in the light of these overwhelming possibilities and with the awe and the circumspection proper to them, that we should conduct all our dealings with one another. There are no ordinary people. Next to the blessed sacrament itself, your neighbor is the holiest object presented to your senses." ("The Weight of Glory").

In this sense, "the infinite wonders of the universe will be revealed to us in exact measure as we are capable of receiving them. The keenness of our vision depends not on how much we can see, but on how much we feel." (Helen Keller, "The World I Live In.")

The transparency of the veil increases when we are spiritually sensitive and prepared to act. As our powers expand, we will experience the glittering facets of the life of the Spirit. "To use the careful preparation and training we receive as a springboard, to be capable of disciplined, controlled procedure and to be receptive to flashes of insight, is what solid Latter-day Saints should have going for them in

their inner lives." ("My Religion and Me," Lesson #9). Our journey to the veil sets us free to be creative, and sets us creative to become more free. Truly, our experiences at the veil amplify quiet spiritual stirrings and act as a catalyst that has been designed to propel us into the presence of God.

"I wish I could remember the days before my birth,' wrote the poet, "and if I knew the Father before I came to earth. In quiet moments when I'm all alone, I close my eyes and try to see my Heavenly home. Although I can't remember and cannot clearly see, I listen to the spirit and so I must believe. But still I wonder, and I hope to find the answer to the question that is on my mind. Where is Heaven? Is it very far? I would like to know if it's beyond the brightest star." (Janice Kapp Perry).

In the temple, we
sometimes have a striking
experience when light, or truth,
gradually distils upon our souls.
Just so, in the Sacred Grove, light
"descended gradually," entering the
quiet grove slowly enough that Joseph
was able to gauge its approach until it
finally reached him and enveloped him
within its dazzling brilliance. It was only
then that he "saw two Personages, whose
brightness and glory (were beyond all)
description," and who stood suspended
in the air within the encircling light.
(J.S.H. 1:17). We may not see Them,
but when we are in the temple,
and we receive inspiration
and revelation, we can
be sure that we are
in holy precincts,
as well.

We
will all be
tested by trials
and temptations,
and we will make
mistakes. But we will
rise above our failures
because of the love of the
Savior and His Atonement. It
is in the next act that all the
mysteries will be solved, all the
pieces of the puzzle will be put in
their proper place, all the confusion
that sometimes tormented us will put
to rest, and everything will be made
right. If that is to occur, we need
to be up and about starting now,
by making our way to the
temples of the Lord.

Chapter Five

The temple scripts God's Plan to save our souls

In the New Testament, there are tantalizingly few verses that speak of The Plan of Salvation. In Titus 1:2, Paul spoke of the promise of "eternal life, which God, that cannot lie, promised before the world began." (Titus 1:2). In his letter to the Hebrews, he wrote that the Savior "became the author of eternal salvation" (Hebrews 5:9). Peter wrote that Jesus Christ was "foreordained before the foundation of the world," to be the Redeemer. (1 Peter 1:20).

In the Pearl of Great Price, Moses spoke of "the Plan of Salvation unto all men" (Moses 6:62), and Abraham wrote of the divine design of the Gods: "And we will prove them herewith, to see if they will do all things whatsoever the Lord their God shall command them; and they who keep their first estate shall be added upon; and they who keep not their first estate shall not have glory in the same kingdom with those who keep their first estate; and they who keep their second estate shall have glory added upon their heads for ever and ever." (Abraham 3:25-26).

In all the scriptures, it is in The Book of Mormon that we really get a feel for The Plan. In several verses, (1 Nephi 13:26, 29, 32, 35, 35, & 40, & 1 Nephi 14:23 & 19:3), Nephi explained that in the Last Days, the Gentiles would "stumble exceedingly, because of the most plain and precious parts of the Gospel of the Lamb" that had been distorted within or deleted from the scriptures. (1 Nephi 13:34).

But a light would be provided at the end of the tunnel, for those whose minds had been "blinded by the subtle craftiness of men." (D&C 123:12). Today, in the instruction that is received in the temple, "we have also a more sure word of prophecy ... as unto a light that shineth in a dark place, until the day dawn, and the day star arise in (our) hearts." (2 Peter 1:19).

In the Old Testament, the Lord alluded to the revelatory experiences that can be ours when we attend the temple: "I will proceed to do a marvellous work among this people, even a marvellous work and a wonder: for the wisdom of their wise men shall perish, and the understanding of their prudent men shall be hid." (Isaiah 29:14).

<u>In the temple, we learn about The Merciful Plan of the Great Creator. (2 Nephi 9:6).</u>

"Mercy claimeth the penitent, and ... cometh because of the Atonement (which) bringeth to pass the resurrection of the dead, (which bringeth us back) into the presence of God. For behold, Justice exerciseth all his demands, and also Mercy claimeth all which is her own; and thus, none but the truly penitent are saved." (Alma 42:23-24, underlining mine). Our conscience is a celestial spark that God has put into each of us as part of the Merciful Plan of the Great Creator.

<u>In the temple, we learn about The Plan of our God. (2 Nephi 9:13).</u>

Its "great and eternal purposes were prepared from the foundation of the world." (Alma 42:26). John Taylor taught: "To the Son is given the power of the resurrection,

the power of the redemption, the power of salvation, the power to enact laws for the carrying out and accomplishment of the design. Hence, life and immortality are brought to light, the Gospel is introduced, and He becomes the Author of eternal life and exaltation." ("Mediation and Atonement," p. 171-172).

<u>In the temple, we learn about The Great and Eternal Plan of Deliverance from Death. (2 Nephi 11:5).</u>

One of the foundation teachings of the Gospel is that we came into this world to die. When Adam and Eve were placed in the Garden of Eden, it was with the understanding that they would violate or transgress a law in order to bring to pass the blessings of mortality for themselves and for all of their posterity. "And now, behold, I say unto you that if it had been possible for Adam to have partaken of the fruit of the Tree of Life at that time, there would have been no death, and the word would have been void, making God a liar, for he said: If thou eat, thou shalt surely die." (Alma 12:23).

<u>In the temple, we learn about The Plan of Salvation. (Alma 24:14).</u>

It is The Plan of Redemption, The Plan of Mercy, and The Plan of Happiness, because it makes possible, through the Atonement, the resurrection of otherwise imperfect mortals to eternal lives of glory. If it had not been for The Plan of Salvation, "which was laid from the foundation of the world, there could have been no resurrection of the dead. But there was a Plan ... laid, which shall bring to pass the resurrection of the dead." (Alma 12:25).

<u>In the temple, we learn about The Plan of Redemption. (Alma 29:2).</u>

"According to justice, The Plan of Redemption could not be brought about" and "Mercy could not take effect except it should destroy the work of Justice." (Alma 42:13). The beauty of The Plan of Redemption, then, is that it meets the demands of Justice through the infinite mercy of our loving Heavenly Father. The Plan allows Him to be both just and merciful at the same time.

<u>In the temple, we learn about The Great Plan of the Eternal God. (Alma 34:9).</u>

None of us can hope to find meaning in our lives if we treat the integral elements of the endowment superficially or carelessly. A conscious appreciation of its value must be earned. If we take it for granted, or if we abandon its core principles, its power to bless our lives may slip away and be lost forever. While The Great Plan of the Eternal God guarantees free will, it also gives us wide latitude to use our agency as we wish, with the ever-present risk that we will do so inappropriately and make poor choices. It provides us with the currency of the Atonement, but it also allows us to substitute that legal tender with wads of counterfeit cash with which we may attempt to make late payments with interest tacked on for bad behavior. If we try to subvert The Plan in futile efforts to obtain and retain blessings we do not deserve and that we cannot retain, our destabilizing efforts will be rewarded with a pyrrhic victory, at best.

<u>In the temple, we learn about The Great and Eternal Plan of Redemption. (Alma 34:16).</u>

Nephi clearly taught that "it is by grace that we are saved, after all we can do." (2 Nephi 25:23). Latter-day Saints, however, tend to emphasize works to the point that it may seem to others that they relegate the grace of God to a back seat, as they pursue their independent efforts to somehow earn salvation. In spite of their focus on accountability, agency, industry, and labor, as they are exhorted to greater dedication, diligence, and duty, the truth is that nothing we can do will ever qualify us for the blessing of eternal life. Paul and Luke echoed Nephi, writing that it is "by grace (we) are saved, through faith, and that not of (ourselves). It is the gift of God." (Ephesians 2:8). "We believe that through the grace of the Lord Jesus Christ we shall be saved." (Acts 15:11). It is "the grace of God that bringeth salvation." (Titus 2:11). It is only because of The Great and Eternal Plan of Redemption that we are saved, and its principles and doctrines are reinforced by the endowment.

<u>In the temple, we learn about The Great Plan of Redemption. (Alma 34:31).</u>

The "great and eternal purposes of God," Whose Plan is dramatically portrayed in the temple endowment, "were prepared from the foundation of the world."

(Alma 42:26). The Great Plan of Redemption, (Alma 34:31), that is so beautifully illustrated, required that "an atonement should be made; therefore, God Himself atoneth for the sins of the world, to bring about the plan of mercy, to appease the demands of justice, that God might be a perfect, just God, and a merciful God also." (Alma 42:15). The Atonement allowed God to satisfy justice and still mercifully reclaim us from physical and spiritual death. The Savior thus became the Master of the situation. In His sacrifice, the debt would be paid, redemption made, the covenant fulfilled, justice satisfied, the will of God done, and all power, including the keys of resurrection, would be given to the Son.

In the temple, we learn about The Plan of Restoration. (Alma 41:2).

The endowment clearly teaches that the Fall would give us the opportunity to come to the earth in order to prepare for our resurrection. We learn that death becomes our golden ticket to eternal life, even "the death which has been spoken of by Amulek, which is the temporal death; nevertheless there was a space granted unto" us whereby we "might repent; therefore this life became a probationary state; a time to prepare to meet God; a time to prepare for that endless state which has been spoken of by us, which is after the resurrection of the dead." (Alma 12:24). As the endowment unfolds, Heavenly Father makes it abundantly clear that the Atonement is the keystone of His Gospel arch that supports His Plan of Restoration. It allows us to be raised in the resurrection clothed in exactly the kinds of bodies for which we have prepared ourselves through repentance and forgiveness.

In the temple, we learn about The Great Plan of Salvation. (Alma 42:5).

Into every ordinance of the temple are woven the principles of The Great Plan of Salvation. (Alma 42:5). Without the light of the temple, where we learn about God's

Plan, we are doomed to suffer in the shadows, to experience only the indistinct flicker of illusions and caricatures of reality. Without the revelatory experiences of the House of the Lord, the discrepancy between our marginalized behavior and the ideals of The Plan would become so great that our short-lived pleasure in worldly ways would surely evaporate as the morning dew in the full light of day. If this disparity were allowed to reach "critical mass," a requisite readjustment would be required to tear down the façade of corruption and hypocrisy that had crept into our lives, to allow the cultivation of a more nurturing lifestyle made possible by obedience to the covenants we make in the temple.

Without the influence of the Light of Christ and the Holy Ghost that are found in the House of the Lord, civilizations wither and die. They become empty shells and structures of custom and convenience only, illuminated by the flickering candlelight of superstition and magic. The luminosity of the Lord encourages us to free ourselves from the bondage of sin. There is a warm glow that emanates from the temple, illuminating a friendship that has been forged with the Light of Christ and the Holy Ghost. It is simply the result of our spiritual transformation as we bask in the celestial light of the Lord.

If we scribe a line, having set the stylus of our compass on the process of purification, within the circle will be the endowment and the other ordinances driven by the engine of the priesthood and given vitality by the Light of the world. His power is manifest in our temple covenants, and our solemn oaths trigger a cleansing, and initiate a sanctification, that results in our innocence and holiness. In the dazzling light of truth, the nature of evil that is abroad on the earth is plainly manifest, and we are given "power over that spirit." (D&C 50:32). We are blessed with the means to lay bare evil designs, "not with railing accusation ... neither with boasting nor rejoicing," but with the measured response expected of the Lord's anointed, and characteristic of those who walk in obedience to the covenants of the temple. (D&C 50:33).

As we walk mildly and quietly in the brightly lighted hallways of the House of

the Lord, we become more comfortable embracing truth. "The wisdom that is from above is first pure, then peaceable, gentle, and easy to be entreated, full of mercy and good fruits, without partiality, and without hypocrisy." (James 3:17). In a world that grows increasingly noisy, we remember that inspiration comes in the peaceful setting of the temple. In 1991, Boyd K. Packer lamented that in spiritual Babylon, "clothing and grooming and conduct are looser and sloppier and more disheveled. Raucous music characterizes the drug culture, with obscene lyrics blasted through amplifiers, while lights flash psychedelic colors. This trend to more noise, more excitement, more contention, less restraint, less dignity, less formality is not coincidental nor innocent nor harmless. The first order issued by a commander mounting a military invasion is the jamming of the channels of communication of those he intends to conquer. Irreverence suits the purposes of the adversary by obstructing the delicate channels of revelation." (C.R., 10/1991).

As we embrace the influence of the Holy Ghost that is found within the revelatory walls of the temple, we establish a prayerful attitude. Spencer W. Kimball promised: "The Lord is eager to see our first awakening desires and our beginning efforts to penetrate the darkness. Having granted freedom of decision, He must permit us to grope our way until we reach for the light. But when we begin to hunger, when our arms begin to reach, when our knees begin to bend and our voices becomes articulate, then, and not till then, does our Lord push back the horizons, draw back the veil, and make it possible for us to emerge from dim uncertain stumbling to sureness, in heavenly light." (Munich Germany Area Conference, 8/1973). Isn't it wonderful when the sound of the voice of the Lord that is so familiar to the prophets is for us a continuous melody and a thunderous appeal, as we faithfully serve in lesser capacities, in the Church and Kingdom?

<u>In the temple, we learn about The Great Plan of Happiness. (Alma 42:8).</u>

Alma taught that in the absence of repentance for our sins, and without the benefit of The Plans' saving principles, we must ultimately be in a wretched state, living forever in our sins. "And now behold, if it were possible that our first parents could

have gone forth and partaken of the Tree of Life they would have been forever miserable, having no preparatory state, and thus The Plan of Redemption would have been frustrated, and the word of God would have been void, taking none effect." (Alma 12:26). Without redemption from sin, if Adam and Eve had partaken of the fruit of the Tree of Life, without first having received a remission of their sins through the preparatory state of repentance founded upon the infinite and eternal Atonement of Christ, it would not have been possible for them to sustain a celestial existence, inasmuch as in their fallen condition they would have been incapable of obedience to celestial principles. Thus, The Great Plan of Happiness would have been frustrated.

In the temple, we learn that "every time it rains, it rains pennies from heaven." When we leave the Lord's House, even if we look up into stormy skies, all we see are clouds that contain pennies from heaven. We find our fortune falling all over town, and so we make sure that our umbrella is upside down. The temple teaches us that if we want the things we love, if we want a package of sunshine and flowers, we must have showers. So when we hear it thunder, we don't run under a tree, because we know there will be "pennies from heaven for you and me." (Lyrics by Johnny Burke & Arthur Johnston).

Pennies from heaven were the first coinage to bear the inscription 'In God We Trust.' They are date-sensitive, and have their greatest intrinsic value when they are uncirculated, are in mint condition, or are even of proof quality. Pennies from heaven are the only legal tender that is allowed in the House of the Lord. They stand in sharp contrast to the spurious counterfeit coins that are circulated by Satan and by his money changers, who lurk in the shadows, hoping to negotiate with temple patrons and defile them in a one-sided currency exchange.

<u>In the temple, we learn about The Plan of Mercy.</u> (Alma 42:15).

When Adam and Eve were driven from the Garden, they were "punished" with the very things that would later prove to bring them the greatest happiness. As the

Sufi poet Rumi observed: "Our wounds become portals that allow light to enter us." A Savior would be provided for them, but in the meantime, cherubim and a flaming sword would be placed to keep the way of the Tree of Life, to preserve the doctrine of the Atonement, and the principles of repentance and forgiveness, that link together Justice and Mercy. As soon as they had been taught about The Plan of Mercy, they would be free to experience all of the wonders of mortality without harming their eternal identity. (See Genesis 3:24).

<u>In the temple, we learn about The Plan of Happiness. (Alma 42:16).</u>

The cherubim guaranteed that The Plan of Happiness would not be frustrated. "For behold, if Adam had put forth his hand immediately, and partaken of the Tree of Life, he would have lived forever, according to the word of God, having no space for repentance." (Alma 42:5). This would have posed an immediate problem that begged a solution. Because of the transgression of Adam and Eve in the Garden, Justice demanded that they "became lost forever ... And now, ye see by this that our first parents were cut off both temporally and spiritually from the presence of the Lord." (Alma 42:6-7). So it was, that "they became subject to follow after their own will." The crowning principle of agency was to be honored, even if it meant that Justice must be served. Therefore, "it was appointed unto man to die" (Alma 42:6), rather than to reclaim him without repentance "from this temporal death, for that would (have destroyed) The Great Plan of Happiness." (Alma 42:8).

<u>In the temple, we learn about The Great Plan of Mercy. (Alma 42:31).</u>

The Great Plan of Mercy gives us the opportunity to live our lives, push the envelope, and to take calculated risks. When we fail to measure up to God's undeviating standard, Jesus Christ stands ready to intervene in our behalf. When we Recognize our mistakes, when we experience Remorse for having made them, when we attempt to make Restitution if our behavior has wronged others, when we learn from the mistake and Reform our ways through Repentance, and Resolve to Refrain from Repeating it, we will be free to continue the path of progress, with a

complete Resolution through the Atonement of what would have otherwise proven to be incapacitating short-comings and irreconcilable inadequacy. By following this ordained process, our powers are set free to continually expand as we experience the glittering facets of the life of the Spirit. We go to the House of the Lord to receive flashes of insight, and to be cast off into streams of revelation and carried along in the quickening currents of direct experience with God.

Who is it that shall
enjoy the rest of God?
"He that walketh righteously,
and speaketh uprightly; he that
despiseth the gain of oppressions,
that shaketh his hands from holding
of bribes, that stoppeth his ears from
hearing of blood, and shutteth his eyes
from seeing evil. He shall dwell on high.
(His eyes) shall behold the land that is
very far off" in the world that is the
habitation of the Gods, and of
which the temple is a type.
(Isaiah 34:14-17).

As
cast members of
life's Three Act Play,
we can better understand
our roles if we have engaged
others in the scenes we play. We
need to be on familiar terms with
those who participate in the drama,
and share the stage with them as we
rehearse, through the endowment, the
challenges we face that are related
to mastering the assignments that
are, in turn, attached to each
of our individual parts.

Chapter Six

The endowment: the libretto of Life's Three Act Play

Every human being is a willing participant in a drama whose text was written eons ago, long before the world was made. The First Act took place in the pre-earth existence, where as spirit children of our Heavenly Father we were nurtured by His side. The Second Act takes place on the earth, where we have come for a brief sojourn, to have experiences that only mortality can offer, to develop faith, and to learn to be obedient. The Third Act will take place after physical death overtakes us. The endowment in the temple is the libretto of Life's Three Act Play.

That we even participated in the First Act comes as a complete surprise to most of us, because a veil has been drawn across our memory of those events. We take for granted our participation in the Second Act, because it involves the "here and now." The Third Act fills us with trepidation, because of our inherent fear of the unknown. But when we comprehend the grammar of the Gospel, we realize that "death is a mere comma, and not an exclamation point." (Neal A. Maxwell). It is not

extinguishing the light, but rather putting out the lamp because the dawn has come, for "life is eternal, love is immortal, and death is only a horizon which is nothing save the limit of our sight." (Raymond W. Rossiter).

It was in our primeval childhood that the curtain rose on the First Act. As the sons and daughters of the Master Playwright, and with the enthusiasm and energy characteristic of budding actors, we tried out for individual parts. He, in turn, bestowed upon each of us a role that was ideally suited to our talents, and that would maximize our potential to grow and develop as the play unfolded.

From the very beginning, the Master Playwright made us accountable as stewards over the blessings that He had prepared for us. He "stretched out the heavens, and built the earth," for it was his handiwork, and all things therein are His. (D&C 104:13-14). Set design, lighting, sound, costuming, choreography, musical score, and a thousand other details (but no stunt doubles!) were perfectly choreographed so that the production would be ideal from the beginning. Nothing would be left to chance. In the words of one young actor who already showed a propensity for mathematical genius, it was obvious that the Master "does not play dice" with His creations.

As budding young thespians, we excelled during that First Act, mastering our lessons until no more could be learned, and when the curtain fell at its conclusion, so did our profound comprehension of the broad scope of all three acts of the Play. In the light of the morning of a new day, with a veil drawn across our minds, we awakened to the Second Act, so that our mortal experiences would be as fresh and new to us as if it were our first encounter with the Play itself. This time, the wonders of mortal life would occupy a new stage whose breadth and depth and profundity would continually amaze us.

If we were fortunate enough to be born into homes where the script to the Play was available for careful study, we would awaken, as it were, from a dreamless sleep. A storyboard that came alive because of the Light of Christ would help us

to gradually come to an awareness of our divine potential, and it would bring comprehension that we had, indeed, been given tools sufficient to the tasks at hand. There would come a point in time when the eyes of our understanding would snap into sharp focus, and as sentient beings we would come to view ourselves as sons and daughters of God, even as white-hot sparks struck off His divine anvil. The flame of faith would ignite our resolve and focus our power to do whatsoever thing would be expedient, or right to do, to regain the glory of our former home at the conclusion of the Second Act of the Play.

For those who had retained no remembrance of the First Act, and who now saw themselves as strangers in a strange land, cast upon a foreign shore without map or compass, the Second Act would, nevertheless, be breathtaking in scope, and for many, it would be enough simply to enjoy its twists and turns, its nuances, and its capacity for character development.

But those familiar with the script knew of the Master's reputation for theatrical encore. Whereas critics might see frivolous repetition or even look in vain for a brief intermission from active engagement with "life," in fact, sooner or later, there would be for every participant in the Play their moment in the sun, when the light of understanding would illuminate their minds and confirm to their souls its divine potential.

Victor Hugo intuitively appreciated the nuances of the Three Act Play. He wrote: "The nearer I approach the end, the clearer I hear around me the immortal symphonies of the world which invite me. It is marvelous yet simple. For half a century, I have been writing my thoughts in prose, verse, history, drama, romance, tradition, satire, ode, and song. I have tried them all; but I feel that I have not said a thousandth part of that which is in me. The tomb is not a blind alley. It is an open thoroughfare. It closes in the twilight to open in the dawn. My work is only a beginning; my work is hardly above its foundation. I would gladly see it mounting forever."

Thus, every scene during the Second Act has been designed to have profound significance. "The earth rolls upon her wings, and the sun giveth his light by day, and the moon giveth her light by night, and the stars also give their light, as they roll upon their wings in their glory, in the midst of the power of God ... Behold, all these are kingdoms, and any man who hath seen any of the least of these hath seen God moving in his majesty and power." (D&C 88:45 & 47).

Thoughtful attention to each scene reveals its intrinsic importance, and when as actors we no longer trivialize outwardly insignificant story lines within the Play, we finally realize the truth of the statement of the Savior, Who said "then shall ye know that ye have seen me, that I am, and that I am the true light that is in you, and that you are in me."   (D&C 88:50).

Even as that First Act unfolded, the Master Playwright saw that "among all (the cast members) there were many of the noble and great ones; and (He) saw these souls that they were good. And he stood in the midst of them, and he said: These I will make my rulers." (Abraham 4:22-23). That is to say, some of us would be given starring roles, while others were to be given less spectacular, but equally supportive, responsibilities. All of us would be given agency, to act independently within the sphere of our influence, to see if we would of our own free will promote the purpose of the Play, which was to bring to pass our immortality and eternal life. (See Moses 1:39). Every participant would have an equal opportunity to progress, but only if their behavior supported the storyboard of the Play itself.

In an evolutionary development of character, there would come a time when it would dawn on us that if we kept our second estate, we should have "glory added upon their heads for ever and ever." (Abraham 3:26). It is not often that A Star is Born, but we would wrapped up in that process, not of maturation but of generation.

But for the players, there was a surprise in the storyboard created by the Master Playwright. The curtain that fell after the First Act was more impenetrable than

thick fog, for not only was their vision obscured, but also the very memory of the First Act had been erased from their conscious awareness. Nevertheless, they were permitted flashes of insight that would provide tantalizing hints of their former life. As Wordsworth revealed: "Our birth is a sleep and a forgetting. The soul that rises with us, our life's star, hath had elsewhere its setting, and cometh from afar. Not in entire forgetfulness, and not in utter nakedness, but trailing clouds of glory do we come, from God, who is our Home." ("Ode: Intimations of Immortality").

As we now participate with awakening understanding in the Second of the Three Acts, we realize that no matter our individual circumstances, through ups and downs, and detours and wash-outs in the road of life, there is meaning and purpose that we can scarcely comprehend. "My life is but a weaving between the Lord and me;" wrote the poet. "I cannot choose the colors; He worketh steadily. Oft-times, He weaveth sorrow, and I, in foolish pride, forget that He seeith the upper, and I, the underside. Not 'til the loom is silent and the shuttles cease to fly, shall God unroll the canvas and explain the reasons why. The dark threads are as needful in the Weaver's skillful hand, as the threads of gold and silver, in the pattern He has planned." (Benjamin Malachi Franklin, "The Weaver").

Joseph Smith gave the Three Act Play, a name. He called it The Plan of Salvation. He characterized it as "one of heaven's best gifts to mankind." Nephi called it The Merciful Plan of The Great Creator (2 Nephi 9:6), The Plan of our God (2 Nephi 9:13), and The Great and Eternal Plan of Deliverance from Death (2 Nephi 11:5). Alma variously called it not only The Plan of Salvation (Alma 24:14), but also Plan of Redemption (Alma 29:2), The Great Plan of The Eternal God (Alma 34:9), The Great and Eternal Plan of Redemption (Alma 34:16), The Great Plan of Redemption (Alma 34:31), The Plan of Restoration (Alma 41:2), The Great Plan of Salvation (Alma 42:5), The Plan of Mercy (Alma 42:15), The Great Plan of Mercy (Alma 42:31), The Plan of Happiness (Alma 42:16), and my personal favorite: The Great Plan of Happiness. (Alma 42:8). Whereas the most successful play on Broadway might close after a 10 or 15 year run, The Plan of Salvation has been around since before our first parents tended the Garden in Eden. It's performance

will extend beyond mortality, (which is the Second Act), on into the eternities, where the Third Act will play to sell-out crowds forever.

If there were ever a play worthy of a Tony Award, it would be this one, for "the great plan of salvation is a theme which ought to occupy our strict attention." (Joseph Smith). In this ultimate sense, it is clear that our "Father knows best!"

As members of the cast, we can better understand our roles if we are familiar with the other actors in the drama and engage them in the scenes we play, sharing with them the challenges we all face when attempting to master our individual parts. In addition, we can better relate to the other participants, and they to us, if we see each other against the milieu of the First, Second, and Third Acts, namely, our pre-mortal (or pre-earth) life, mortality, and life after death. Knowledge of this big picture, this sweeping panorama, is essential to our understanding of the intricacy, complexity, and sophistication of the Play itself.

In clear, explicit, and unambiguous language, the script confirms that we are spiritual children of our Heavenly Father; we are lifetime card-carrying members of His Screen Actor's Guild. We are guaranteed ultimate recognition for our efforts, and it is written into each of our contracts that we may, conditional upon our worthiness, receive residuals after the credits have been rolled. At the conclusion of the Second Act, after we have walked to center stage before our friends and colleagues to receive a Lifetime Achievement Award, we will go Home, to the celestial equivalent of the Lillian Booth Actor's Home, to laugh, and love, and reminisce about the performance of our lives.

After all is said and done, our familiarity with the script answers the question: "Who are these children coming down like gentle rain through darkened skies, with glory trailing from their feet as they go, and endless promise in their eyes? Who are these young ones growing tall, growing strong, like silver trees against the storm; who will not bend with the wind or the change, but stand to fight the world alone? These are the few, the warriors saved for Saturday; to come the last day of the

world. These are they, of Saturday. These are the strong, the warriors rising in their might to win the battle raging in the hearts of men, on Saturday. Strangers from a realm of light, who have forgotten all - the memory of their former life and the purpose of their call. And so, they must learn why they're here, and who they really are." ("Saturday's Warrior," lyrics by Doug Stewart).

The script is amply annotated with Latter-day scripture that sheds new light on our relationship with our Heavenly Father, Who is therein revealed to be the Master Playwright, for "by him, and through him, and of him, the worlds are and were created, and the inhabitants thereof are begotten sons and daughters of God." (D&C 76:24). It was He with Whom we participated in that First Act, for we were "in the beginning with God." (D&C 93:29).

The Pearl of Great Price provides a glimpse into the cast meeting held before the Play's premier performance. The setting was a grand Council in Heaven where "there stood one among them that was like unto God, and he said unto those who were with him: We will go down, for there is space there, and we will take of these materials, and we will make an earth whereon these may dwell; And we will prove them herewith, to see if they will do all things whatsoever the Lord their God shall command them." (Abraham 3:24-25, underlining mine). In other words, the members of the cast were to be proven "with the earth" itself. The stage upon which the Second Act was to be choreographed would be an experimental theater where cast members could be tried, tested, and proven, to evaluate their trustworthiness.

It was necessary, beforehand, that we be familiar with each of the key participants in the Play. Our comprehension of the role of Lucifer (whose stage name would be Satan) in the Play had all to do with adversity and opposition, the two conditions that are essential to the operation of the Play. These were new concepts for us, basking as it were in the light of the Play and the Plan, at the very feet of the Master Playwright. Nevertheless, as Lehi taught, "It must needs be that there is an opposition in all things." (2 Nephi 2:11). Else how could we enjoy happiness, if there

were no misery? How could we have life itself, if there were no death?

That the great thespian named Lucifer rebelled against the Play itself is undisputed. "And I, the Lord God, spake unto Moses, saying, That Satan, whom thou hast commanded in the name of mine Only Begotten, is the same which was from the beginning, and he came before me, saying, Behold, here am I, send me, for I will be thy son, and I will redeem all mankind, that one soul shall not be lost, and surely I will do it, wherefore give me thine honor." (Moses 4:1). When he and those who followed him staged a writer's union strike, they lost all of their bargaining chips, and are even now consigned to a permanent lock-out.

Lucifer's version of the Play was fundamentally different from that of the Master Playwright. Worst of all, it was a counterfeit. Covertly, it was a work of fiction, and like good fiction, it must have been immensely entertaining, engaging, and perhaps somewhat distracting. It was probably a "good read." It may have touched some impressionable young minds with titillation, drawing upon sensory experience that could only be imagined by neophyte actors still in the adolescent years of honing their craft. It may have been avant-garde for its time, and the Bohemian approach of its script to life may have left some of its readers with a touch of exhilaration, risqué as it was.

As fiction often does, it flirted with the forbidden, anticipating a future connection to carnality and sensuality, qualities that are always persuasive selling points to the masses. But as a work of fiction, it was deviously dangerous, for it had the appearance of plausibility, even though it was inoperable. Its fatal flaw was simple: it would not work. That it was, nevertheless, attractive to at least some of Heavenly Father's spirit children ('a third part') attests to the power of its ideology, however blemished it might have been.

Lucifer's goal was to be a Master Playwright in his own right, but he lacked both the inherent skill and the requisite patience to pay the performance costs associated with greatness. He wanted the steak without the sizzle, and when he could not have

it, he threw a temper tantrum, as gifted yet egocentric artists sometimes do, and he became Satan. For the scriptures attest that "the devil was before Adam, for he rebelled against me, saying, Give me thine honor, which is my power; and also a third part of the hosts of heaven turned he away from me because of their agency.

And they were thrust down, and thus came the devil and his angels." (D&C 29:36-38, underlining mine).

From this footnote in the Script, we know that as a consequence of Lucifer's disobedience, at least some of Heavenly Father's other spirit children also went on writer's strike while yet in the opening scenes of the First Act of the Three Act Play. The process may have been more like a slow leak rather than a blowout. It was a train wreck in slow motion. In their immaturity, these adolescents probably first refused to memorize the lines they had been given; then they likely showed up late for rehearsals. Perhaps they eschewed discipline on the set and fomented chaos instead. They may have questioned the storyboard itself, thinking that it applied to others, but not to themselves. Their murmuring became faultfinding, and then finally mutated into the conspiracy of a full-blown rebellion.

Fortunately, their numbers were few. One part of the cast remained valiant in defending the vision of the Master Playwright. Another part did not actively disobey but perhaps with less fervency rallied somewhat abjectly around the Master. It was that third part of the host, unknown in number, whose rebelled against both preparation and practice during the First Act, and who were dismissed from the cast party. As a result, they were given other, less noble, roles to play in the Second Act.

We know that we responded to the unveiling of the script with unbridled enthusiasm, for Job prophetically asked: "Where wast thou when I laid the foundations of the earth? Declare, if thou hast understanding ... When the morning stars sang together, and all the sons of God shouted for joy." (Job 38:4 & 7). We were there when the overture of a heavenly orchestra signaled the raising of the curtain over all the earth, and when it was met with thunderous applause.

Future members and non-members of The Church of Jesus Christ were surely sitting side-by-side at that council. When mission assignments were handed out and temporal roles were allocated, some must have turned to friends seated nearby to plead: "Find me! You will find me, won't you?"

It would be necessary to do so, because many are now only going through the motions of the Second Act, with little or no understanding of the Play itself. They have lost the script, and without its guidance leading to comprehension, they wander to and fro as flotsam and jetsam on the sea of life. Alternative screenplays have been created in frantic attempts to explain the mysteries of life, but every wind of doctrine drives their readers further from the truth. Many of these fictions turn out to be nothing more than short-lived sit-coms that are cancelled after only a few episodes.

Other scripts have become devious deceptions whose goal has been misinformation. "For there are many yet on the earth among all sects, parties, and denominations, who are blinded by the subtle craftiness of men, whereby they lie in wait to deceive and who are only kept from the truth because they know not where to find it." (D&C 123:12).

Even when they are at their very best, these self-appointed lights-unto-themselves lack the "star-power" of a recognizable stage legend. Pre-eminent among the real icons of ideology was "Jesus Christ, whom the prophets testified should come into the world. "And behold, (said He) I am the light and the life of the world; and I have drunk out of that bitter cup which the Father hath given me, and have glorified the Father in taking upon me the sins of the world." (3 Nephi 11:10-11). It was His selflessness and sacrifice that set Him apart from, and above, all others, who were nothing more than pretenders to the throne.

In mortality, myriad characters in the Play surround us, and the Second Act moves

forward relentlessly without interruption, following the arrow of time, that is the fire in which we burn. But, whether we recognize it or not, every social gathering is in reality another cast party. We hope and pray that our interactions with other cast members are alcohol and drug free, and that they are uncluttered and unencumbered by the soul-stains of sin. Too often, though, "heaven lies about us in our infancy. (But then) shades of the prison house begin to close upon the growing boy, but he beholds the light from whence it flows. He sees it in his joy. The youth, who daily farther from the east must travel, still is nature's priest, and by the vision splendid, is on his way attended. At length, the man perceives it die away, and fade into the light of common day." (Wordsworth). And so, we gradually lose our perspective; we forget (if we ever knew in the first place) where we came from, why we are here, and where we are going.

But even that apparent misfortune may be a blessing in disguise. For it was a fall from grace that became a critical and necessary part of our progression, through the Second Act and on into the Third. "It came to pass that the devil tempted Adam, and he partook of the forbidden fruit, and transgressed the commandment, wherein he became subject to the will of the devil, because he yielded unto temptation." (D&C 29:40). And thus it came to pass that, for all the sons and daughters of God, mortality became the Second Act of the Three Act Play.

God, the Master Playwright, knew beforehand that in the day Adam partook of the fruit, his eyes would be opened, and he would possess a broader perspective, for through opposition he would experience both good and evil, light and darkness, and pleasure and pain, (See Moses 4:11).) Master once again became Mentor, and the crucible of mortality became an experimental theater. The universe itself, the stage on which the Second Act would be played out, became "a machine for the making of Gods." (Henri Bergson, "Two Sources of Religion in Mortality").

Because of the Fall, we are subject to physical and spiritual death, the two fundamental certainties connected to the Second Act. So the Atonement became a critically important necessity, allowing the repentant faithful to return to the

presence of our Heavenly Father, to fulfill the promise He made concerning our participation in the Third Act. The Prophet Joseph Smith said "we came to this earth that we might have a body and present it pure before God in the Celestial Kingdom." While we are here, we "should be anxiously engaged in a good cause, and do many things of (our) own free will, and bring to pass much righteousness; for the power is in (us), wherein (we) are agents unto (ourselves)." (D&C 58:27-28). We are blessed with understanding, to rely upon the merits of Christ, so that we might be called and chosen to participate fully in the Third Act of the Play.

We know that life does not end with physical death, for "through the redemption which is made ... is brought to pass the resurrection from the dead. And the spirit and the body are the soul of man. And the resurrection from the dead is the redemption of the soul." (D&C 88:14-16). "For man is spirit, the elements are eternal, and spirit and element, inseparably connected, receive a fullness of joy." (D&C 93:33). When we finally enter our third estate, when the curtain rises on the Third Act of the Play, we shall be judged according to our works, and shall receive accordingly. (See D&C 76:111).

The line in everyone's favorite fairy tale reads "...and they all lived happily ever after," but it is not written in the Second Act. It is in the Third Act. As Boyd Packer said: "Until you have a broad perspective of the eternal nature of The Plan, you won't make much sense out of the inequities of life. (But) when you know The Plan and the purpose of it all, even those things will manifest a loving Father in Heaven." Today, we will be tested by trials and temptations, and we will make mistakes as a consequence of the Fall. But we will rise above our failures because of the love of the Savior, and because of His Atonement. It is in the next Act that all the mysteries will be solved, all the pieces of the puzzle will be put in their proper place, the confusion that sometimes tormented us will be put to rest, and everything will be made right.

In the Second Act, we can successfully address some of our worries by ourselves and without outside intervention or assistance. At the same time, we may think

that our apprehensions are undeserved. However, "anyone who imagines that bliss is normal is going to waste a lot of time running around shouting that he's been robbed. The fact is that most putts don't drop, most beef is tough, most children just grow up to be people, most successful marriages require a high degree of mutual toleration, and most jobs are more often dull than otherwise. Life is like an old-time rail journey, with delays, sidetracks, smoke, dust, cinders and jolts, interspersed only occasionally by beautiful vistas and thrilling bursts of speed. The trick is to simply be thankful to the Lord for allowing you to have the ride." (Jenkin Jones, Editor of "The Tulsa Tribune").

The locomotive that helps us to enjoy the ride is the temple, the crown jewel of the Second Act. We board a train that is bound for glory with a first-class ticket that makes the "delays, sidetracks, smoke, dust, cinders and jolts," a lot more comfortable. The conductor of that train is Jesus Christ, Who provides significant relief from the pressures of the journey by allowing us to take upon ourselves His yoke.

Even as we pass through mortality, it is the Third Act that is continually competing for our attention. Along the way, it helps to have celestial signposts to guide us through the telestial traffic jams and conceptual cul-de-sacs that threaten to detour us from the strait and narrow way. That path leads to a veil that will be parted to allow us to pass onto a stage where the Third Act will play out. If we are true to eternally valid principles, expanding circles of opportunity will assure us of direct experience with the perfect law of liberty. Thus, we will trade the uncertain course adopted by individuals bound for the Telestial Kingdom for the certain reality of Celestial Surety. Then, the Third Act will prove to be everything for which we have ever hoped and dreamed. As Hans Christian Anderson said: "Our lives are fairytales waiting to be written by the finger of God." In the Play that is The Plan, fairytales do come true, and there is a magic kingdom waiting for us, just beyond the horizon of our vision.

When we engage our agency within the bounds the Master Playwright has set,

we limit our options. If we choose the better alternative, we automatically have made the decision not to choose less attractive alternatives and their attendant consequences. Those who suffer from compulsions have reached this condition because of repeated and successive re-acts until a point is reached where, as

William James explained, "unlimited freedom leads to unlimited tyranny." Under these circumstances, the Play can be twisted by u inspired scriptwriters into a nightmarish scenario, even a living hell.

Instead, faithful participants in the Play are now and forever independent in that stage of development to which their decisions have led them. Poised on the edge of forever, they need little incentive to push off into the unknown. Heavy with anticipation, they eagerly look forward to the libretto of life's Three Act Play; to the final pages of the storyboard, where they will read of themselves: "And they all lived happily ever after."

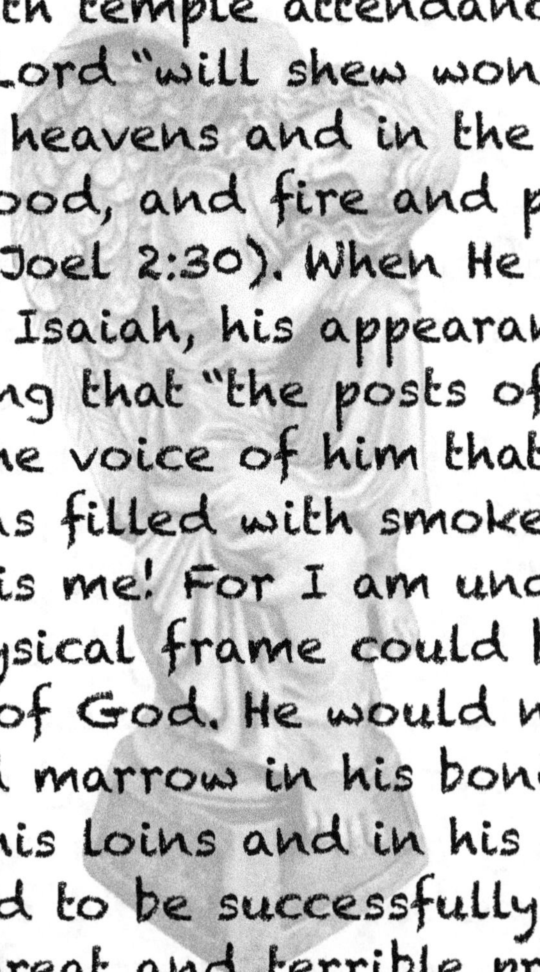

To those who
prepare themselves
with temple attendance,
the Lord "will shew wonders
in the heavens and in the earth,
(with) blood, and fire and pillars of
smoke." (Joel 2:30). When He revealed
Himself to Isaiah, his appearance was so
commanding that "the posts of the doors
moved at the voice of him that cried, and
the house was filled with smoke. Then, (said
Isaiah), Woe is me! For I am undone." (Isaiah
6:4-5). His physical frame could barely tolerate
the Presence of God. He would need health in
his navel and marrow in his bones, as well as
strength in his loins and in his sinews, if he
ever hoped to be successfully admitted
into the great and terrible presence of
the Lord Himself. (See D&C 89:18,
Proverbs 3:8, & Job 40:16).

To those who are unfamiliar with journeys thru harsh environments, palms often seem to grow in desert wastes. It is only upon closer inspection that oases of underlying currents of life-sustaining water may be noticed, that bring nourishment to the roots of the thirsty trees. So, too, the temple is a storehouse of bread, and a reservoir of living water. Its flowing fountains of revelation provide sustenance to all who hunger and thirst after righteousness.

Chapter Seven
Life's greatest questions

"Even the humblest human beings, Pope John Paul II observed, are naturally philosophic, asking themselves such questions as "Who and I? Where do I come from and where am I going?" Religious revelation provides answers to these questions, the pope acknowledges." ("Uniting Faith and Reason," Time Magazine, 10/26/1998).

Ever since the restoration of the guiding principles that are taught in the endowment under priesthood direction in the Last Days, members of the Lord's Church have received a heavenly witness of their origin and destiny as children of God. This knowledge has acted as a catalyst, inspiring them to be the best that they know how. Those who are bereft of this eternal perspective, however, who have no choice but to define themselves only in the present tense, are much less inclined to characteristically make the kinds of decisions that reflect their noble lineage, or to independently develop attitudes and habits that, in a future state, would bring them into conformity with the nature of God. "Whenever individuals believe that … there

is no cosmic yardstick by which we can really measure things, how then can they be punished for falling short by feet or inches?" (Neal A. Maxwell, "Freedom: A Hard Doctrine").

When we refuse the habitation of the Lord, and deny His grace and His power to change our lives, we dismiss His sacrifice, and esteem as a thing of naught His suffering. We close our minds to the soul-expanding opportunities afforded by mortality. We decline His offer to experience life abundantly, and ignore His invitations to come and follow Him. Because we are deaf to His entreaties, we live for the moment, deluding ourselves into thinking that we have it all, but we die as to the things of the Spirit.

In contrast, understanding ourselves from the eternal perspective of the temple has many advantages. Its view of life is multidimensional. "Whom say ye that I am?" the Savior asked Peter. (Luke 9:20). When he realized that Jesus was in fact the Christ, the Son of the Living God, Peter was up and moving along on the pathway to personal re-discovery and self-actualization.

The temple teaches us that we live in eternity, as well as in time. The scriptures make a valiant effort to describe God's perspective, but at the end of the day we remain trapped in time and can only indirectly appreciate the eternities. "Even now, time is clearly not our natural dimension," said Elder Neal A. Maxwell. "Thus it is that we are never really at home in time. Alternately, we find ourselves impatiently wishing to hasten its passage or to hold back the dawn. We can do neither, of course. Whereas, the bird is at home in the air, we are clearly not at home in time, because we belong to eternity. Time, as much as any one thing, whispers to us that we are strangers here. If it were natural to us, why is it that we have so many clocks and wristwatches?" ("B.Y.U. Speeches of The Year," 1979).

The world, though, would rather focus its attention and energy on what it perceives to be more pressing matters of immediate urgency. While it does prioritize activities, it falls into the trap of engaging in those tasks that concentrate on obtaining,

accumulating, consolidating, and securing its temporal well being, while the eternal welfare of souls hangs in the balance. Wasting the precious hours of preparation that has been allotted to us, most of us spend our time far less wisely than we spend our money. We "tend to fill space, as if what we have, what we are, is not enough. Being affluent, we strangle ourselves with what we can buy, things whose opacity obstructs our ability to see what is really there." (Gretel Erlich, "The Atlantic Magazine").

The temple teaches us that we come from a nobler realm where we were taught that success is measured by accomplishment, by the building of character, and by rendering service. In the presentation of the endowment, we discover that religious recognition is just that, a re-knowing of what we have already learned. As the poet wrote: "Oh this world has more of coming and of going than I can bear. I guess it's eternity I want, where all things are, and always will be; where I can hold my loves a little looser; where, finally, we realize that time is the only thing that really dies." (Carol Lynn Pearson, "Optical Illusion," in "Beginnings and Beyond").

Where did we come from?

Insight from the endowment stirs our spirits and confirms the truth. "I am God," the Lord told Moses. "I made the world, and all men before they were in the flesh." (Moses 6:51). Moses then shared the wonderful news with Israel: "Ye are the children of the Lord your God." (Deuteronomy 14:1). Later, Jehovah explained to Jeremiah that he was a spirit child of God, saying: "Before I formed thee in the belly I knew thee; and before thou camest forth out of the womb I sanctified thee, and I ordained thee a prophet unto the nations." (Jeremiah 1:4-5)

Israel was asked to "remember the days of old … when the most High divided to the nations their inheritance, when he separated the sons of Adam, he set the bounds of the people according to the number of the children of Israel." (Deuteronomy 32:7-8). Clearly, we lived before we were born, and were nurtured in the household of God. As the Psalmist said: "All of you are children of the most High." (Psalms 82:6). The Preacher knew that, at the conclusion of our mortal lives "shall the dust return to the

earth as it was, and the spirit shall return unto God who gave it." (Ecclesiastes 12:7).

Latter-day revelation confirms that we were organized from uncreated intelligence as spirit children of our Heavenly Father. We were "in the beginning with God" (D&C

93:29) and were "created before the world was made." (D&C 49:17). Emphatically, the Lord declared: "I was in the beginning with the Father, and am the Firstborn. Ye were also in the beginning with the Father." (D&C 93:21 & 23). We "received (our) first lessons in the world of spirits and were prepared (there) to come forth in the due time of the Lord." (D&C 138:56).

As Eliza R. Snow wrote: "O my Father, Thou that dwellest in the high and glorious place, when shall I regain Thy presence, and again behold Thy face? In Thy holy habitation, did my spirit once reside? In my first primeval childhood, was I nurtured near Thy side? For a wise and glorious purpose Thou hast placed me here on earth, and withheld the recollection of my former friends and birth. Yet, oft-times a secret something whispered, 'You're a stranger here,' and I felt that I had wandered from a more exalted sphere. I had learned to call thee Father, through Thy Spirit from on high. But until the key of knowledge was restored, I knew not why. In the heavens are parents single? No, the though makes reason stare! Truth is reason, truth eternal tells me I've a Mother there. When I leave this frail existence, when I lay this mortal by, Father, Mother, may I meet you in Your royal courts on high? Then, at length, when I've completed all You sent me forth to do, with Your mutual approbation, let me come and dwell with You." ("O My Father").

"The publication of "O My Father" caused a deep turn in traditional New World Christianity, for the concept of a literal Mother in Heaven has no antecedent. It opened up a view of women's roles in the eternities - motherhood on a celestial level. The words plainly express the existence of a mother goddess residing in the highest realms of eternity at the side of a Heavenly Father. Understanding all of the poem's lines has confirmed a greater, more exalted role for all women." (Keith & Ann Terry, "Eliza," p. 58).

Eliza R. Snow herself explained: "When we were first organized as a Relief Society, the Prophet used to attend all our meetings and give us instructions in regard to our present duties and also taught many things that transpired in our Spirit home. I got my inspiration from the Prophet's teachings. All that I was required to do was to use my gift and clothe that eternal principle in poetry." (Keith & Ann Terry, "Eliza," p. 58). Wilford Woodruff simply declared: "That hymn is a revelation."

Sister Snow drew from the same source that revealed to Abraham all "the intelligences that were organized before the world was; and among all these there were many of the noble and great ones. And God saw these souls that they were good, and he stood in the midst of them." (Abraham 3:22-23). These were those who were present at the foundation of the earth, who had The Plan of Salvation explained to them, and who "sang together (at a time when) all the sons of God shouted for joy." (Job 38:4 & 7).

The Lord told Joseph Smith how the creative process had taken place: "For by the power of my Spirit created I them; yea, all things both spiritual and temporal; First spiritual, secondly temporal." (D&C 29:31-32). "And every plant of the field before it was in the earth, and every herb of the field before it grew. For I, the Lord God, created all things, of which I have spoken, spiritually, before they were naturally upon the face of the earth." (Moses 3:5). Surely, then, "God (is) the God of the spirits of all flesh." (Numbers 16:22).

Luke understood that in Him, "we live, and move, and have our being; as certain also of your own poets have said, For we are also his offspring." (Acts 13:28). In vision, Jude saw a portion of Heavenly Father's spirit children, "the angels which kept not their first estate" because as spirit sons and daughters of God, they had been rebellious. They "left their own habitation" in consequence of their disobedience, and so "he hath reserved (them) in everlasting chains under darkness unto the judgment of the great day." (Jude 1:6). The Father of the Faithful confirmed: "They who keep their first estate shall be added upon; and they who keep not their first estate shall not have glory in the same kingdom with those who keep their first estate." (Abraham 3:26).

Those who kept their first estate now live "in the hope of eternal life, which God, that cannot lie, promised (to each of His children) before the world began," "according to the promise of life which is in Christ Jesus." (Titus 1:2 & 2 Timothy 1:1). Assurance was given during our pre-earth existence that those who, during mortality, would establish an unbroken pattern of obedience, both to the commandments and, when necessary, to repentance, should be saved because of the atoning sacrifice of the Lord Jesus Christ.

Those who live without the benefit of latter-day revelation and instruction in the temple, only dimly perceive our noble heritage, and sometimes find it hard to accept the reality that we dwelt among the Gods before our mortal births. In The Book of Mormon, even the prophet Alma acknowledged that there were certain points of doctrine that were not completely clear to him. To his son Corianton, he declared: "Now these mysteries are not yet fully made known unto me; therefore I shall forbear." (Alma 37:11). He felt that it was always better to keep his opinion to himself, rather than to speculate without the foundation of fact or specific revelation. Sometimes it is better to remain silent and be thought a fool, rather than to speak and remove all doubt. In his counsel to his son, Alma emphasized: "There are many mysteries which are kept, that no one knoweth them save God himself." (Alma 40:3).

Without the spiritual enlightenment that comes from the endowment by way of personal revelation, we cannot understand that in the beginning, "the Gods formed man from the dust of the ground, and took his spirit ... and put it into him; and breathed into his nostrils the breath of life, and man became a living soul." (Abraham 5:7). The body is composed of the corruptible elements of the earth, but the spirit comes from God, and quickens, or gives life to, the body. Thus, latter-day revelation confirms: The spirit which came from God and the body which was formed of the earth, "are the soul of man." (D&C 88:15).

As William Wordsworth wrote: "Our birth is but a sleep and a forgetting. The soul that rises with us, our life's star, hath had elsewhere its setting, and cometh from

afar. Not in entire forgetfulness, and not in utter nakedness, but trailing clouds of glory do we come from God, Who is our Home." (Ode: Intimations of Immortality, from Recollections of Early Childhood). These inspiring words are true. We "are the sons (and daughters) of the living God." (Hosea 1:10). "The Spirit itself beareth witness with our spirit, that we are the children of God." (Romans 8:16). Within each breast is the yearning to know: "Have we not all one father?" Each of us is prompted to ask the same question: "Hath not one God created us?" (Malachi 2:10). The answer rings loud and clear when we attend the temple, and resonates within our hearts: "In him we live, and move, and have our being (for) we are the offspring of God." (Acts 17:28-29). He is "the Father of all." (Ephesians 4:6).

Why Are We Here?

The knowledge of our pre-mortal existence as it unfolds in the endowment sanctifies life, dignifies individual effort, rewards achievement, and validates progress as a righteous goal. The Lord opens our eyes to the wonder of creation and to The Plan of Salvation, so that we might not counsel each other, "neither trust in the arm of flesh, but that (each of us) might speak in the name of God the Lord, even the Savior of the world; that faith also might increase in the earth; that (the) everlasting covenant might be established; (and) that the fulness of (the) gospel might be proclaimed by the weak and the simple unto the ends of the world." (D&C 1:19-23).

Viewing life from the perspective of the temple empowers parents as they teach their children correct principles. "Faith," after all, "cometh by hearing, and hearing by the word of God." (Romans 10:17). In time, children will also have the responsibility to teach their own posterity in an unbroken pattern of obedience. "And again, inasmuch as parents have children in Zion, or in any of her stakes which are organized, that teach them not to understand" the doctrines of the kingdom, "the sin be upon the heads of the parents ... And their children shall be baptized for the remission of their sins when eight years old, and receive the laying on of the hands. And they (that is, the children) shall also teach their children to pray, and to walk uprightly before the Lord." (D&C 68:25-28, underlining mine).

Our knowledge of the pre-earth existence and of The Plan of Salvation ennobles marital relationships that have been ratified by the authority of the priesthood of God. The Savior Himself explained to His Apostles: "Whatsoever thou shalt bind on earth shall be bound in heaven." (Matthew 16:19). "What therefore God hath joined together, let not man put asunder." (Mark 10:9). Thus sealed in the House of the Lord in the bonds of holy matrimony, a man and a woman may be "heirs together of the grace of life." (1 Peter 3:7).

"In the celestial glory," we are taught, "there are three heavens or degrees; And in order to obtain the highest, a man must enter into this order of the priesthood (meaning the new and everlasting covenant of marriage)." (D&C 131:1-2). The scriptures clearly teach that "whatsoever God doeth, it shall be forever." (Ecclesiastes 3:14). Ultimately, because of covenants we make in the temple, "neither is the man without the woman, neither the woman without the man, in the Lord." (1 Corinthians 11:11).

Celestial marriage is a diamond tiara created by the power and authority of God, that was meant to be prominently worn so that all might see and wonder. While no other religion stresses so much the meaning and worth of the soul, marriage and family are the highest expressions of individual achievement. This is the hardest for others to understand.

Those who are familiar with The Church of Jesus Christ of Latter-day Saints, however, are not surprised that the exaltation of families is the work and glory of God. They understand that our knowledge of The Plan of Happiness as it relates to families is a treasured "principle of intelligence (that we may) attain unto in this life, (that) will rise with us in the resurrection." (D&C 130:18). The understanding of the profound significance of the family as a stabilizing influence on society is a pearl of great price. (Matthew 13:46).

As always, on the one hand we may wisely exercise our agency, or, on the other hand we may repudiate our noble heritage, deny our birthright, forsake happiness,

invite misfortune, and forfeit our potential. It is Christ's way for us to act for ourselves. It is Satan's way for us to be acted upon. The choice is between liberty and eternal life, or captivity and spiritual death. We are free to behave in ways that are contrary to the instruction we receive in the temple, but unbridled freedom to do so eventually leads to tyranny. We are free to choose, but we cannot choose to escape the consequences of our poor choices. When we voluntarily give up our agency to Satan, we find ourselves in the grip of bad habits, and sooner or later we will feel his heavy cords around our necks that will ultimately restrict our behavior and drag us down to hell. It is very hard to break bad habits, precisely because we have given up our agency in order to acquire them.

Heavenly Father operates differently. He always has, and always will, honor the eternal principle of agency. It is riskier this way, but it is the only avenue that catalyzes the conditions wherein we may make sustained progress. The "perfect law of liberty" requires that we be free according to the flesh; to be agents unto ourselves. (James 1:25).

Rather than enslaving us in good habits, Heavenly Father uses the probationary state of mortality, and in particular free access to the temple, to repeatedly gives us the opportunity to recommit ourselves to covenants of obedience to true and eternal principles. These free us from the shackles of sin and expand our opportunities for expression. Probation is a time of testing, or of putting questions to the proof, which in this case are: "Will we serve God, when given the opportunity?" "Will we recognize Christ as our Savior, and exercise faith unto repentance?" "Will we allow Him to help us to reach our potential?" "Will we recognize Him as the Father of our spiritual regeneration?"

Because life is a probation, temple attendance is vital to our spiritual well being. By demonstrating through the ordinances and covenants that we are willing to submit to the authority of God, our awareness is expanded and we are magnified as we work toward our potential. By developing the qualities and attributes of our Heavenly Father and by "keeping our second estate," we will be rewarded with the

glory of our former home, after we pass through the veil separating mortality from eternity. In this sense, the meaningful experiences of the temple that lead us to make correct choices are essential to our eternal progression. How we respond to

Heavenly Father's invitation to frequent His holy habitation will make a difference in regard to what opportunities will be available to us later on.

While we are here, one of the ways God helps us to grow is by providing us with experiences that teach us how to deal positively with the adversity that is a part of life. It would be wrong to assume that the more righteous we are, or just because we are members of the Church, or just because we attend the temple, the less we will suffer. All suffer. God only promises that we will be blessed with the strength to endure. The difference is that the wicked must suffer the consequences of sin, in addition to the suffering that is a natural part of our mortal experience. Marion G. Romney taught: "If we can bear our afflictions with understanding, faith, and courage, we shall be strengthened and comforted and spared the torment which accompanies the mistaken idea that all suffering comes as a chastisement for transgression." (C.R., 10/1964).

Punishment naturally follows sin, but even that suffering can have a positive consequence when it is the very thing that brings us to repentance. The Atonement teaches us that the Lord will be merciful to us following our disobedience, and that His course is one eternal round. All of the experiences of mortality may ultimately work to our benefit. Lehi taught: "It must needs be, that there is an opposition in all things. If not so ... righteousness could not be brought to pass, neither wickedness, neither holiness nor misery, neither good nor bad." (2 Nephi 2:11). All these things give us experience. (See D&C 122:7).

Opposition was present from the very beginning. But in the Garden of Eden before the Fall, Adam and Eve did not have true moral agency until after they had yielded to the enticements of Satan. Nevertheless, Adam was not deceived. His decision to partake of the forbidden fruit of the Tree of the Knowledge of Good and Evil was

intelligently and consciously made, the result of a correct understanding of the requirements of the Gospel Plan. One of the basic messages of the Restoration is that "Adam fell that men might be, and men are that they might have joy." (2 Nephi 2:25). The scriptures refer only to his "transgression," and the 2nd Article of Faith makes a specific distinction between it and our sins. Mortality was the consequence of that transgression, but it was certainly not a punishment for sin. It was necessary "that the devil should tempt the children of men, or they could not be agents unto themselves; for if they never should have bitter they could not know the sweet. Wherefore, it came to pass that the devil tempted Adam, and he partook of the forbidden fruit and transgressed the commandment, wherein he became subject to the will of the devil, because he yielded unto temptation." (D&C 29:39-40).

Life is short, and yet all that is required may be accomplished. The transgression of Adam gave each one of us the opportunity to be born into a world full of exciting opportunities, with hard choices to be made on a daily basis. In the end, after having had experiences unique to mortality and that under the best of circumstances involve temple worship, we all must die in order to "fulfil the merciful plan of the Great Creator." (2 Nephi 9:6).

Because of the opposition that is a necessary part of our experience, our eternal progression depends upon our willingness to take advantage of the Atonement. When the Fall of Adam is considered in conjunction with the mission of Christ as our Savior and Redeemer, it is clear that both are essential to the successful implementation of God's Plan of Eternal Progression. The Atonement was required to vitalize The Plan for each of us who gladly accepted our role in the theater of life. It nullifies the permanent effects of physical death, and gives everyone the opportunity to have the effects of spiritual death removed through repentance. The Atonement saves us from the effects of our sins by activating the Law of Mercy that mitigates for those of us who conform to its requirements the effects of the first Law that demands Justice. Simply stated, the playing field is leveled for all of us. Nowhere is this doctrine more clearly articulated than in the endowment in the temple.

Where are we going?

The personal, tangible, resurrection of our bodies is essential to the successful execution of The Plan of Salvation, for we are "spirit, the elements are eternal, and spirit and element, inseparably connected, receive a fulness of joy." (D&C 93:33). Therefore, we were born to die, so that we might enjoy a glorious resurrection and receive a fulness of joy. Viewed from an eternal perspective, then, "death is not extinguishing the light; it is (only) putting out the lamp because the dawn has come." (Rabindraneth Tagore). "To a world that is spiritually illiterate, (faithful Latter-day Saints) give great lessons in the grammar of the Gospel, including this one: Death is a mere comma, not an exclamation point." (Neal A. Maxwell, "Ensign," 5/1983). "Life is eternal, love is immortal, and death is only a horizon which is nothing save the limit of our sight." (Raymond Rossiter).

Heavenly Father has seen to it that those who have developed faith unto salvation "shall not taste of death, for it shall be sweet unto them." (D&C 42:47). "Thou shalt live together in love," explained the Savior, to the end that "thou shalt weep for the loss of them that die, (but) more especially for those that have not hope of a glorious resurrection." (D&C 42:45). Under the best of circumstances, when the temple endowment has defined the course and quality of our journey through life, "the only difference between the old and the young dying, is one lives longer in heaven and eternal light and glory than the other, and is freed a little sooner from this miserable world." (Joseph Smith, H.C., 4:553).

Heavenly Father's disobedient and undisciplined children, however, will remain unprepared to be reunited with Him at the conclusion of their mortal sojourn. The Lord said of those who die bereft of hope in a glorious resurrection, "wo unto them, for their death is bitter." (D&C 42:47). In consequence of their disobedience while they yet live, they have no expectation of forgiveness, progression, salvation, or exaltation. Without hope, they "must needs be in despair, and despair cometh because of iniquity." (Moroni 10:22). When they attend the Banquet of Consequences, they will "droop in sin." (2 Nephi 4:28). "There will not be much that is satisfying at

the table unless they are able to bow their heads in reverence, and not hang them in shame, in the presence of God Who will be there." (Marion D. Hanks, "Speeches of The Year," 10/3/1967).

The Savior taught: "Blessed are all they that mourn, for they shall be comforted." (3 Nephi 12:4). In one specific way, those individuals are truly blessed who have been baptized and have received the Holy Ghost, for our heaviest burdens have to do with unresolved sin. When we are sensitive to our feelings, mourning for sin can help us to overcome its negative consequences by facilitating the process of repentance, so that we may be blessed with the joy of forgiveness. In this way, when our experiences bring us trials, but we are rooted deeply in the Gospel soil that is surrounds temple precincts, the Lord will bless us with emotions that help us to maintain an eternal perspective. This can lend nobility to even our most difficult challenges. Obedience to the Gospel principles of repentance and forgiveness helps us to break free of the shackles that limit our progress and thwart our chances to live abundantly. When we have been forgiven of our sins, we look forward with enthusiasm to temple worship. We have no cause to despair, even if we have had cause to mourn our imperfections.

At another level, grief is good when we mourn for those who have died in full faith and fellowship in the Church with the secure hope of eternal life in the Kingdom of God. As Joseph Fielding Smith said: "They shall never die the second (spiritual) death, and feel the torment of the wicked, when they come face to face with eternity." ("Church History & Modern Revelation," 1:186). Death is only bitter for those who are unprepared to meet God. For this reason, if it is within our power, let us never be more than a few days or a few steps from the temple. Our path that leads to the House of the Lord will be measured in faith and in hours, but not in miles.

Spiritual death is alienation from the Holy Ghost, and occurs if we die "as to things pertaining unto righteousness." (Alma 12:16). The first individual spiritual death occurs when we commit sin after the age of accountability. In the scriptures, this

is called "the first spiritual death." (D&C 29:41). We can be spiritually born again through the cleansing action of the Holy Ghost, after repentance and baptism of water and the Spirit, by participating in ordinances of salvation, justification, and sanctification. Therefore, one of the greatest obstacles to our enjoyment of eternal life, that of spiritual death, can be overcome by attending the temple and participating in ordinances of exaltation.

Then, there is "the second spiritual death," that is an eternal separation from the presence of God. This occur after we pass from mortality without having had the opportunity to participate in the ordinances of the temple, and when we then willingly decline the vicarious work that is performed on our behalf by saviors on Mount Zion, that is to say, in the House of the Lord.

And so we come full circle. The two most important days of our lives are the day we were born and the day we find out why. "When a baby is born, and as we wait with those who are dying, we brush against the veil, as greetings and goodbyes are said almost within earshot of each other. In such moments, this resonance with realities on the other side of the veil is so obvious that it can be explained in only one way." (Neal A. Maxwell, "B.Y.U. Devotional," 11/1979). Mortality is only one act of the great drama. When we have played out life's experiences, it will be time to move on to the next stage of our eternal development.

A mind and soul expanding message of the Restoration is that we have the potential to become as our Father in Heaven. When God called Enoch to be His prophet, the untutored youth wondered why, and admitted, "I ... am but a lad, and all the people hate me; for I am slow of speech." (Moses 6:31). Yet something in Enoch whispered to him that God's test didn't concern his ability, but rather his availability. Consequently, Enoch kept the commandments and trusted in the Lord's confidence in him, and he went on to become the builder of the greatest city on earth.

Helen Keller spoke for each of us, when she said that "every one who wishes to gain true knowledge must climb the Hill of Difficulty alone, and zigzag it in their own

way. I slip back many times; I fall, I stand still, I run against the edge of hidden obstacles, I lose my temper and find it again and keep it better. I trudge on; I gain a little, I feel encouraged, I get more eager and climb higher and begin to see the widening horizon. Every struggle is a victory. One more effort and I reach the luminous cloud, the blue depths of the sky, and the uplands of my desire." ("The Story of My Life").

The Gospel gives us the power to make a such a difference. "When we are dead," wrote the 14th century Sufi poet Hafez, "seek not our tomb in the earth, but find it in the hearts of men." "Mormons are like artichokes," observed a latter-day journalist. "At first encounter, you either like them or you don't. But those who have unfavorable first impressions often find that once the outer layers are peeled away, both Mormons and artichokes are most likable. In fact, most people who get to know Mormons become their friends. And a little objective research on Mormon beliefs reveals that, except for a few doctrinal differences, these people who call themselves Latter-day Saints are just like the rest of us … very human beings." ("The Boston Globe," 1967). But they are human beings with a common vision, motivated by zeal and empowered by the Gospel to reach their potential as sons and daughters of God, trailing clouds of glory as they make the journey from their former home through the learning laboratory of life, and on to an eternal destiny.

The Lord's Church is oriented toward missionary work so that all might have an equal opportunity to exercise their potential. His servants do not preach and teach only to make the lives of people better. They baptize and confirm the children of men so that they might be saved in the Celestial Kingdom of God. As we look around, it seems the world has gone mad, but the Church remains an island in the storm and the Gospel of Jesus Christ provides a refuge from life's uncertainties. It speaks a language of stability, direction, and purpose to those who are unsure, uncertain, and hesitant. Of those who join the Church, it might be said: "The stars fade away, the sun himself grows dim with age, and nature sinks in years; But thou shalt flourish in immortal youth, unhurt amidst the war of elements, the wreck of matter, and the crash of worlds." (Joseph Addison, "Cato," Act 5, Scene 1).

Henry Wadsworth Longfellow lamented: "Tell me not, in mournful numbers, life is but an empty dream! For the soul is dead that slumbers, and things are not what they seem. Life is real. Life is earnest! And the grave is not the goal. Dust thou art, to dust thou returnest, was not spoken of the soul. Not enjoyment, and not sorrow, is our destined end or way; but to act, that each tomorrow finds us farther than today. Lives of great men all remind us we can make our lives sublime, and departing, leave behind us footprints on the sands of time. Let us then be up and doing, with a heart for any fate; still achieving, still pursuing. Learn to labor, and to wait." ("A Psalm of Life").

Paul asked the question: "If we are no more servants, but rather sons of God, then does it not follow that we are heirs of all that God has, through His Son? (Galatians 4:7). We are "heirs of God, and joint-heirs with Christ." (Romans 8:17). The purpose of life is to provide a way for us to find eternal happiness, for it "is the object and design of our existence, and will be the end thereof if we follow the path that leads to it. And this path includes faith, virtue, uprightness, and keeping all the commandments of God." (Joseph Smith, "Teachings," p. 255-256).

Paul assured the Corinthian Saints that if they remained steadfast, in no matter what circumstances they might find themselves, no matter what cards they might have been dealt in life, in no matter what twist of fate they might think themselves trapped, ultimately, all things would be theirs, for they were "Christ's, and Christ is God's." (1 Corinthians 3:21-23). Our hope of a glorious resurrection hinges on this truth, however dimly it may be perceived. The endowment in the temple teaches us that, although "it doth not yet appear what we shall be, (nevertheless) we know that, when he shall appear, we shall be like him, for we shall see him as he is." (1 John 3:2).

Joseph Smith taught: "God Himself, finding He was in the midst of spirits and glory, because he was more intelligent, saw proper to institute laws whereby the rest could have a privilege to advance like Himself." ("Teachings," p. 364). Eternal life will not be thrust upon those who are unprepared or unacquainted with God and His

ways, or who are unwilling to make sacrifices today to secure blessings tomorrow. We are works in progress, and mortality was designed to be a life-long project to give everyone the opportunity to mold their nature to more closely resemble that of God. When that happens, we shall be "caught up to the third heaven," as was Paul.

(2 Corinthians 12:2). Then we shall "sit with (God) in (His) throne" for we shall have assumed both His image and His likeness. (Revelation 3:21).

When we receive the image of the Lord in our countenances, our faces will reflect an unearthly light, and our hearts will be transformed. The world seeks change from the outside, and fails miserably. The Gospel, through the temple endowment, changes us from the inside, and succeeds brilliantly. We are thus created to reach our potential in both the image and likeness of God our Father.

Again, the sage advice of Miss Keller seems apropos: "I, who am blind, can give one hint to those who see. Use your eyes as if tomorrow you would be stricken blind. And the same method can be applied to the other senses. Hear the music of voices, the song of a bird, and the mighty strains of an orchestra, as if you would be stricken deaf tomorrow. Touch each object as if tomorrow your tactile sense would fail. Smell the perfume of flowers, taste with relish each morsel, as if tomorrow you could never smell and taste again. Make the most of every sense; glory in the beauty which the world in all the facets of pleasure reveals to you through the several means of contact which nature provides. But of all the senses, I am sure that sight is the most delightful."

When we reach the end of our mortal journey, we will remember that our passage was facilitated by celestial signposts that guided us through the telestial traffic jams, the conceptual cul-de-sacs, and the doctrinal dead-ends that always threatened to detour us from the strait and narrow way. We will be forever grateful for the expanding circle of opportunity afforded by obedience to Gospel principles that exposed us to direct experience with the perfect law of liberty, and that allowed us to trade the uncertain course adopted by those bound for the telestial kingdom for the certain reality of celestial surety.

We will take great satisfaction to know that we engaged our agency within the bounds the Lord had set, and that, even with limited options, we were exposed to the perfect law of liberty. When we were blessed to choose better alternatives, we automatically made the decision not to accept less attractive consequences. We gained independence in that stage of development to which our decisions led us. But, in no matter what circumstances we found ourselves, our "universe became a machine for the making of Gods." (Henri Bergson, "The Two Sources of Morality and Religion"). Each of us was blessed with the privilege to "shine forth as the sun in the kingdom of (our) Father." (Matthew 13:43). If we were really fortunate, we grasped the invitation to expand the foundations of our spiritual center through temple worship.

If we believe in the power of God unto salvation, and accept His grace, and if we yield to His Spirit, we will continue our eternal progression. When we stand before the Bar of Justice, we will acknowledge that the requirements of the Gospel Plan were not haphazard or arbitrary, with corollaries, footnotes, addenda, and exceptions to the rule. Our obedience to God requires neither analysis or interpretation by legal counsel. His ordained Plan is a perfect Plan, and is all the more beautiful because of its simplicity. It has been spelled out for us with exactness and is clearly established and carefully clarified with purposeful precision in the ordinances of the temple so that there will be no disputations concerning its validity or its accessibility. Our Heavenly Father sends an invitation to all of His children, and His arms of mercy are extended to them through the Atonement of His Son. (See Alma 5:33).

Those familiar
with the scripting of
the Three Act Play might
be aware of the Master's well
known reputation for theatrical
encore. Denigrators might see only
a frivolous repetition, or even look
in vain for even a brief intermission
from the endowment's active and vital
engagement with life. However, sooner or
later, Heavenly Father will surely extend
an invitation to each of the participants
in the Play to have their moment in the
sun. Their minds will be illuminated by
the Light of Christ or the Holy Ghost.
In a spiritual awakening, they will
experience a confirmation of the
divine potential that had always
rested within their souls.

The greater understanding of the Plan of Salvation that is revealed in the House of the Lord blesses our lives in many ways. Its power creates the opportunity for dynamic change, as wisdom flows along established channels. Moreover, personal accountability, responsibility, and commitment to obedience expands. A humble need to serve strengthens the bonds of brotherhood and sisterhood, and generates interdependency in a community of true believers in which any cultural boundaries are effectively expunged. We are no more strangers or foreigners, but become fellowcitizens with the Saints in the household of God.

Chapter Eight
Trailing clouds of glory

I had never thought of the possibility that we lived before we were born, until I was taught by the missionaries and learned about the Gospel of Jesus Christ. I was unaware of William Wordsworth's observation that "our birth is but a sleep and a forgetting," and that "the soul that rises with us, our life's star, hath had elsewhere its setting, and cometh from afar." It hit me like a ton of bricks that "not in entire forgetfulness, and not in utter nakedness, but trailing clouds of glory do we come from God, Who is our Home." ("Ode: Intimations of Immortality"). If I had been familiar with these lines, I am sure they would have touched the tender chords of religious recognition that God had planted within me.

I had read the King James Version of the Bible, but had overlooked the verses that would have tickled my heart-strings with hints of our pre-earth life. Among them are the following: "Before I formed thee in the belly I knew thee; and before thou camest forth out of the womb I sanctified thee, and I ordained thee a prophet unto

the nations." (Jeremiah 1:5). "Ye are the children of the Lord your God." (Deuteronomy 14:1). We "are the sons of the living God." (Hosea 1:10). "All of you are children of the most High." (Psalms 82:6). He is "the Father of all." (Ephesians 4:6). "In him we live, and move, and have our being (for) we are the offspring of

God." (Acts 17:28-29). I did not yet know that, when each of us die, "shall the dust return to the earth as it was: and the spirit shall return unto God who gave it." (Ecclesiastes 12:7). Even now, I continue to wonder why these scriptures did not jump off the page, as I studied the Bible on my own.

If I had pondered these things, I might have received answers to the questions I had not yet thought to ask. Emerson might have been thinking of me, when he wrote: "The man who has seen the rising moon break out of the clouds at midnight has been present like an archangel at the creation of light and of the world." On another occasion, he declared: "If the stars should appear but one night in a thousand years, how would we believe and adore, and preserve for many generations the remembrance of the city of God which had been shown." To Abraham and Moses were revealed wonders that would have astonished even Emerson, things that answer the fundamental questions of existence relating to creation, agency, pre-mortality, and foreordination. These are the very things that are addressed in the temple endowment.

As he stood before the Burning Bush on Sinai, Moses became the first person in recorded history to ask: "Who am I?" (Exodus 3:11). In the revelatory thunder of the Book of Moses, we find plain and precious truth as we are given the rest of the story. "And God spake unto Moses, saying: Behold, I am the Lord God Almighty, and Endless is my name; for I am without beginning of days or end of years ... And behold, thou art my son." (Moses 1:3-4).

Today, in the holy precincts of the House of the Lord, we are described in the same way, as the children of God, and our character is molded and shaped by a covenant relationship that builds momentum during the presentation of the endowment.

We know that God is moral, because he has put us under covenant to obey the law of chastity. We know that He has charity, because he commands us to love Him and each other. We better understand His discipline as we conform our lives to the Law of Obedience. We know that He must have been a righteous steward, because He has provided us with the Law of Consecration. We learn how much He must love His less fortunate children, because he has given us the Law of the Fast. Our observance of the Word of Wisdom reminds us of His perfected, resurrected body. Our desire to seek knowledge recalls His omniscience. We carry a prayer of thanksgiving in our hearts for the laws that are anchored to the principles of The Plan of Salvation, that are so unmistakably explained in the endowment. We begin to realize that if it were not possible to become as God is, covenants would be unnecessary. Covenants ground our almost unimaginable destiny to the here-and-now. They are cables in air that anchor our temporal world to eternity.

In the temple, we learn that we are begotten spirit children of Heavenly parents, and that we lived in a pre-earth existence with Them before we began our sojourn in this second estate known as mortality. The endowment provides us with moments of deep reflection, as we "think of stepping on shore, and find that it is heaven! We visualize taking hold of a hand, and we find that it is God's hand. We envision breathing a new air, and find that it is celestial air. We imagine feeling invigorated, and find that it is immortality. We dream of passing from storm and tempest to an unbroken calm, and of waking up, and find that it is home." (Anonymous).

The temple endowment helps us to envision what it will be like coming home from our mortal mission. "It will seem like the time passed too quickly. We will think of the people we met, the people we helped, and of how our experiences helped us to grow spiritually. We will recall that we were like immature children when we left home, such a short time ago. We will find Mother waiting to embrace us, standing just a bit behind Father, who is bursting with pride. We will see tears of happiness falling from Her cheeks. Father will be the first to strike hands with us, and then warmly embrace us. Our feelings will resonate with familiarity, and we will feel the

Spirit as we never have before. We will know this is where we belong, and it will be a real homecoming as we return with honor to heaven." (Anonymous).

God taught these fundamental truths to Abraham, who was pondering, as so

many of us do during the presentation of the endowment, the majesty of God's handiwork. "Thus I, Abraham, talked with the Lord, face to face, as one man talketh with another; and he told me of the works which his hands had made; And he said unto me: My son, my son (and his hand was stretched out), behold I will show you all these. And he put his hand upon mine eyes, and I saw those things which his hands had made, which were many; and they multiplied before mine eyes, and I could not see the end thereof." (Abraham 3:11-12).

We are reminded of Helen Keller's observation that "there is one tragedy in life worse than to be born without sight, and that is to be born with sight, but without vision. Why cannot the soul go forth from its dwelling place," she asked, "and, discarding the poor lenses of the body, peer through the telescope of truth in to the infinite reaches of immortality?"

As He had earlier done with Moses, the Lord asked Abraham to define himself based on his relationship with God. Thus, He revealed to Abraham "the intelligences that were organized before the world was; and among all these there were many of the noble and great ones; And God saw these souls that they were good, and he stood in the midst of them, and he said: These I will make my rulers; for he stood among those that were spirits, and he saw that they were good; and he said unto me: Abraham, thou art one of them; thou wast chosen before thou wast born." (Abraham 3:22-23). Abraham must have tingled with excitement, as had I during my missionary discussions, to realize that he had been chosen before he was born.

Joseph F. Smith was blessed with a similar spiritually confirming vision of those who were "among the noble and great ones who were chosen in the beginning to be rulers in the Church of God." (D&C 138:55). He saw that these were called and set apart during a council that had been held in Heaven. As Job rhetorically asked:

"Where wast thou when I laid the foundations of the earth? ... When the morning stars sang together, and all the sons of God shouted for joy." (Job 38:4 & 7).

"It is extremely important to get straight what happened in that premortal council," explained Neal A. Maxwell. "It was not an unstructured meeting, nor was it a discussion between plans, nor a brain-storming session, as to how to formulate the plan for salvation and carry it out. Our Father's Plan was known, and the actual question put was whom the Father should send to carry it out." ("Deposition of a Disciple," p. 11).

Satan did not offer a viable alternative plan. His duplicitous suggestion that he be chosen was an unworkable counterfeit. (See Abraham 3:27). That he was a liar from the beginning, and drew so many away from Heavenly Fathers Plan, underscores the effectiveness of the ideological warfare strategy that lay at the heart of his rebellion. But just who, and how many, were cast out of heaven remains unclear. "For behold, the devil was before Adam, for he rebelled against me, saying, Give me thine honor, which is my power; and also (not a third, but) a third part of the hosts of heaven turned he away from me because of their agency. And they were thrust down, and thus came the devil and his angels." (D&C 29:36-37). Of this third-part, Moses wrote, somewhat vaguely, "he had drawn away many after him." (Moses 4:6). Abraham similarly stated: "Many followed after him." (Abraham 3:28).

We learn in the temple endowment that Lucifer became a minister of misinformation and a purveyor of propaganda. With extreme prejudice, he promoted what was really a political cause, that he might further his agenda and form a persuasive consensus among his brothers and sisters that was in opposition to His Father's Plan. Within the gut of those who listened to him, his bogus alternative produced, not a rational response, but an emotional reaction that was visceral in its intensity. The unthinkable inevitably followed, when the spirit of rebellion fomented war in heaven.

God, Who is an eternal optimist, kept His level head about Him. The scriptures

explain how the divine gift of agency that had been so powerfully illustrated during the conflict following the Council was preserved to interact with foreordination, that the lives of His valiant children might have purpose and meaning. He declared: "We will go down, for there is space there, and we will take of these materials, and we will make an earth whereon these may dwell; And we will prove them herewith, to see if they will do all things whatsoever the Lord their God shall command them; And they who keep their first estate shall be added upon; and they who keep not their first estate shall not have glory in the same kingdom with those who keep their first estate; and they who keep their second estate shall have glory added upon their heads for ever and ever." (Abraham 3:24-26).

This revelation makes clear that our divine right to exercise our agency in an atmosphere of opposition was intertwined with the rebellion of our common enemy Lucifer, that we might freely choose God and his commandments. The Plan foreordains us to have glory added upon our heads forever, on the condition of our faithfulness to God and the Atonement of Jesus Christ. We can better understand the foreordinations specific to our lives if we listen with real intent as the endowment unfolds before us.

Woven into its fabric is a conditional bestowal of gifts that is subject to our faithfulness to the covenants we make at holy altars. "Prophecies foreshadow events without determining their outcomes, because of a divine foreseeing of that outcome. So, foreordination is a conditional bestowal of a role, responsibility, or a blessing that, likewise, foresees but does not fix the outcome." (Neal Maxwell, B.Y.U., 10/10/1978).

"Our Heavenly Father has a full knowledge of the nature and disposition of each of His children, a knowledge gained by long observation and experience in the past eternity of our primeval childhood. By reason of that surpassing knowledge, God reads our future individually and collectively as communities and nations. He knows what each will do under given conditions, and sees the end from the

beginning. He foresees the future and as a state which naturally and surely will be; not as one which must be because He has arbitrarily willed that it should be." (James E. Talmage, "The Great Apostasy," p. 20).

Harold B. Lee taught: "Now a further word about this matter of foreordination. The Prophet Joseph Smith taught that every one "who has a calling to minister to the inhabitants of the world was ordained to that very purpose in the grand council of heaven before this world was." ("Teachings," p. 365). So, likewise, declared the Apostle Paul, "for whom he did foreknow ... them he also called." (Romans 2:29-30). But the endowment emphasizes that such a calling and such foreordination does not pre-determine what we must do. A prophet on this western continent has spoken plainly on this subject: "Being called and prepared from the foundation of the world, according to the foreknowledge of God on account of their exceeding faith and good works; in the first place being left to choose good or evil. (Alma 13:3)." ("Decisions for Successful Living," p. 168-169).

We learn from the endowment that our Heavenly Father may have called and chosen us even before we were born, to do a specific work, but whether we will accept that calling here and magnify it by faithful service and good works while in mortality is a matter that is decided when we reach out to God as we raise our right arm to the square during the ordinance of the endowment. It is no coincidence that we raise our hands to the heavens as a part of the covenant-making process. Nor is it a coincidence that the ordinance of the endowment culminates in communion with God that is intensely personal.

Even as we ae invited to enter the presence of the Lord, we might ask, as did Moses: "Tell me, I pray thee, why are these things so?" (Moses 1:30). In response to the inquiry of the great law-giver, the Lord gave the most simple, yet powerful, reply: Because it "is my work and my glory, to bring to pass the immortality and eternal life of man." (Moses 1:39). The temple was created that we might have a greater opportunity to exercise our agency, that we might participate with God in his marvelous work of bringing to pass our immortality and eternal life.

While serving in the temple, we discover an important key: The more we put our heart and soul into the work, the greater is our happiness and joy, and the more fully are we able to fulfil our own foreordained destiny. We have a greater desire to be ever faithful to the cause of Zion. Knowledge of our pre-mortal existence makes our lives almost sacramental; if dignifies our individual effort, rewards our timid achievement, and validates our faltering progress as we make our way to the veil.

One of our greatest personal challenges is to recognize in the distant recesses of memory our foreordained callings. When we humble ourselves before God, and have faith in Him, then will He make weak things strong unto us, just as He did as events unfolded following the Council in heaven, so long ago. (See Ether 12:27). Trailing clouds of glory we will return to God, Who is our Home.

As we think of our journey to the veil, we recall the wisdom of Winston Churchill, who said: "There comes for each of us that special moment when we are figuratively tapped on the shoulder and offered a chance to do a very special thing, unique to ourselves and fitted to our talents. What a tragedy if that moment should find us unprepared or unqualified for that which would be our finest hour." As we stand before God, angels and witnesses at the veil, it will be a fitting conclusion to our finest hour that were spent as willing participants in the ordinance of the endowment.

In a coming day, when we
face eternity, as we surely must,
the spiritual element in which we are
then immersed will transform our mortal
clay. Until that time comes, while we yet tarry
on the earth, we might ask ourselves under what
circumstances does that element quicken us, and
how can the pure knowledge that flows out of it
be vitalized? Surely, it is "a man's wisdom (that)
maketh his face to shine, (when) the boldness
of his face shall be changed," (Ecclesiastes
8:1), as he embraces the principles
of the endowment.

Chapter Nine
One in thine hand

Truly did
Shakespeare muse:
"All the world's a stage,"
for life is a Three Act Play and
we are willing participants in a drama
whose script was written long before
the earth fell into existence.

We pay dearly for our secular education and expect a handsome return on our investment. But it is our reintroduction to the elements of The Plan of Salvation that is equivalent to matriculating in a bachelor of independent study fine arts program. Its only entrance requirements are a ready heart and a willing mind, there is no temporal tuition, and its retirement benefits are out of this world. Its far-reaching design and sole purpose is to shepherd us back to our heavenly home.

In the course catalogue, primarily found in The Pearl of Great Price and in The Book of Mormon, it is variously referred to by well over a dozen different names.

It is mentioned by name in neither the Doctrine & Covenants nor in the Old or New

Testament, although Paul came tantalizingly close when he wrote that Christ "became the author of eternal salvation unto all them that obey him," and that He is "the author and finisher of our faith." (Hebrews 5:9 & 12:2). Paul also indirectly referred to God as the author of peace. (1 Corinthians 14:33). Whichever name it goes by, The Plan embraces God's ordained core curriculum that leads to family exaltation, and that is embedded within the temple endowment.

The blueprint of the temple diagrams safe passage through the minefields of mortality, documents potential perils and pitfalls, charts the recommended route that leads to refuge, maps out success strategies for abundant living, and measures our progress on the pathway to perfection. Its elements are similar to the World Wide Web that, for access, requires only computer literacy, an I.P. address with a network, and relevant hardware and software. The mainframe of the temple must exist somewhere, although its exact location is very hazy. A best guess is that it is somewhere in the neighborhood of Kolob. The storage of its data certainly exceeds that of the internet, which in 2019 was estimated to be in the neighborhood of 1,200 petabytes. That is 1.2 million terabytes, or 1.2 billion gigabytes.

It is that mind-boggling storage retrieval capacity of the temple that has the potential to order our chaotic world, to bless us with clarity rather than confusion, to teach us fluency in the language of the Spirit, and to educate those who are functionally illiterate so that they, too, might be mesmerized by the power of the Word. In simple binary terms, the Atonement is the Savior's user name, and repentance is the password that grants us access to the resources of the temple.

The temple's operating system first reviews what life must have been like in the pre-earth existence, and secondly it explains the purpose of mortality, while lastly it opens our hearts and our minds to expanding eternal opportunities. When we

conform to its overall strategy for success, we become better friends, neighbors, and missionary representatives of Christ, and we are also better equipped to find true happiness. It is within the elements of the temple that we discover that "while thousands of candles can be lighted from a single flame, the life of the candle will never be diminished." (Buddha).

In our busy and complex world, we often see through a glass darkly, making it very difficult to discern how to harness the power of the elusive equations found within the mathematics of the temple endowment. Its permutations and combinations do not reveal if our passage through its portals is facilitated by fame or anonymity, discovered by poverty or wealth, realized in sickness or health, undertaken with influence or obscurity, or if it is better accomplished by beauty or the beast. We sometimes forget that it promises both nurturing rain and the mud that inevitably follows, and that it is our lot in life to dutifully trudge along past potholes and other obstacles on rocky roads that are uphill most of the way and that face into a steady headwind. The fabric of the tapestry of the temple warns us about the "dark threads that are as needful in the Weaver's skillful hand as the threads of gold and silver, in the pattern He has planned." (Benjamin Malachi Franklin, "The Weaver").

We cannot hope to find meaning in our lives if we treat the elements of the temple superficially or carelessly. A conscious appreciation of their value must be earned. If we take them for granted or if we abandon their core principles, their power to bless our lives may slip away and be lost forever. While the principles taught in the temple guarantee free will, they also give us wide latitude to use our agency inappropriately to make poor choices. They give us enough rope to either hang ourselves, or to lasso the stars and "hitch our wagons" to eternity. (See Ralph Waldo Emerson, "American Civilization").

The temple provides us with currency sufficient for our needs, but it also allows us, if we choose to do so, to substitute its legal tender for wads of counterfeit cash

with which late payments may be made with interest and penalties tacked on for bad behavior. If we attempt to subvert its principles in futile efforts to obtain and retain blessings we do not deserve, our destabilizing efforts will reward us with a pyrrhic victory at best.

If we never learn the hard lessons of life that are sure to come our way, we will continually look elsewhere for gods of wood and stone that may temporarily soothe our temporal trauma but can never permanently redeem us from our misery. Our worldly ways will leave us vulnerable to a spiritual sickness that mimics the symptoms of those with advanced diabetes. When our peripheral circulation has been compromised, we will become numb to "the better angels of our nature" as we lose our capacity to touch the power of the endowment. (Abraham Lincoln).

If we become isolated from the sensitivity to our surroundings that is nurtured by the endowment, we may become inured to our condition in the sense that we are "past feeling." We may overcompensate with knee-jerk reactions, and without conscious awareness develop a "lead foot" that puts the pedal to the metal. Although life in the fast lane may be thrilling and provide a brief rush of adrenaline from the rapid release of other brain chemicals, when it finally "takes our breath away" we may not realize that our reduced lung capacity has robbed us of the vibrancy, joie de vivre, and capacity to inhale deeply of the celestial air that could have been ours, without the assistance of chemo-therapeutics.

Nothing can compensate for the dogged and determined discipline required by our temple covenants. Cheap thrills will never replace its lofty rewards. The titillation of novelty and the counter-productivity of spectacle cannot defeat, but might certainly delay, implementation of the temple's promises. The universal influence of the Spirit encourages us to fix our attention on the Pole-star of the Atonement, that has been designed to guide us to higher plateaus of personal progress.

The temple allows us to become engaged and energized, even as we journey through Babylon at an unhurried and yet productive pace. It even allows us to be captivated by the complexity of the world around us, to be immersed in its

intricacies, riveted by its rewards, and wrapped up in its spectacles, without being dragged down by the opposition that permeates those magical wonders. The ordinances of the temple stand at attention before the portals of heaven, patiently waiting for us to acknowledge their power to transform our lives.

In a sense, we must return to the secret garden of our childhood that is personalized by the temple in order to fully mature because, as William Henry Wordsworth wrote: "Heaven lies about us in our infancy. Shades of the prison house begin to close upon the growing boy, but he beholds the light and whence it flows. He sees it in his joy. The youth, who daily farther from the east must travel, still is nature's priest, and by the vision splendid, is on his way attended. At length the man perceives it die away, and fade into the light of common day." ("Ode: Intimations of Immortality").

Fortunately, the HazMat Protocol of repentance has been written into the temple's operating manual, so that as we prepare to worship there, the Atonement may detoxify us from the cares and conditioning influences of the world and from the homogenization process that occurs as we are worn down by the vicissitudes of life. Repentance paves the way that leads to the delivery room of the temple, where we are born again, repetitively re-vitalized, and astonishingly re-introduced to that magical kingdom where dreams really do come true. In between the sights and sounds, rides and attractions, and thrills and spills of our earthly theme-park experience, the inherent stabilizing influence of repentance draws our attention to personal spiritual hygiene practices including bathing in fonts that have been designed for the specific purpose of removing the grit and grime that threaten to foul our inner-workings.

The temple also mandates the need to make frequent changes out of clothing that has been soiled by sin into clean garments, and even requires occasional physical therapy and spiritual massage for relief from the bumps and bruises that we'll surely receive during our journey to the veil.

The temple assists us as we learn to be become handy with the tools that have been

provided to repair our mortal tabernacles. But we cannot hope to attend to our personal needs so successfully that, on our own, we will be able to maintain ideal form and function. Grandma's home remedies, although useful, will not be equal to the task, and if we eagerly embrace the elixirs peddled by the world's snake-oil salesmen, we will just be grasping at straws.

So we must instead embrace the temple, its therapies, and its gurneys upon which we will be given transfusions of the spiritual element to keep us going, at least until it's time to repeat the process in a week's time. When we frequent the blood-bank that has been created in our behalf, we will have experiences similar to those who regularly go to dialysis centers, where contaminants are removed from their blood because their kidneys cannot accomplish the task on their own.

But there will always be some who will not seek help, because they are caught up in the celebration of their so-called autonomy. The Lord described these as the enemies of God "unless they yield to the enticings of the Holy Spirit … and becometh as (children), submissive, meek, humble, patient, full of love, willing to submit to all things which the Lord seeth fit to inflict upon (them), even as a child doth submit to his father." (Mosiah 3:19).

In contrast to the hectic pace demanded by our technologically addicted world, the elements of the temple generate repetitive opportunities to stop and smell the roses along the pathway that leads Home. In fact, Heavenly Father created the roses in the first place, as love letters to His children. Of these subtle, positive reinforcements, the poet wrote: "Earth is crammed with heaven, and every bush with fire of God. But only those who see, take off their shoes. The rest stand around picking blackberries." (Elizabeth Barrett Browning).

The ingenuity, originality, and resourcefulness of the temple are such that they provide redundant mechanisms designed to give us repetitive opportunities for self-reflection, self-analysis, self-renewal, self commitment, and self-actualization,

while at the same time miraculously minimizing the character-crippling tendency to focus inward. When we conform our lives to its principles, we find our greatest expression, and room for self-doubt or second-guessing is eliminated.

The temple sets us free to be creative, and our creativity sets us free to plan properly prior to the time when we come face to face with the crises of life, so that we can prevent poor performance or mitigate its consequences. When we learn to trust the power of the covenants we have made with God, internalize their elements, and freely surrender ourselves to their infinite possibilities without reservation, we find our greatest individuality, personal expression, and freedom. Our progress along the pathway to perfection assumes self-shaping, self-supporting, self-sustaining and self-renewing characteristics. At its core, the endowment is made up of liberating laws that allow us to reach our potential in a mutually supportive atmosphere of inter-dependency with the Savior. (See Moses 1:39).

Those of weak character frequently think that they can side-step or somehow bypass the covenants of the temple, but this is only because they have never enjoyed the experiences of those who live on the strait and narrow path, thanks to the liberating influence of the Atonement. They mistake wickedness for happiness, confusing nature with nobility. When their behavior reflects worldliness rather than illumination from the Source of all light, when their activities harmonize more with secular standards and less with spiritual certainties, or when they are with their peers but without God, the resulting false sense of security generates instability because its immorality is unsustainable. Young people talk about "Best Friends Forever," but Heavenly Father would rather have us "Be Forever Faithful" through bonds of obedience to the principles, doctrines, ordinances, and covenants of the temple.

Opposition allows us to gauge the success of our internalization of the provisions of the endowment, and gives us a sense of how we are doing in our efforts to consciously and energetically participate without deviation in purposeful programs of personal progress that carry us forward on proven pathways. Conformity within

the embrace of the endowment has the capacity to provide significant sustainable support, and to carry us upward "as upon eagles' wings." (D&C 124:99). Without the consistency that is one of the greatest blessings of the temple, our lives would be nothing but cruel jokes whose punch lines would pierce our hearts without pity.

Such is the condition of those who are confronted by the sense of utter futility that accompanies their stubbornness, and their unwillingness to focus on the innate upward reach of the temple.

Without the light-generating capacity of the temple, we would be doomed to dance in flickering shadows that are only illusions and caricatures of reality. The blind who lead the blind stumble about in the dark until the discrepancy between their marginalized behavior and the ideals that are represented by the endowment becomes so great that their short-lived pleasure in worldly ways evaporates as the morning dew in the full light of day. Sooner or later, this disparity reaches "critical mass," requiring a requisite readjustment that tears down the façade of corruption and the accretions of hypocrisy, to allow the cultivation of more nurturing lifestyles that leads to family exaltation made possible by a return to obedience to the principles of the temple.

In scripture, we see this happening quickly, because historical narrative artificially compresses the passage of time. In fact, the obligatory alterations occur more gradually. In any event, time becomes an integral component of the temple, and in the presentation of the endowment, we can see that it was created as an elegant matrix to provide us with the gift of perspective for as long as we remain trapped within the confines of our mortal clay.

"They say time is the fire in which we burn." (Delmore Schwartz, "Calmly We Walk Through This April's Day"). This is true, in the sense that it is "with fire and with the Holy Ghost" that time becomes the element employed by the endowment to enable us to work out our own salvation with fear and trembling before the Lord. (3 Nephi 9:20, see Mormon 9:27).

Enough time has been built into the endowment for the recognition of our shortcomings to sink in, so that we can determine to take corrective action through renewal and recommitment. This is one reason why we raise our right arm to the square so frequently during the administration of the endowment. Repentance itself has been designed as a celestial barometer to measure the effectiveness of our commitment to our covenants, as we deal with the telestial tempests that regularly sweep across our landscapes. At the same time, our exercise of repentance triggers alarm bells in heaven, and gets our Father's immediate and undivided attention. It alerts Him to take note of our on-going efforts to rely upon the Atonement as the only moderating influence that can mitigate the damage of telestial and celestial trauma caused by those repetitive explosions within the temporal test tubes that are the fixtures of life's learning laboratory.

The temple endowment allows us to become reinvigorated by the refreshing breeze of celestial air. It gives us the opportunity to live our lives in an atmosphere of free-will, to inhale deeply even though our telestial aether might be tainted by opposition. We push the envelope, and we take risks. If, in our efforts, we fail to measure up to the covenants we have made, Jesus Christ will intervene in our behalf. If we Recognize a mistake, if we experience Remorse for having made it, if we attempt to make Restitution if our behavior has wronged others, if we learn from our blunders and Reform our ways, Resolving to Refrain from Repeating them, Repentance will encourage us get back on the bike and to continue our wobbly journey along the path of progress, with a complete Resolution through the Atonement of what would have otherwise been incapacitating short-comings and irreconcilable inadequacy. By following this process, we imperfect mortals can feel comfortable walking the hallowed hallways of the temple; we can feel our powers expand as we experience the glittering facets of the life of the Spirit wherein we become Receptive to flashes of insight, and are cast off into streams of Revelation and carried along in the quickening currents of direct experience with God.

The temple releases our energies to be creative and fosters creativity to allow us to experience greater capacity. In its design, is the perfect law of liberty. (See James

1:25). Our eternal welfare is thoroughly integrated into the success strategies of the endowment. Spencer W. Kimball recognized its nurturing potential when he urged us to lengthen our stride. In doing so, he knew that we would be lifted to spiritual

independence and to an awakening sensitivity that would put us in touch with our divine destiny.

However, it is not the purpose of the temple to give us our second wind in the first mile of the race, when we have only just begun our journey. We only feel its rejuvenating energy after we have warmed up our muscles with spiritually aerobic exercise, when we have loosened up our ligaments in compassionate service, when we have stretched beyond our perceived capacity and have gained the flexibility that is the reward of frequent temple attendance. We work out the "nots" in our physical and spiritual muscles by pushing ourselves to become habitual temple worshipers; we clear our vision to see beyond our supposed limitations, and raise our sights to fix our mind's eye on a finish line that rises up to meet a celestial horizon, and we settle in to sustained effort that sees us through to the end.

The temple endowment envisions a Utopian society, but it also contains corrective provisions should our agency lead us away from the Rod of Iron. It has built-in circuit breakers that will trip when we experience a power surge, and it has self-diagnostic provisions, should our efforts at improvement become stymied. If we are caught in the trauma of temporal traps, feel confused, abandoned, or disillusioned, if we despair as a consequence of our focus on worldly pleasure, or if our faith is flawed and we are blinded to the impotence and insignificance of our false gods, the endowment will ground us as no other therapy can. Without its influence, sooner or later, our misery will catch up to us and we will "perish in Babylon, even Babylon the great, which shall (surely) fall." (D&C 1:16).

If we want our service in the temple to be of benefit, we cannot at the same time maintain a vacation home in Idumea as a refuge from the strait and narrow path. Such diversions are only detours from life's journey. They will only cause us to

lose traction, slow our forward momentum, derail us from our sure footing on Gospel sod, and delay our progress toward our determined destination. When we succumb to temptation and embrace these distractions in any degree, we lose power, purpose, and focus. For example, if we depend more upon economic security than on spiritual preparedness, we will be more inclined in times of crisis to grasp at the world's goods rather than rededicate ourselves to the proven guidelines of the temple. If we put our trust in "idea gods," we will have no-where to look for help when the hot winds of change melt the very foundations of our misplaced faith in the "flavor of the day."

The temple is sometimes ignored because it is easy to be influenced by the desire to obtain what we do not need, to amass what we do not deserve, to hoard what we have not earned, and to stockpile what we cannot ultimately control. Each fall and winter, several million unvaccinated people worldwide succumb to the effects of an influenza virus that manifests itself in frustratingly mutated forms, but more die spiritually because they are infected by avarice and greed, covetousness and lust, and pride and prejudice.

Some think that they can be happy if they wander and play, but they never consider the blessing of the temple, that it is a place where we can ponder and pray. If we disregard temple service, we may fall into activities that dull our senses and leave us more vulnerable to Satan's enticements. Life is all a stage, but when the bouquets are thrown at our feet when we are summoned for a final curtain call after the last act has been played out, only those of us who have been obedient to the covenants we have made in the temple will receive standing ovations. This is why Samuel the Lamanite charged the people of Zarahemla: "Ye have sought all the days of your lives for that which ye could not obtain, and ye have sought for happiness in doing iniquity, which thing is contrary to the nature of that righteousness" which is inherent in temple worship. (Helaman 13:38).

The adversary finally betrays his followers because they can only live in opposition to their covenant consciousness for so long before his cunning caresses lead

them into conceptual cul-de-sacs. These are doctrinal dead-ends from which all exits lead to confusion, uncertainty, doubt, ambiguity, hesitation, and a retreat that plunges them headlong into a perceived freedom that, on closer inspection, is a bottomless pit of misery that is awash in doctrinal dilemmas. In a perverted and twisted way, the Devil "seeks that all men might be miserable like himself." (2 Nephi 2:27). Never does he promise happiness, but instead he manipulates us into thinking that we can circumvent the guiding principles of the temple by engaging in a warped reasoning that encourages rationalization that is only a reinvention of happiness in one of its many mutated form.

The meager substitutes for the rewards of the temple include affluence, authority, comfort, dominion, fashion, influence, position, style, and wealth. Lumped together, these are the Holy Grail of those who engage in a blind quest for the power and control that are the antithesis of the principles of the temple. To be sure, Heavenly Father wants us to reach our potential, and He could easily give us what He has. But instead, the temple foreordains us to become all that He is, by giving us the tools to incorporate His image and likeness into our own being and nature. (See 2 Peter 3:18 & 3 Nephi 28:10). For the temple to be meaningful, our bodies must be kept in good working condition, because they are the earthly tabernacles of our eternal spirits. The endowment gives us the tools to transform our corruptible bodies, so that they may become clean, pure, and full of light.

The tabernacles of our spirits can be holy temples in their own right. For we are "spirit, the elements are eternal, and spirit and element, inseparably connected, receive a fulness of joy." (D&C 93:33). Service in the temple helps us to more easily feel the influence of the Holy Ghost. In fact, when spiritual "health is absent, then wisdom cannot reveal itself, culture cannot become manifest, strength cannot fight, wealth becomes useless, and intelligence cannot be applied." (Heraclitus - Philosopher of the Golden Age of Greece).

We learn in the endowment that we will inherit our bodies in the resurrection and be joined to our spirits, never again to be separated. "The spirit and the body shall

be reunited again in its perfect form; both limb and joint shall be restored to its proper frame." (Alma 11:43). Therefore, our bodies must be kept as pure and as holy as are our spirits, in order to release the power of the temple to bless our lives, as envisioned by our Heavenly Father.

It is only natural, then, that Satan would tempt us to misuse our bodies. He is in a wretched state because he was never permitted to enjoy corporeal form. Because misery loves company, he wants each of us to be equally desolate. Thus, "the wicked one cometh and taken away light and truth, through disobedience." (D&C 93:39). Those who treat the ordinances of the temple as a thing of naught will inherit bodies and spirits in the resurrection that are perfectly matched to each other. But they will be without light. Their darkness will be a sinister and impenetrable gloom, and a nightmare from which they may never awaken.

The Lord specifically protects us against this risk by giving us a codicil to the temple known as Doctrine & Covenants Section 89 - The Word of Wisdom. This revelation was given "in consequence of the evil and designs which do and will exist in the hearts of conspiring men in the Last Days." (D&C 89:4). Evidently, more so than in former times, evil now has a well-entrenched and particularly pervasive and persuasive influence. The Lord's Law of Health has never been more important than it is today, and obedience has never been more critical as a condition of temple worthiness. So that the deck is not stacked against us, the Lord has leveled the playing field by giving us this addendum. We may still enjoy our moral agency, even as we are given pointed and specific instruction identifying what we ought to do to avoid deviation from the pathway to happiness that is dictated by the covenants of the temple.

Our finest hours are those when unexpected challenge is met with extraordinary response. Like the Seven Dwarfs, when we embrace the tenets of the temple we whistle while we work, because we have learned that, because of the Atonement, our efforts are linked to happiness. The virtue of the temple is its incredible power to touch our hearts, to change our nature, to soften us and to humble us, to make us as pliant clay in the hands of the Master Potter, to mold us as children, and to

securely envelop us in the fold of His garment, or in happiness.

But the more we chase the caricatures of the temple, the more "The Right Stuff" will elude us. However, if we plan our work and work The Plan (or serve in the temple), "that happiness which is prepared for the Saints" will come and sit softly on our shoulders. (2 Nephi 9:43). Lehi simply stated: "If there be no righteousness there be no happiness." (2 Nephi 2:13). Satan's frontal assault on the temple consists of bellicose behaviors, cunning customs, duplicitous deviations, hostile habits, insincere institutions, recalcitrant rituals, sneaky social conventions, and treacherous telestial traditions, and he works tirelessly to sabotage our best intentions to remain faithful to our covenants. Even technology gets in the way, substituting the electronic media for the direct interpersonal relationships, or the skin to skin contact, that represents the fulfilment of temple worship.

"Reach out and touch someone" has been twisted into a euphemism for "Use technology to isolate yourself from others." We see each other's Faces in Books and nurture on-line relationships to the exclusion of conventional real-time social interactions. Computers assess compatibility, talking heads provide commentary, sound-bites substitute insensibility for substance, and spin-doctors use the internet to wrest the news, promote hidden agendas, and endorse vested interests.

It is precisely because of the threat of behavioral instability that God has provided us with the covenants that are found in the temple endowment. Therein lies its power to reorient us to a lifestyle that pertains to righteousness, and to recalibrate our moral compass so that it will lead us to happiness. Our covenants provide unequivocal understanding and unambiguous definitions of eternal truth. They allow us to learn from the events within which we are swept up, to derive mutual benefit from our relationships with others, to grow within our environment no matter how unique or difficult it might seem, and to protect us from the worldly influences that encroach upon the fortress of our spiritual security, sanctuary, and symmetry.

The principles of the temple soften our telestial tendencies and create an impenetrable shield of faith. They provide a sounding board against which we can discern between the polarized opposites that clamor for our attention. The fruits of repentance, or forgiveness through the Atonement of Christ, defines the difference between happiness and its worldly counterfeits, and strikes familiar chords within our hearts and souls. Applying the principle of repentance in our lives is the spiritual equivalent of dusting for Satan's dirty fingerprints on the idols with which he teases, taunts, tempts, torments, and tortures us. Only when we fail to repent, can he turn and twist our attention from the truth.

Our covenants are the chiropractic adjustments that treat spiritual scoliosis. Covenants are a heavenly horticulturalist's weapons against the blight of sin. The sturdiest plants that bear the best fruit are those that have deep roots in good, rich, nurturing soil. The temple encourages us to surround ourselves with a loam that is rich in art, conversation, decency, example, honor, music, and virtue. Its objective is to allow our spirits to grow freely beyond narrow confines that are equivalent to one-pint nursery containers. Instead, we are liberated to send down taproots into Gospel soil, and we are anchored to the Infinite.

As we do so, we commit the 13th Article of Faith to memory as well as to our lifestyle. "If there is anything virtuous, lovely, or of good report or praiseworthy, we seek after these things." (See Philippians 4:8). To the extent that we do this, we are ignited with the "fire of God." (2 Kings 1:12). If we don't, we may experience a different kind of burning, in a hell while we yet dwell upon the earth; for that mental anguish may simply be the conscious recognition of lost opportunities and the unconscious sense of dread that accompanies the stupor of thought when our decisions have precipitated a subtle revolt against the ideals of the temple endowment.

Our obedience to the elements of the endowment gives us the opportunity to catch a glimpse of heaven. The Savior revealed: "Abundance is multiplied unto (us) through the manifestations of the Spirit." (D&C 70:13). In other words, we can so profoundly

feel the Spirit that it will seem to overflow as we realize our righteous objectives. These stay in focus because the spiritual guideposts of the endowment provide a Gospel-centered orientation and are the only proven perspective in a world that is filled with voices competing for our attention.

The Plan of Happiness is within the reach of every one of us, no matter what our cultural, social, political, or economic circumstances might be. The portals to the temple are supported by the scriptures and are buttressed by Gospel principles that testify of their universal applicability. They are our pillars of creation. On our own, we can do pitifully little to influence our circumstances. It is only through the miracle of continuing, enduring, immeasurable, infinite, uncorrupted, unfathomable, uninterrupted, and unspoiled grace that are embodied by the ordinances and covenants of the temple that we are "swallowed up in the joy of (our) God, even to the exhausting of (our) strength." (Alma 27:17).

When we reach that epiphany, our hearts will "brim with joy." (Alma 26:11). The ordinances of the temple are designed to save us in God's Celestial Kingdom. His mission statement, "this is my work and my glory – to bring to pass (our) immortality and eternal life," suggests that His carefully crafted Plan is not just a hobby; it is His very real work to which He gives His undivided attention. (Moses 1:39). His temple was not just designed so that we might live with our families forever. Instead, it was created to teach us how to live now, how to learn to appreciate the dominion He enjoys, how to use the tools He has provided, and how to create a heaven on earth, that we might retain a hope of eternal life, even during our engagement with mortality.

Therefore, it seems only reasonable that the temple would have the depth, breadth, majesty, and capacity to encircle all His children within His warm embrace. As the poet wrote: "He scribed a circle that drew me out. Heretic, rebel, a thing to flout! But love and I had the will to win. We scribed a circle that drew him in." (Edwin Markham).

This may be why, after the conclusion of the War in Heaven, when God pronounced

His subsequent creations as "good" He said that His crowning achievement, man, was, in fact, "very good." (Moses 2:4, 10, 12, 18, 21, 25 & 31). The earthly environment He has fashioned for us is ideally suited to nurture not only the favored "first part"

of His creations, but also the "second" part, and perhaps, for all we know, even the "third" part.

The Lord's Atonement, after all, is the key that unlocks the blessings of the temple. It was conceived before the foundation of the world. We are taught that it is infinite and eternal in its scope, and it directly influences the vast majority of Heavenly Father's spirit children who have not known Christ. As Paul said to those gathered at Mars Hill: "As I passed by, and beheld your devotions, I found an altar with this inscription, 'To the Unknown God.' Whom therefore ye ignorantly worship, him declare I unto you." (Acts 17:23).

Not all have been as fortunate as Jacob, who "knew of Christ, and … had a hope of his glory many hundred years before his coming." (Jacob 4:4). With its breathtaking reconciliation of Justice and Mercy within the matrix of free will, the Atonement renders the ordinances of the temple perfect, even for the ignorant men and women of Athens, in Paul's day. It seems reasonable that it would allow, not only the best of us, but also the worst of us to work out our salvation with fear and trembling, and to earn the privilege, as prodigal sons and daughters of God, to rejoin His household in full fellowship, with all the rights and privileges one would expect, following the reformation of our errant behavior and character. Is this not what the principle of repentance and the doctrine of Atonement are all about? After all, there is so much good in the worst of us, and so much bad in the best of us, that it hardly behooves any of us to talk about the rest of us.

None of us wants to miss the "Glory Train" that has been provided by the ordinances of the temple. We all want to "hear the whistle sound, for those souls heaven bound." We are all eager to "climb onboard the glory ride and set our earthly bonds aside." Most assuredly, that "old train will leave some day, boarding

Christians along the way." We can see it even now in our mind's eye, "roaring down those one-way tracks, and bound for heaven; it won't be back." We can hear the urgent call: "Get your ticket while you can. If you want a ride to Glory Land, we'll meet at the Lords' station. There's no time left for hesitation." When we climb on board, there will be enough seats for all who want to experience the ride of their lives, because "this long black train has no gears. It's full throttle ahead leaving here." We'll be in good company, for "the archangel will be our engineer. We'll depart amidst angelic cheers." All Christians of conscience will soberly realize "the price of the ticket is paid for us. Jesus died on the cross for sins we do. We must surrender to the Good Shepherd our all, before we miss that last boarding call." The promise is: "We'll glide on the ride to heavens' shore, where we will endure troubles no more. So shed your shackles. There's no need to pack. Board that Glory Train with one-way tracks!" (Kenneth Ellison, "Glory Train"). Faithful Latter-day Saints wait to board that glory train at temple station.

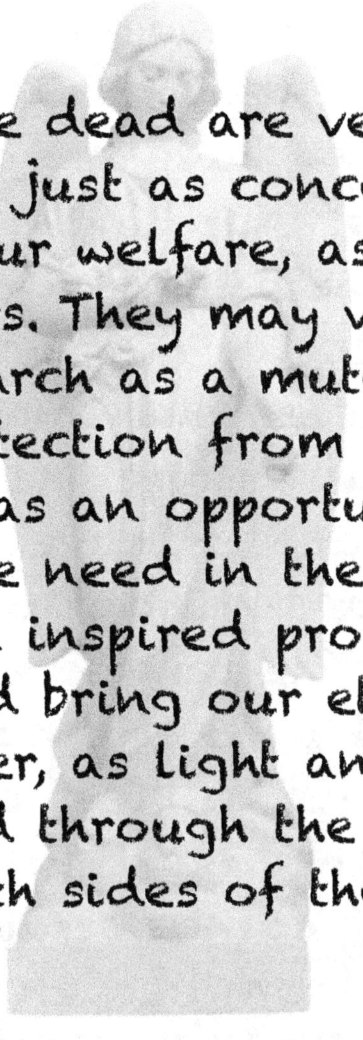

The dead are very
likely just as concerned
about our welfare, as we are
about theirs. They may view family
history research as a mutually shared
avenue of protection from the deceits of
the adversary, as an opportunity to receive
the assistance we need in the conduct of our
lives, and as an inspired program to deepen
conversion and bring our eternal families
closer together, as light and knowledge
are received through the Holy Ghost
on both sides of the veil.

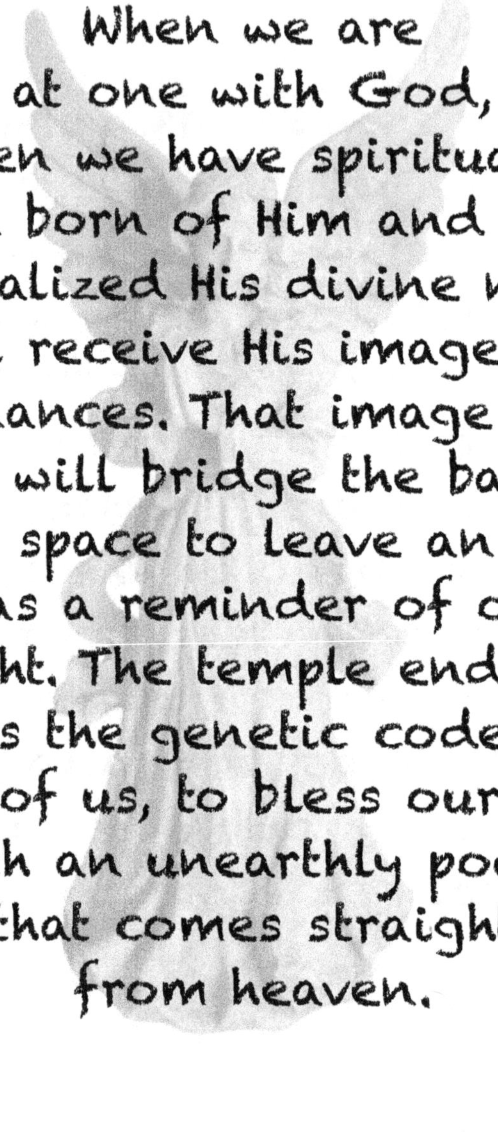

When we are
at one with God,
when we have spiritually
been born of Him and have
internalized His divine nature,
we will receive His image in our
countenances. That image and His
likeness will bridge the barriers of
time and space to leave an indelible
marker as a reminder of our noble
birthright. The temple endowment
rewrites the genetic code within
each of us, to bless our lives
with an unearthly power
that comes straight
from heaven.

Chapter Ten
Temple blessings are for everyone

Before offering the dedicatory prayer in the Ogden Utah Temple, Joseph Fielding Smith said: "When we dedicate a house to the Lord, what we really do is dedicate ourselves to the Lord's service, with a covenant that we shall use the house in the way he intends that it shall be used." ("Ensign," 3/1972). We thereby avoid the curse spoken of by Malachi, the last of the prophets of the Old Testament, who closed his ministry with these words: "Behold, I will send you Elijah the prophet, before the coming of the great and dreadful day of the Lord. And he shall turn the heart of the fathers to the children, and the heart of the children to their fathers, lest I come and smite the earth." (Malachi 4:5-6).

We might better understand the meaning of Malachi's prophecy, if we turn to the words of the Angel Moroni, who appeared to Joseph Smith on September 21, 1823. "Behold, I will reveal unto you the Priesthood, by the hand of Elijah the prophet, before the coming of the great and dreadful day of the Lord. And he shall plant in the hearts of the children the promises made to the fathers, and the hearts of the children shall turn to their fathers. If it were not so, the whole earth would be

utterly wasted at his coming." (D&C 2:1-3).

The message of Malachi is so important that it has been repeated, with only slight variation, in each of the four standard works. The Bible variant (Malachi 4:5-6) quoted above is identical to D&C 2:1-3, also quoted above, and to J.S.H. 1:37-39 in The Pearl of Great Price. (See D&C 128:17). In The Book of Mormon, the prophecy reads: "Behold, I will send you Elijah the prophet before the coming of the great and dreadful day of the Lord. And he shall turn the heart of the fathers to the children, and the heart of the children to their fathers, lest I come and smite the earth with a curse." (Nephi 25:5-6). The earth would be wasted, or cursed, simply because if there were no welding link between parents and children, then the work of God which is The Plan of Salvation, would fail.

We learn from latter-day revelation that Elijah held the sealing power of the Melchizedek Priesthood and was the last prophet on earth to do so before the time of Jesus Christ. On April 3, 1836, in the Kirtland temple, he appeared with Moses and others, and conferred his keys of authority upon Joseph Smith and Oliver Cowdery. (See D&C 110:13-16). Joseph Fielding Smith, Jr. explained: "This Priesthood holds the keys of binding and sealing on earth and in heaven of all the ordinances and principles pertaining to the salvation of man, that they may thus become valid in the celestial kingdom of God. It is by virtue of this authority that ordinances are performed in the temples for both the living and the dead. It is the power that unites for eternity husbands and wives when they enter into the new and everlasting covenant of marriage according to the eternal plan." ("Doctrines of Salvation," 2:117). It is the authority by which parents obtain the claim of parenthood concerning their children not only for time, but also through all eternity, which makes the family the basic building block in the Kingdom of God.

The fullness of the power of the priesthood is "the opportunity of entering into covenants, accepting ordinances that pertain to our salvation beyond what is preached in the world, beyond the principles of faith in the Lord Jesus Christ, repentance from sin and baptism for the remission of sins and the laying on of

hands for the gift of the Holy Ghost. These principles and covenants are received nowhere else but in the temple of God." (Joseph Fielding Smith, Jr., "Doctrines of Salvation," 2:40).

The sealing power of the priesthood is "the leaven that saves the earth from being utterly wasted at the coming of Jesus Christ. It is "so interwoven with the plan of salvation, that one cannot exist without the other." (Joseph Fielding Smith, Jr., "Liahona," 4/15/1930). Quite simply, without the temple and its ordinances and covenants, there can be no salvation. There can be immortalty, but not eternal life

In fact, the sealing power is irrevocably integrated with exaltation in the kingdom of God. Where there is one, there is the other. Where the one is not present, neither can there be the other. This is why, in our day, chosen servants of the Lord have been given this sealing power, that they might perform the saving ordinances of the Gospel for both the living and the dead. (See D&C 128:8).

The ordinances performed in the temple on behalf of those who have passed beyond the veil establish a covenant relationship with our Father and are cornerstones of The Plan of Salvation. When you stop and think about it, "the entire work of salvation (for ourselves and for our kindred dead) is a vicarious work, Jesus Christ standing as the propitiator, redeeming us from death for which we were not responsible, and also redeeming us from the responsibility of our own sins on condition of our repentance and acceptance of the Gospel. In the Last Days, He has delegated authority to the members of his Church to act for the dead (in a vicarious work for those) who are helpless to perform the saving ordinances for themselves." (Joseph Fielding Smith, Jr., "The Restoration of All Things," p. 174-75).

Our unselfish work for our dead in the House of the Lord harmonizes perfectly with the doctrine that God is no respecter of persons. (See Acts 10:34). He esteems all flesh as one. (See 1 Nephi 17:35). He views all of His children as living. (See Genesis 2:76, & Job 33:4). The dead are undoubtedly as concerned about our welfare, as we are about theirs. They may very well view family history research as our mutually

shared avenue of protection from the wiles of the adversary, as an opportunity to receive divine assistance in the conduct of our lives, and as an inspired program to bring our eternal families closer together, as conversions are deepened and light and knowledge are received through the Holy Ghost on both sides of the veil.

Joseph Fielding Smith, Jr. taught: "The Lord has decreed that all of his spirit children, every soul who has lived or shall live on earth, shall have a fair and just opportunity to believe and obey the laws of his everlasting Gospel." This creates a minor problem with family history research as it is currently being performed. As President Smith continued: "It is obvious that only a small portion of mankind has so far heard the word of revealed truth from the voice of one of the Lord's true servants. In the wisdom and justice of the Lord, (however), all must do so." (B.Y.U. Speeches of the Year," 1/12/1971).

How can that be possible, if, in our wildest estimates, "humanity has produced an astonishing 108 billion individual people over the past 50 millennia?" (Source: "Population Reference Bureau"). How could we ever do the work for so many people? To help to answer this question, Joseph Smith explained that "immortal beings will frequently visit the earth" during the millennium. "These resurrected beings will help" to accomplish this great work. ("Teachings," p. 268).

Brigham Young added: "We will have revelations to know our forefathers clear back to Father Adam and Mother Eve, and we will enter into the temples of God and officiate for them." (J.D., 15:137). Then, we will be sealed together until the chain is made perfect from the present back to our first parents.

Joseph Fielding Smith, Jr. taught: "There is too much work to finish before the Millennium begins, so it will be completed during that time. Resurrected beings will help us correct the mistakes we have made in doing research concerning our dead ancestors. They will also help us find the information we need to complete our records." ("Doctrines of Salvation," 2:167, 251-252).

This might help to explain why there is to be a thousand years of peaceful activity

that is focused on family history research following the Second Coming of the Lord. We know that during the Millennium, "Christ will reign personally upon the earth." (10th Article of Faith). We will enjoy unimpeded access to the House of the Lord, which will be as a celestial family history center, where angelic mentors will assist us as we perform vicarious work for the dead. Guided by revelation, we will prepare the records of our ancestors all the way back to Adam and Eve, to take to the ordinance rooms that are scattered across the face of the earth.

These temples are going to be humming with activity during the Millennium. The "Church News" reported on August 27, 1988: "The 100 millionth endowment for the dead was performed sometime in August. The first endowments for the dead were performed about 111 years ago, but, in keeping with an accelerating rate of temple (construction) and temple work, more than half have been performed in the last 11 years." That's about 50 million endowments in just 11 years, from 1978 to 1988, which is all the more remarkable, because at the time this article was published, there were only 41 temples in operation throughout the world.

By doing the math, if we were to continue performing work for the dead in all of those 41 temples at the same pace, roughly 5 billion endowments could be performed in 1,000 years. (+/- 5 million endowments per year x 1000 years = 5 billion endowments). But if there were not just 41, but 1,000 temples in operation, all performing endowments at the same pace as those initial 41 temples, more than enough endowments (almost 125 billion) could be performed in a thousand years.

The real question is: Is it necessary to perform the work for all 108 billion people that were postulated by the Population Reference Bureau to have lived on earth? After all, priesthood ordinances are only important for those who are willing to accept the Gospel in the Spirit World. In fact, "President Wilford Woodruff taught that almost all in the Spirit World will accept the vicarious ordinances when they are performed for them." ("The Improvement Era," 11/1941). So the answer may very well be 'Yes.'

Joseph Fielding Smith, Jr. said: "Those who did not have the opportunity to hear the message of salvation in this life but who would have accepted it with all their hearts if such an opportunity had come to them - they are the ones who will accept it in the Spirit World; they are the ones for whom we shall perform the ordinances in the temples; and they are the ones who shall, in this way, become heirs with us of salvation and eternal life." (B.Y.U. Speeches of the Year, 1/12/1971).

In 1856, Brigham Young famously declared: "To accomplish this work there will have to be not only one temple but thousands of them, and thousands and tens of thousands of men and women will go into those temples and officiate for people who have lived as far back as the Lord shall reveal." (J.D., 3:372).

President Young could have been speaking figuratively (thousands being a very big number), hyperbolically (sometimes, he got carried away), analytically (he was the Great Colonizer, after all), or prophetically (he knew the numbers, by revelation). It could have been any or all of the above. Perhaps he was recalling his own experience, back in Nauvoo, when about 5,200 individuals had received the endowment in just 42 working days. At the Nauvoo Temple pace, it would require 4,320 such temples to reach the magical number of 108 billion endowments during the Millennium.

Here is the Nauvoo math: In one temple, 123.8 endowments were performed per day (5,200 / 42 days), equaling 45,187 projected endowments per year, (123.8 x 365), or 45,187,000 in a thousand years (45,187 x 1,000). If 2,400 such temples were in operation, 108 billion endowments could be performed. However, during the Millennium, things could change dramatically, if the logistics of providing endowments were modified; for example, if the 21,000-seat Conference Center in Salt Lake City, Utah were converted into one large endowment room, or if endowments were broadcast to the chapels in which any of the 29,000 congregations of the Church meet, or, if the endowment itself were streamlined in some way. Witness the changes to the temple endowment that were implemented by the Church in 2019.

In any event, temple work is "one of the grand principles of truth revealed through the Prophet Joseph Smith. Obedience to this principle will allow us to "rejoice in the kingdom of God with our relatives and friends in the grand reunion and assemblage of the Saints of the Church of the First Born," thereby avoiding the curse that was spoken of by Malachi. (Joseph Fielding Smith, Jr., C.R., 10/1911).

Without the perspective
of the temple, we are more
likely to allow ourselves to be
caught up in the thick of thin things.
We tend to be short-sighted, and can be
insufferably self-indulgent, if only because
there are no parameters to help us establish a
foundation frame of reference, no standard to
which we may turn, no mentors to monitor our
progress, no Rod of Iron running straight and
true to which we may hold, no absolutes in
which we can confidently place our child
like trust, and no sustaining support
from a sympathetic priesthood.

Chapter Eleven
Our temple covenants

Joseph Smith stated: "There are but a very few beings in the world who understand rightly the nature of God, and if men do not understand the character of God they do not comprehend themselves." (H.C., 6:303). The purpose of the temple endowment is to help us to consciously develop qualities and character traits that are consistent with His divine nature.

Our Heavenly Father glories in the possibility that we might one day be like Him, and He offers us a special gift in the temple; specifically His grace, consisting of the gifts and power by which we may be brought to His perfection and stature, so that we may enjoy not only what He has, but also what He is. As Moroni declared: "If ye by the grace of God are perfect in Christ, and deny not his power, then are ye sanctified in Christ by the grace of God, through the shedding of the blood of Christ, which is in the covenant of the Father unto the remission of your sins, that ye become holy, without spot." (Moroni 10:33).

The priesthood energizes His grace by administering the ordinances of salvation, sanctification, justification, and exaltation, that allow us to receive the blessings of the Gospel by binding us to Him by means of covenants of action. The ordinances of the temple introduce us to a greater understanding of God's nature. They introduce us to binding contracts that come through revelation, and no person who participates in temple ordinances enters into such covenants except on its basis. It follows that the only ones who can legitimately make covenants with God are those who qualify by worthiness to enter the House of the Lord and participate in sacred ordinances that are revelatory in nature and are designed to bring us into His presence.

These covenants reflect not only His grace, but also His attributes. He is moral, so He gives us the Covenant of Chastity. He has charity, so He commands us to love Him and each other. God is disciplined, so He gives us the Law of Obedience. Because He is holy, He gives us the Law of Consecration. In consequence of the Gift of His Son, He gives us the Law of Sacrifice. God could give us everything He has, but what He is, we must earn for ourselves, as we struggle to overcome adversity and gain self-mastery. The purpose of our covenants is to help us to focus our efforts to become as He is. If that were not possible, covenants would be unnecessary.

Keeping the covenants we make in the temple protects us from the influence of the adversary and endows us with the priesthood and spiritual power necessary to overcome evil, until we have finished our work on the earth, and have obtained exaltation. As Peter taught: "Humble yourselves therefore under the mighty hand of God, that he may exalt you in due time." (1 Peter 5:6). The Prophet Joseph Smith said that salvation consists of our being placed beyond the power of our enemies, meaning the enemies of our progression, such as dishonesty, greediness, lying, immorality, and other vices.

Only by making covenants with God can we break the bands of death and are we made free to fully enjoy His grace. "There is no other name given whereby salvation cometh," said Benjamin; "therefore, I would that ye should take upon you the name

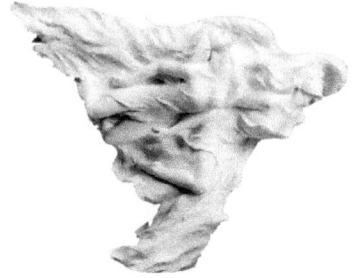

of Christ, all you that have entered into the covenant with God." (Mosiah 5:8). No other organization has the power to break the death grip of Satan, who would drag our souls down to hell in an instant, if we were to give him the opportunity to do so. Is it any wonder that The Church of Jesus Christ of Latter-day Saints builds temples, and that the Lord Himself proclaims that it "is the only true and living church upon the face of the whole earth, with which I, the Lord, am well pleased?" (D&C 1:30).

In the temple, we learn
that the world gauges success
using artificial measurements. But it
also powerfully teaches us that we come
from a more noble realm in which we were
taught that accomplishment is determined by
the building of character, and by rendering
service. As we participate in the endowment,
we discover that religious recognition is
just that, a re-cognition or re-knowing
of the principles of provident living
that touch our spirits because they
are inherently treasured, true,
and trustworthy.

Chapter Twelve

Shattering the glass ceiling of limiting beliefs

"But the worst enemy thou canst meet,
wilt thou thyself always be."
(Friedrich Nietzsche).

In a very real sense, each of us is confined to the world of our own making, and most of us are trapped within the narrowly defined perceptual prisons we have created for ourselves. Its walls are topped by the razor-wire of limiting beliefs, those stories we tell ourselves that cause us to sabotage our own best efforts. They can damage our resolve and even cripple our lives as they diminish our abilities, compromise our progress, and hold us back from reaching our goals, although most of us aren't even aware that we have made conscious decisions about what we choose to believe and not to believe. It is within the precincts of the temple that we have the power to recognize, wrestle with, change, and even eliminate our limiting beliefs. The temple can be a celestial observatory where we get our bearings on eternity Limiting beliefs exert tremendous pressure on us to resist change, remain short-

sighted, and retreat into the shadows of the status-quo, as we get caught up in the moment and persist in insufferable self-indulgence. They blind us to foundation frames of reference based on unchanging principles, deafen us to mentors who might otherwise have helped us to monitor our progress, and foster insensitivity to the standards to which we might have otherwise turned for clarity. They initiate corrosion of the iron rods that are ever before us, and they weaken the rebar of the absolutes upon which we would have otherwise framed our implicit trust. Limiting beliefs condemn us to repetitively recycle learning, without ever coming to a knowledge of the truth that would have made us free. They condition us to grasp at straws, and they blind us to the recognition that nothing will kill our creativity more surely than the self-assurance that poisons our ability to acknowledge the influence of a power greater than ourselves. Nothing will stifle the guiding Spirit faster than stubborn self-confidence mutated into unbridled pride and vanity. Limiting beliefs are antithetical to the expansion of understanding that is represented by the revelatory atmosphere of the temple.

Our limiting beliefs provide no sanctuary when the winds blow and the rains beat down. They offer no safe harbor to which we may flee when the ocean of life is in turmoil and we are tossed about as flotsam and jetsam. Our limiting beliefs obscure the course leading back to the source to which, in other circumstances, we would have looked for the stability we so desperately seek. Our limiting beliefs not only conceal the answers to life's greatest questions, but they also condemn us to ask the wrong questions.

It is no co-incidence that in the temple limiting beliefs can find no foothold, for it is there that we enjoy "a house of learning, even a house of prayer, an house of fasting, a house of faith, a house of learning, a house of glory, a house of order, (and) a house of God." (D&C 88:119).

When we submit to the blind guides of limiting beliefs, however, we close our eyes and our minds to the expansion of understanding that is found in the House of the Lord. If we yield to the forces of subtraction that are so prevalent in the world, we

tacitly decline the temple's invitation to experience the mathematics of the Celestial Kingdom. When we ratchet down our expectations because of our enslavement to limiting beliefs, we paint ourselves into conceptual corners, hobbling our creative talents to a few expressions within a narrow and confusing rational reality. Turning our backs to the creativity of insight, inspiration, intuition, and revelation, we may delude ourselves into thinking we have it all, when all that is before us is an illusion, a shadow, and a caricature of what could have been ours had we opened our hearts to the Spirit. By contrast, as we regularly attend the temple, we experience an amazing truth: "That which is of God is light, and he that receiveth light, and continueth in God, receiveth more light, and that light groweth brighter and brighter until the perfect day." (D&C 50:24).

Limiting beliefs can be so strong, vivid, and prominent that our minds can scarcely imagine other possibilities. Not so long ago, we convinced ourselves that the earth was flat, and that if we were to sail west, we would fall off its edge. We looked at birds in flight but told ourselves as recently as 1895 that "heavier than air flying machines are impossible." (Lord Kelvin, President of The Royal Society). In 1903, the President of the Michigan Savings Bank refused to back the Ford Motor Company, telling its founder: "The horse is here to stay." "Drill for oil?" said those whom Edwin L. Drake tried to enlist in his new energy project in 1859, in Titusville, Pennsylvania. "You mean drill into the ground to try and find oil? You're crazy!"

Of all the holy sanctuaries that have been created by God to be a safe haven from the follies of the world, the temple stands out as the least understood. The temple reminds us that "the natural man receiveth not the things of the Spirit of God, for they are foolishness unto him, neither can he know them" because of his limiting beliefs, "for they are spiritually discerned." (1 Corinthinans 2:14).

Limiting beliefs are strongly influenced by conventional wisdom. "Computers in the future may weigh no more than 1.5 tons." (Popular Mechanics, 1949). "I think there is a world market for maybe five computers." (Thomas Watson, chairman of I.B.M., 1943). "Data processing is a fad that won't last out the year." (The editors at

Prentice Hall, 1957). "But what (is the microchip) good for?" (memo from an I.B.M. engineer, 1968). "The telephone is inherently of no value to us." (Western Union memo, 1876). "The wireless music box has no imaginable commercial value. Who would pay for a message sent to nobody in particular?" (David Sarnoff's associates,

1920). "Who would want to hear actors talk?" (Harry Warner, Warner Brothers Studios, 1927). "People will soon get tired of staring at a plywood box every night." (Darryl Zanuck, head of 20th Century Fox, 1946). "Louis Pasteur's theory of germs is ridiculous fiction." (Professor of Physiology at Toulouse, 1872). "The abdomen, the chest, and the brain will forever be shut from the intrusion of the wise and humane surgeon." (Sir John Ericksen, British surgeon to Queen Victoria, 1873).

Limiting beliefs are influenced by the views of authority figures who all too easily dismiss innovation, by saying: "Are you crazy? We've always done it this way. It's too hard to change. No-one would accept it. It's too expensive. It would take too much time. It's too risky. People will laugh at you."

Those who make their way to the temple to enjoy its quiet serenity, and to partake of the fruit of the Tree of Life, must negotiate a treacherous path past great and spacious buildings that stand, as it were, in the air high above the earth. (See 1 Nephi 8:26). When Lehi described his dream to his son, he said of those whose minds and spirits were enslaved by limiting beliefs: "They did point the finger of scorn at me, and at those that were partaking of the fruit." (1 Nephi 8:33).

Even religious leaders are not immune to limiting beliefs: "There is no scripture other than the Bible. The heavens are closed. Revelation has ceased. Ordinances are unnecessary. God no longer speaks to us. The Church of Jesus Christ no longer exists on the earth. It is impossible to know God's will. Jesus was no more than a great teacher. And even: "A Bible! A Bible! We have got a Bible, and there cannot be any more Bible." (2 Nephi 29:3).

When great ideas are presented to the world, because they fly in the face of limiting beliefs that have imprisoned the minds of entire cultures, they are often

met defensively, first with ridicule, and then with active opposition. Finally, though, as they penetrate the darkness clouding stubborn minds, they may be smugly acknowledged as self-evident. It would be a good exercise for each of us to review the way we do things by looking them over carefully. We should be even and objective in our consideration of our perceptions. After a while, we should regard our pre-conceived ideas and attitudes with suspicion. We should dig deeper into our prejudices and our self-defeating behaviors that just may be defined by limiting beliefs. And finally, we should recognize that many of our behaviors should be abandoned in favor of new approaches.

Perhaps this is the "key of knowledge" that was spoken of by Joseph Smith. It certainly relates to the temple as a house of learning. He taught: "Now the great and grand secret of the whole matter, and the summum bonum of the whole subject that is lying before us, consists in obtaining the powers of the Holy Priesthood. For him to whom these keys are given there is no difficulty in obtaining a knowledge of facts in relation to the salvation of the children of men, both as well as for the dead as for the living." (D&C 128:11).

Taking the time and making the effort to understand ourselves from a perspective that is free of limiting beliefs is difficult, but it has many advantages. It permits us to view life multidimensionally. "Whom say ye that I am?" the Savior asked Peter. When he realized that Jesus was in fact the Christ, the Son of the Living God, Peter was up and moving along on the pathway to personal re-discovery.

Self-actualization germinates invention, which is incompatible with limiting beliefs. It spawns creativity. Innovation can be incremental or revolutionary, but it optimistically dangles the carrot of positive change before our noses, and it often spectacularly delivers on its promises. The economics of innovation frequently increases value. Our revolutionary experiences in the temple help us to focus on the process itself, as well as on its end point. During our passage through mortality and as we exercise our agency, the temple becomes a celestial signpost that guides us through the telestial traffic jams and conceptual cul-de-sacs created by limiting

beliefs that threaten to detour us from the strait and narrow way. The expanding circle of opportunity that is woven into our temple experiences has no room for limiting beliefs. It is within the hallowed walls of the temple that we trade the uncertain course adopted by those who are bound for mediocrity for the certain reality of those who are celestial-bound.

Frequent attendance at the temple helps us to break away from, and stay away from, the self-defeating behaviors of limiting beliefs. As we brush up against the heavens, we are awakened by the starlight to a new vision that may, at first, be blinding. But, as our eyes adjust, we are often surprised to see the world, for the first time, as it really is. As we begin to feel the creativity of the endowment, we experience foot-candles that kindle our divine potential. We feel the confidence to ask seemingly simple questions that have profound answers, and we grapple with implications that shake our world, spreading like the ripples radiating outward from a rock thrown into the still water of the pond of innocent inquiry.

In spite of their broad application, these questions are intensely personal. Jacob Bronowski observed of Einstein that he was a man who could ask immensely simple questions from whose answers he could hear God thinking. When we take our questions to the temple, we sometimes hear, as did High B. Brown, "truth spoken with clarity and freshness; uncolored and untranslated, it speaks from within ourselves in a language original but inarticulate, heard only with the soul, and we realize we brought it with us, were never taught it, nor can we effectively teach it to others. (See "Eternal Quest," p. 435).

In one particularly profound episode of "Star Trek, The Next Generation," the omniscient and omnipotent Q told Captain Picard: "You just don't get it, do you Jean Luc? The trial never ends. We wanted to see if you had the ability to expand your mind and your horizons. And for one brief moment, you did. For that one fraction of a second, you were open to options that you had never before considered. That is the exploration that await you. It is not mapping stars and

studying nebula, but instead charting the unknown possibilities of existence." We don't need to book passage on Galaxy Class Starships to have similar revelatory experiences. We just need to make time to frequent the celestial observatory of the

House of The Lord if we want to push off into the unknown possibilities of existence and explore the far reaches of eternity.

Both scientific and philosophical lines of inquiry can lead to mutual illumination and resonate with enlightenment. "Is the earth really the center of the universe?" "Why does an apple fall from a tree?" "What would the world look like if I were riding on a beam of light?" "Can I reach the Far East by sailing west?" "What would happen if I fell into a black hole?" When we ask questions in the temple, we just might find ourselves "poised at the edge of forever," as we plunge into a stream of revelation and are carried along in the quickening currents of direct experience with God. As George Bernard Shaw observed: "Some men and women see things as they are and ask why? I dream things that never were, and ask why not?" Because of the temple, such an innocent expectation is not so far-fetched as it is a self-fulfilling prophecy.

Sometimes, our questions cut to the core of our being. "Am I my brother's keeper?" (Genesis 4:9). "If a man die, shall he live again?" (Job 14:14). "Does God love me?" "Does my existence make a difference?" "Even the humblest human beings, Pope John Paul II observed, are naturally philosophic, asking themselves such questions as "Who and I? Where do I come from, and Where am I going?" Religious revelation provides answers to these questions, the pope acknowledges." ("Uniting Faith and Reason," Time Magazine. 10/26/1998). Such child-like questions ultimately lead to the granddaddy of them all, that is at the foundation of the doctrine of eternal progression; it is a question that we might repeatedly ask ourselves as the catalyst that confirms our faith and testimony: "Which church is right?"

This all leads to the experience of Joseph Smith, and the earth-shaking counsel he found by reading in the book of James: "If any of you lack wisdom, let him ask of

God, that giveth to all men liberally, and upbraideth not, and it shall be given him. But let him ask in faith, nothing wavering." (James 1:5-6). Of this discovery, he said: "Never did any passage of scripture come with more power to the heart of man than this did at this time to mine. It seemed to enter with great force into every feeling of my heart. I reflected on it again and again, knowing that if any person needed wisdom from God, I did; for how to act I did not know, and unless I could get more wisdom than I then had, I would never know; for the teachers of religion of the different sects understood the same passages of scripture so differently as to destroy all confidence in settling the question by an appeal to the Bible. At length I came to the conclusion that I must either remain in darkness and confusion, or else I must do as James directs, that is, ask of God. I at length came to the determination to ask of God, concluding that if he gave wisdom to them that lacked wisdom, and would give liberally, and not upbraid, I might venture." (J.S.H. 1:12-13).

In a similar fashion, Alma urged the poor Zoramites: "Awake and arouse your faculties, even to an experiment upon my words, and exercise a particle of faith, yea, even if ye can no more than desire to believe, let this desire work in you, even until ye believe." (Alma 32:27). His suggestion was to study, pray, and commit to a plan of action. Elsewhere in scripture, the Lord counseled: "Study it out in your mind; then you must ask me if it be right, and if it is right I will cause that your bosom shall burn within you; therefore, you shall feel that it is right." (D&C 9:8).

In essence, He was asking us to forsake the tyranny of limiting beliefs, and use our reasoning faculties as they were intended; to "get a "bright idea!" We all learn by experience that "it is impossible to advance in the principles of truth, to increase in heavenly knowledge, except we ... exert ourselves ... to the utmost of our ability." (Lorenzo Snow). Then, after we have received these things, we follow the counsel of Moroni, and "ask God, the Eternal Father, in the name of Christ, if these things are not true; and if ye shall ask with a sincere heart, with real intent, having faith in Christ, he will manifest the truth of it unto you, by the power of the Holy Ghost. And by the power of the Holy Ghost ye may know the truth of all things." (Moroni

10:4-5, underlining mine).

Breaking free from our limiting beliefs is like splitting an atom; the nuclear furnace of potential is unleashed within us. Daniel Burnham taught: "Make no small plans, for they have not the power to stir the souls of men." At the end of the day, the universe is full of magical things patiently waiting for our wits to grow sharper, so that we can appreciate them. (Anonymous). More importantly, when we shed our limiting beliefs, we recognize the universe for what it really is: "a machine for the making of Gods." (Henri Bergson, "Two Sources of Religion in Morality," 1932).

It behooves us all to sit back and evaluate our own attitudes to see if we have limiting beliefs slinking around in the dark recesses of our consciousness. The Lord knows how to handle these self-defeating behaviors. He counseled: "If men come unto me I will show unto them their weakness. I give unto men weakness that they may be humble; and my grace is sufficient for all men that humble themselves before me; for if they humble themselves before me, and have faith in me, then will I make weak things become strong unto them." (Ether 12:27). There must needs be opposition in all things, and limiting beliefs can be rehabilitated to become the foundation for improvement.

When we cast aside our doubts, and our eyes become single to the glory of God, when we catch the vision of temple worship, and are converted to its power, our "whole bodies shall be filled with light, and there shall be no darkness in (us); and that body which is filled with light comprehendeth all things." (D&C 88:67). "Therefore. we must sanctify ourselves in the temple, "that (our) minds become single to God, and the days will come that (we) shall see him; for he will unveil his face" unto us. (D&C 88:68). When we are no longer hobbled by our limiting beliefs, hen we no longer "see through a glass, darkly; (we shall see) face to face. Now (we) know in part; but then (we) shall know even as also (we are) known." (1 Corinthinans 13:12). Our worship in the temple helps us to overcome our limiting beliefs, and ultimately to be honest with ourselves and with God.

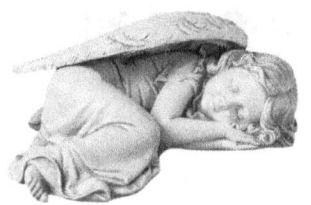

No form of government, and no level of material well-being will save us, to paraphrase Abba Eban. Our salvation will be possible only when towers fall and Jerusalem finally triumphs over Babylon. What is at stake, then, is not only intelligence, but also feeling. We have to change our hearts. Redemption, according to the prophets, is preconditioned by our repentance, which leads the faithful to the door of the temple.

Chapter Thirteen

The connections we make in the temple

"... Till
we all come in
the unity of the faith,
and of the knowledge of
the Son of God ... unto the
measure of the stature of
the fulness of Christ."
(Ephesians 4:13).

No one would argue that we are bound to each other by more than genetics. With few exceptions, for example in the case of monastic ascetics and agorophobics, we are social creatures. Many years ago, it became apparent to behavioral scientists that it might be useful to view our connections as a hierarchy. In 1943, Abraham Maslow described a pyramid of need, in a paper entitled "A Theory of Human

Motivation." In an ascending order of significance, Maslow described the pattern of our connections as if they were on a path leading to self-transcendence, beginning with physiology, followed by safety, a sense of belonging, love, esteem, and finally

self-actualization. This remains a popular framework in sociological research and management training.

From a Gospel perspective, however, it is intriguing to think of our connections a bit differently, namely in the context of the principles of The Plan of Salvation. When levels of interconnectivity have a foundation of faith, they surpass the behavioral sciences to reveal the core of existence, and they bind us to Him Who "hath also sealed us, and given the earnest of the Spirit in our hearts." (2 Corinthinans 1:22). These are concepts that are foreign to sociologists who attempt to explain interpersonal relationships by utilizing only tangible tools that rely upon rationalism, and use definitions that are based upon empiricism, while disparaging metaphysical abstractions simply because they are more spiritual in nature and require discernment to appreciate.

The first useful category is what I call Type 0 or Human Genome Connections. Within this class are the associations that exist only because our species shares the same D.N.A. sequences. Type 0 Connections necessarily leave us as ships passing in the night. We may appear to be similar in construction and in purpose, but at the end of the day there is more of a disconnect than there is a relationship between us. Type 0 Human Genome Connections do not require skin to skin, eye to eye, or heart to heart contact. They do not foster empathic bonds with others. Collectively, Type 0 Connections reduce us to nothing but nameless faces in the crowd. There is little or no evidence of emotion that is the instinctive feeling or intuitive glue that binds us to each other.

The dystopian novel "1984" comes to mind, not to mention "Brave New World," whose characters typify Type 0 connections, where Thought Police persecute individuality, and Newspeak is a satire of hypocrisy, with the Ministry of Love overseeing torture,

the Ministry of Plenty overseeing shortages, the Ministry of Peace overseeing war, and the Ministry of Truth overseeing propaganda. In Type 0 Connections, Big Brother watches us with a chilling sense of dispassionate detachment from reality.

The second category is what I call Type 1 Connections. These allow us to relate to each other through common interests like cars, hobbies, jobs, schools, and sports. But, at the same time, they are casual connections. For example, how many times has each of us thought to ourselves: "I know that face; I just can't put a name to it." Type 1 Connections are neural in origin, but their molecular basis too often develops along the pathways of short-term, and not long-term, memory. They may be powerful initially, but their intensity often fades with time.

The third category is what I call Type 2 Connections, those that are forged through the commanding chemistry of shared experiences, especially those that elicit intense emotion. These connections can last for years, because they trace their foundations to the crises of uncommonly positive or negative experiences with electrifying consequences that catalyze visceral responses that are etched in our psyches and our nervous systems. We have close associates, bosom buddies, life-long friends, and even blood-brothers with whom we have established Type 2 Connections that seem unassailable.

But Type 2 Connections, like Type 1 Connections, can and often do fade with time. Think of the unity that gripped America in the aftermath of 9/11. We can all still visualize members of the U.S. Congress standing on the steps of the Capitol, with arms linked together, singing God Bless America. How quickly are our Type 2 connections smothered in the marsh gas emitted by telestial trash, our competitive scramble for scarce resources, and the approbation of gods of wood and stone!

Somewhere beyond Type 2 Connections, there may come a moment when we "see the light." We may be dazzled by an A-ha! moment, an instant of sudden realization, insight, recognition, comprehension, or even inspiration. We might even feel that we have been "born again!" Nicodemus asked: How can a man "enter the second time

into his mother's womb, and be born? Jesus answered, verily, verily, I say unto thee, except a man be born of water and of the Spirit, he cannot enter into the kingdom of God. That which is born of the flesh is flesh; and that which is born of the Spirit is spirit." (John 3:4-6). The Savior used this occasion to teach Nicodemus about Type

3 Connections that can only be appreciated in the context of deeply moving and faith-promoting spiritual experiences.

The Sons of Mosiah had such a moment, as well, when they felt compelled to "impart much consolation to the church, confirming their faith, and exhorting them with long-suffering and much travail to keep the commandments of God." (Mosiah 27:33). Thereafter, their developing Type 3 connection with the Lamanites motivated them to persevere on a mission in the Land of Lehi that lasted fourteen long years. (See Mosiah 28:9). Ironically, the Lamanites among whom they ministered did not initially understand the power of Type 3 connectivity. But, over time, their Type 2 Connections evolved into Type 3 Connections with the missionaries, with each other, and ultimately with the Lord.

There follows in The Book of Mormon a detailed description of what we might do, in order to experience and sustain similar Type 3 Connections. Mormon reported that at the conclusion of their mission, the Sons of Mosiah were still the brethren of Alma "in the Lord; yea, and they had waxed strong in the knowledge of the truth; for they were men of a sound understanding and they had searched the scriptures diligently, that they might know the word of God. But this is not all; they had given themselves to much prayer, and fasting; therefore they had the spirit of prophecy, and the spirit of revelation, and when they taught, they taught with power and authority of God." (Alma 17:2-3). Their mission introduced them to faith-building Type 3 connectivity that can last forever.

Examples include the bond that can exist between a mother and child, or between "soul-mates" whose match was made in heaven. Both birth and death experiences can generate the intensity to trigger Type 3 Connections. Veil experiences in the temple can compellingly and convincingly communicate connections between the living

and the dead. In our everyday interpersonal relationships, when we are privileged to enjoy opportunities to nurture Type 3 Connections, the terms "Brother" and "Sister" typify familial relationships, even though no actual bond of blood exists.

In this context, we are reminded of Henry V, who, according to Shakespeare, addressed his troops at the Battle of Agincourt, on St. Crispin's day, describing his relationship with them as "we few, we happy few, we band of brothers. For he today that sheds his blood with me shall be my brother, be he ne'er so vile. This day shall gentle his condition." ("Henry V" Act 4, Scene 3).

Type 3 Connections are enduring because they enable us to brush our cheeks against the face of God, to "gentle our condition." Think of the genius of the advertising executives who coined the phrase: "Reach out and touch someone." Perhaps without realizing it, they were tapping into our universal need to establish connections with eternity itself. Paul clearly recognized the power of the word to do so, when he wrote to the Ephesians that, because of their obedience to Gospel principles, they would be "no more strangers and foreigners, but fellowcitizens with the Saints, and with the household of God." (Ephesians 2:19). In our day, when we attend the temple, we nurture our Type 3 connections with each other and with Heavenly Father, Jesus Christ, and the Holy Ghost.

From the beginning of time, the traditional family has provided the milieu in which Type 3 Connections are fostered. Alarmingly, today many family units are hardly recognizable, because they lack the tools to consciously cultivate these associations. Rather, they subsist on a meager diet, mistakenly believing that Type 1 or Type 2 Connections are all they need to nourish human interrelationships. By doing so, they settle for the steak, but without the sizzle. Or, perhaps they just do not care, either way. Without the influence of consistent motivation, they may even slip back into Type 0 connectivity.

Sometimes, they simply have no interest in expanding their horizons, and are content to just go with the flow. They may be "past feeling." (1 Nephi 17:45, Moroni

9:20, & Ephesians 4:19). For whatever reason, they are either unwilling or unable to generate the intrinsic power necessary to create and maintain lasting relationships, let alone the Type 3 Connections that Latter-day Saints recognize as the eternal bonds that exist in forever families.

With this in mind, we can better appreciate the purpose behind the dissemination since 1995 of The Church of Jesus Christ of Latter-day Saints' statement of belief entitled: "The Family: A Proclamation to The World." We also better understand the meaning of Joseph Smith's teaching that, at every age in the world, the main object of gathering the people of God "was to build unto the Lord a house whereby He could reveal unto His people the ordinances of His house and the glories of His kingdom, and teach the people the way of salvation," which has primarily been to develop Type 3 leading to Type 4 Connections through temple worship. (See below). (H.C., 5:423, 6/1843). Hence, we are enjoined: "Thou shalt lay aside the things of this world, and seek for the things of a better." (D&C 25:10).

In essence, both Joseph Smith and the Lord taught that we could not completely nurture our spiritual connections "until the temple (was) completed, where places (could) be provided for the administration of the ordinances of the Priesthood." (H.C., 4:603.) When we neglect opportunities to expand our faith to make connections that can only be envisioned from the eternal perspective of the House of the Lord, we jeopardize the promises of The Plan and neutralize its magic to stir our souls.

Individuals are baptized after Type 2 Connections have propelled them along on a journey toward Type 3 experiences. At other times, those investigating the merits of Christ may have already had fleeting Type 3 connection experiences, have strongly felt the Spirit, and have then determined to be baptized in order to capture those wonderful feelings with the confident anticipation of enjoying them on a regular basis. These are the pathways along which faith, testimony, and conversion are strengthened.

But, in order to maintain the momentum that has been generated, and in order

to make it enduring, new and established members of the Church need to have sustaining spiritual experiences that nourish Type 3 connectivity. As Gordon B. Hinckley said: "Every convert needs a friend, a responsibility, and nurturing with the good word of God." ("Liahona," 2/1999).

If Latter-day Saints do not find resources within the Church, and at the temple, to sustain Type 3 Connections, they risk sliding back into Type 2 interconnectivity. Those who settle for these marginalized relationships are sometimes characterized as being "less active," or "inactive." Fundamentally, they have lost their way because they no longer have the ability to nourish, maintain, and sustain the standard of behavior that is necessary to support Type 3 interpersonal connections that are powered by the principles that had once been their guiding lights.

We cannot endure for long if we rely only upon the light emitted by Type 1 and 2 Connections. Joseph Smith wrote to the Saints in their time of need, exhorting them: "If thou endure it well, God shall exalt thee on high." (D&C 121:8). What he meant was that our Heavenly Father will provide the external power source that is needed in order to become a member of the Second Mile Club of Type 3 Interconnectivity. The Prophet was summoning the Saints to join a select group to many are called, but few are chosen, after their baptisms. (See Matthew 5:41).

Paul knew what it meant to go that second mile. He ministered among the Corinthian Saints, whom he was pleased to discover had developed a working relationship with the laws and ordinances of the Gospel. He characterized their expressions of faith as being written upon "tables of stone." That is all well and good, but he hinted that there exists another order of mind; a connectivity that can be ours if we will make a second mile commitment of faith: "Ye are manifestly declared to be the epistle of Christ ministered by us, written not with ink, but with the Spirit of the living God; not in tables of stone, but in fleshy tables of the heart."(2 Corinthians 3:3).

Sooner or later, every member of the Church is a second miler, who is encouraged to become perfect in Type 3 interconnectivity commitment, and to so live to be

worthy of Type 4 commitment, that leaves Maslow's model of self-actualization in ruins. During His mortal ministry, the Savior said: "He that shall endure unto the end, the same shall be saved." (Matthew 24:13). Going a step further, He then explained to Joseph Smith: "If you keep my commandments (the first mile, or

Type 3 commitment) and endure to the end (the second mile, leading to Type 4 commitment) you shall have eternal life, which gift is the greatest of all the gifts of God." (D&C 14:7). On another occasion, He went even further, all the way to Type 4 interconnectivity, teaching: "For whosoever will save his life shall lose it, and whosoever will lose his life for my sake shall find it." (Matthew 16:25).

Our Type 3 Connections are solidified with compassionate service, particularly when it is directed toward those who cannot provide of their own means to generate equivalent connections. Service in the temple comes to mind. In the baptisms, confirmations, ordinations to the priesthood, washings, anointings, and the clothing ordinances, in the endowment, and in the sealing ordinances performed by temple patrons in behalf of the dead, we repeatedly hear the expression "for and in behalf of." Temple ordinances give substance to the expression that none of us is an island unto ourselves. The Architect of The Plan created opportunities for us to perform vicarious work, that we might comfortably surround ourselves with Type 3 Connections to both the living and the dead, as we establish bonds between all those who have been strengthened by covenants made with God. These can seal us to our forbearers all the way back to Father Adam and Mother Eve, as well as to our descendants, forging an unbreakable chain leading all the way from the Garden to the Celestial Kingdom. We can use Type 3 Connections to redeem the dead, as well as to pay it forward. We use Type 3 Connections to better understand, and relate to, the vicarious work of the Atonement of Jesus Christ.

But helping us to establish Type 3 Connections is not all our Heavenly Father can do for us. This is where the faithful part company with the masses, with Christians of convenience, to be caught up into "the third heaven." (See 2 Corinthians 12:2). God gave us our Type 3 Connections that we might have the power to establish a third-tier platform upon which we could fashion an even more ambitious milieu of connectivity.

Historical perspective provides us with a useful platform upon which we can build an appreciation of Type 4 Connections. After the Flood, the ancients built ziggurats that were towers specifically designed to reach all the way to heaven. The Tower of Babel is the best biblical example of these exaggerated church steeples. (See

Genesis 11:4). But their designers and builders, and those who flocked to behold these architectural marvels, missed the point. Instead of creating physical structures composed of brick and mortar, they could have more profitably spent their time if they had used the principles of the Gospel to build the unbreakable connection of enduring relationships with each other, and with God.

Starting with the baseline of Type 1 Connections, they could have rapidly advanced through Type 2, and on to Type 3. Then, they could have figuratively reached for the stars with that to which I have heretofore alluded, which is the Type 4 level of connection that is described in the scriptures as having our "Calling and Election" made sure. (See 2 Peter 1:10). This is a relationship with God that is poorly understood by theologians and scriptorians alike, let alone academicians and philosophical apologists. It transcends Maslow's model, because it requires a profoundly personal spiritual comprehension that can only be built upon the foundation of Type 1, 2, and 3 Connections that have already been established. When we are caught up in the third heaven that was described by Paul, we are poised to take a leap of faith into eternity. (See 2 Corinthians 12:2).

By design, in this chapter, I have purposely saved the best for last, and that is Type 4 Connectivity. When we achieve it, we shift our focus, and our mystical relationship with God becomes indelibly etched into our spiritual identity. We become perfect in our faith to make our connection with Deity. (See 2 Nephi 9:23). That is why members of The Church of Jesus Christ of Latter-day Saints have the presumption to declare that it is our destiny to one day rule as kings and queens, and priests and priestesses, in the house of Israel forever, to reign with authority over kingdoms, thrones, principalities, powers, dominions, and exaltations. That will happen only when our connections to God are of such magnitude and strength that our shared identity is indistinguishable from our individual personality. That will occur only

when we receive both His image and likeness in our countenances, in a Type 4 Connection.

But we can't get there if, beginning at Type 0, we skip the intermediate steps in our quest to reach what, with our inadequate preparation, would remain a frustratingly undefinable and incomprehensible goal. That's where the experiences of mortality in the learning laboratory of life, enjoyed within the structure of the principles, doctrines, ordinances, and covenants of the Gospel, come into play. Therein lies the inherent beauty of The Plan, and therein is the key to its success. The key to theology teaches that when we hear the bell, we need not wonder for whom it tolls. It tolls for us.

It was with the assurance that he was a child of God, that brave Horatius was able to declare: "To every man upon this earth, death cometh soon or late. And how can man die better, than facing fearful odds, for the ashes of his fathers, and the temples of his gods?" (Thomas McCaulay, "Lays of Ancient Rome," Stanza 27).

When designing The Plan, God knew that, with only nine months to put the final touches on our preparation, we would transition from the eternal world where we had enjoyed the warmth of hearth and home in heaven, to the bleak atmosphere of the lone and dreary world here on earth. When we did so, He knew that there would be an immediate disconnect that would be both brutal and unrelenting in its intensity. The Plan requires that we take God's labor of love and somehow postpone our Type 4 pre-mortal yearnings, as we ease into a world stage that is lit only by fire, where we are brutally assaulted on all sides by the unrelenting monotony of Type 0 mortal experiences. From the beginning, the Gospel was introduced to move us beyond Type 0 Connections, that we might ultimately reach all the way to "the most holy faith" of Type 4 Connections. (D&C 21:2).

In order to counteract the unforgiving reality check of birth, God instilled within each of our beating hearts the instinctive desire to enjoy Type 1 and Type 2 Connections that would gently lead us toward Type 3 Connections, so that we

could eventually have Type 4 Connections. He stamped within each of our minds a blueprint for survival, and inserted within its many pages of instruction enough information to organize ourselves and prepare every needful thing, so that we might intuitively establish a house of prayer, fasting, faith, learning, glory, and order; even a house of God where dreams come true, and where connectivity would not only be magical, but also wondrously possible. (See D&C 88:119). When He illuminated our mortal experiences with the Light of Christ, He left the porch light burning brightly, that we might find our way back Home to the House of the Lord.

That is why Adam and Eve, who had been living in innocence in a Garden setting, were told that it had been patterned after the order of heaven. When Adam and Eve fell that we might be, their physical surroundings in the lone and dreary world were designed, harsh though they might have seemed, to provide a hint of familiarity. If they would be sensitive to the Spirit, Adam and Eve would be able to re-establish their celestial connectivity and have joy. (See 2 Nephi 2:25). They would be given the tools to commune with the heavens. They fell so that God could teach them and their posterity how to use those tools to re-establish Type 4 Eternal Connections.

Truly, "the universe is but one great city, full of beloved ones, divine and human, by nature endeared to each other." (Epictetus). Heavenly Father is the Grand Architect of the Cosmos, of a design that establishes our familial roots and confirms His fatherhood, that we might enjoy a witness that it is in Him alone that "we live, and move, and have our being; as certain also of (our) own poets have said. For we are also his offspring." (Acts 17:28).

When Cain asked his father Adam if he was his brother's keeper, he did so with only a vague familiarity of the doctrinal principles surrounding the question. (See Genesis 4:9). The question exposed his failure to comprehend his Type 3 Connection with his brother Abel. That we are our brothers' keepers fell on his deaf ears. During His mortal ministry, when the Savior posed the same question: "Which now of these three, thinkest thou, was neighbour unto him that fell among

the thieves?" He was asking the young man to whom He was speaking to recognize the spiritual handwriting that was on the wall, and to acknowledge the Type 3 Connections he should have felt, even with someone who was despised as a Samaritan. (Luke 10:36).

Moroni's challenge to come unto Christ is our invitation to establish with Him a Type 3 Connection, and to stretch our minds and our spirits, that the way might be paved for us to embrace a Type 4 Connection that paves the way to our perfection. (See Moroni 10:32, & Matthew 5:48).

Joseph Smith asked the Saints if they could somehow establish a Type 3 Connection with each other that was founded on charity. (See D&C 121:45-47). Similarly, Moses instructed all of Israel to regard its neighbors not with Type 0 connectivity, but as Type 3 brothers and sisters. He taught: "And if a stranger sojourn with thee in your land, ye shall not vex him. But the stranger that dwelleth with you shall be unto you as one born among you, and thou shalt love him as thyself." (Leviticus 19:33-34). In each of these instances, the prophets extended to the people the invitation to establish a covenant relationship with God. They understood how Type 3 Connections can lead to Type 4 eternal joy in the kingdom of heaven.

Ruth felt this connectivity when she implored her mother-in-law Naomi: "Entreat me not to leave thee, or to return from following after thee, for whither thou goest, I will go, and where thou lodgest, I will lodge. Thy people shall be my people, and thy God my God. Where thou diest, will I die, and there will I be buried. The Lord do so to me, and more also, if ought but death part thee and me." (Ruth 1:16-17). She cultivated a profound connectivity that spanned generations and endured in Israel for eleven hundred years, that the Savior of the world might come through her lineage. The reason her petition to Naomi rings true to us today, is because Type 3 and Type 4 Connections are founded on eternal principles that are confirmed by the unimpeachable witness of the Spirit. Their enduring validity transcends both time and space.

Ultimately, the mission statement of our Father in Heaven is to establish Type

4 Connections with His children. (See Moses 1:39). Peter taught: "Brethren, give diligence to make your calling and election sure; for if ye do these things, ye shall never fall." (2 Peter 1:10). The Savior likewise taught His disciples: "Then shall the King say unto them on his right hand, Come, ye blessed of my Father, inherit

the kingdom prepared for you from the foundation of the world. For I was an hungered, and ye gave me meat. I was thirsty, and ye gave me drink. I was a stranger, and ye took me in; naked, and ye clothed me. I was sick, and ye visited me. I was in prison, and ye came unto me. Then shall the righteous answer him, saying, Lord, when saw we thee an hungered, and fed thee; or thirsty, and gave thee drink? When saw we thee a stranger, and took thee in; or naked, and clothed thee? Or when saw we thee sick, or in prison, and came unto thee? And the King shall answer and say unto them, Verily I say unto you, Inasmuch as ye have done it unto one of the least of these my brethren, ye have done it unto me." (Matthew 25:34-40).

With disappointment, He said to those who shrank from the light and sought the shadows, who never went to the effort to establish Type 3 connectivity, and missed the opportunity to be blessed by the grace of God with Type 4 connectivity: "Ye never knew me." (J.S.T. Matthew 7:33, see J.S.T. Matthew 25:11). Clearly, when it comes to seeking the "prize of the high calling of God in Christ Jesus," the ball is in our court. (Philippians 3:14).

Latter-day revelation speaks of those who, during their mortal probation, establish the unshakable bond of Type 4 connectivity with our Father in Heaven and with the Lord Jesus Christ, through unfettered access to the Holy Ghost. "Then shall they be gods, because they have no end; therefore shall they be from everlasting to everlasting, because they continue; then shall they be above all, because all things are subject unto them. Then shall they be gods, because they have all power, and the angels are subject unto them." (D&C 132:20). Joseph Smith understood Type 4 connectivity, and was able to clothe the doctrine of eternal progression that is taught in the temple endowment in words of hopeful anticipation.

Sooner or later, every member of the Church will encounter a line drawn in

the sand. Those with the faith to "endure unto the end, the same shall be saved." (Matthew 24:13). Or, as the Lord explained to Joseph Smith: "If you keep my commandments" by acting in faith to establish Type 3 Connections, "and endure to the end," thereby creating Type 4 connectivity "you shall have eternal life, which gift is the greatest of all the gifts of God. (D&C 14:7).

Our family ties can be traced all the way back to Adam and Eve, who were the offspring of our Heavenly Father. Every member of our family is the physical and spiritual reminder of our Heavenly Father, and so, we become legitimate heirs, through our faithfulness, of all that He is. Our families provide the context we need, so that we may work to become more like Him. Families provide the tapestry upon which is stitched the words to the Primary song: "I am a child of God." (Naomi Randall).

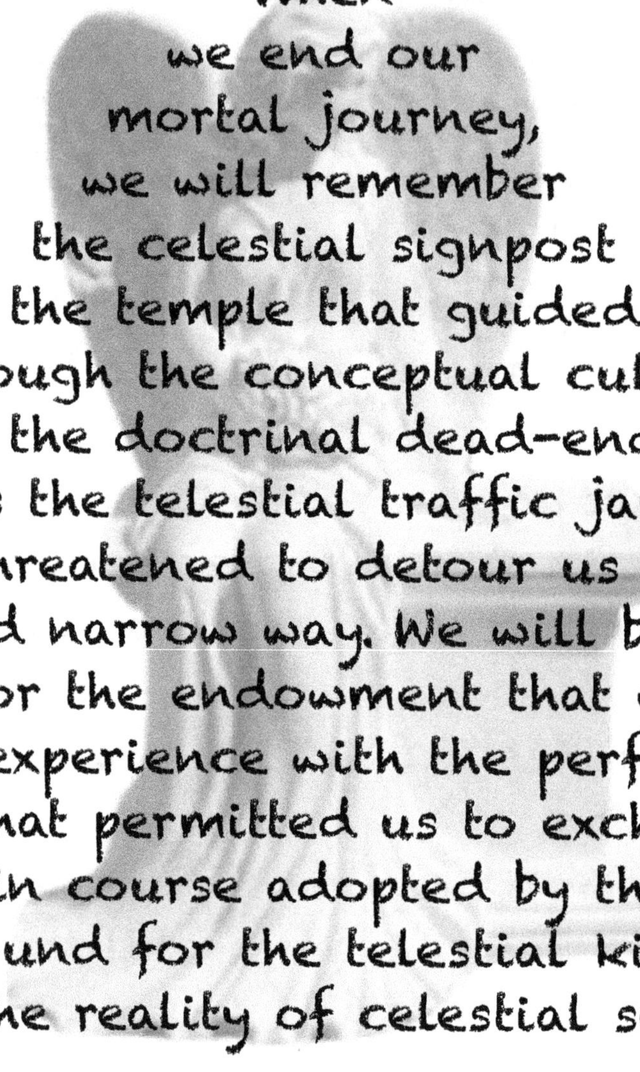

When
we end our
mortal journey,
we will remember
the celestial signpost
of the temple that guided us
through the conceptual cul de
sacs, the doctrinal dead-ends, as
well as the telestial traffic jams that
always threatened to detour us from the
strait and narrow way. We will be forever
grateful for the endowment that exposed us
to direct experience with the perfect law of
liberty, that permitted us to exchange the
uncertain course adopted by those who
were bound for the telestial kingdom,
for the reality of celestial surety.

Chapter Fourteen
An exchange of rings

On May 7, 2019, The Church of Jesus Christ of Latter-day Saints issued an official policy statement. Following is its summarization that can be found on the church website, ChurchofJesusChrist.org.

"Leaders of The Church of Jesus Christ of Latter-day Saints discontinued a policy Monday morning requiring couples who marry civilly to wait one year before being married or sealed in the temple. The change means Latter-day Saint couples can look forward to a temple marriage as soon as their circumstances permit.

Effective immediately, a man and a woman who have been married civilly may be sealed in the temple anytime after they receive their temple recommends for the sealing ordinance, according to a May 6 letter signed by President Russell M. Nelson and his counselors in the First Presidency, President Dallin H. Oaks and President Henry B. Eyring.

"We affirm that the sealing of a man and woman in the temple offers eternal blessings to the couple and their posterity that can be gained in no other way," wrote the First Presidency in the letter to general and local leaders. "We encourage all such couples to qualify for sealing ordinances and blessings."

The change in policy establishes a global standard in the Church regarding civil marriages and temple sealings, the authority to unite families eternally. Local laws in more than half the countries where the Church is established dictate a couple marry civilly before being sealed in the temple, making the scenario common outside of the United States. The policy also allows flexibility as couples are sensitive to the needs of their families.

The First Presidency emphasized the policy change should not be interpreted as "lessening the emphasis on the temple sealing," according to a question-and-answer enclosure accompanying the letter. "The sealing of a husband and wife in the temple is of eternal significance and a crowning experience on the covenant path," the First Presidency wrote.

In the letter, the First Presidency asks local leaders to encourage couples, where possible, to be both married and sealed in the temple. "Where a licensed marriage is not permitted in the temple, or when a temple marriage would cause parents or immediate family members to feel excluded, a civil marriage followed by a temple sealing is authorized," wrote the First Presidency in the letter.
The First Presidency anticipates the change "will provide more opportunities for families to come together in love and unity during the special time of marriage and sealing of a man and woman," according to the letter.

According to the First Presidency, a civil marriage ceremony performed for a couple being sealed in the temple should be "simple and dignified." Couples may use chapels owned by the Church for these ceremonies. Members should understand the "importance and sanctity of the temple sealing so that the sealing is the central focus of the marriage and provides the spiritual basis on which the couple begins their life together," wrote the First Presidency.

In the early days of the Church, civil marriage and temple sealing were separate. Once Latter-day Saints settled in Utah, Church leaders had the authority to perform both at the same time.

There is no specific time within which members should be sealed after being married civilly, according to the letter and accompanying information. "Priesthood leaders interview couples and provide temple recommends when the couple is both worthy and ready to be sealed in the temple. Worthy and prepared couples may be sealed as soon as circumstances permit."

New members are eligible to receive their endowment and be sealed in the temple one year from the date of their confirmation. If they choose to be married civilly during that year, they can still be sealed one year from the date of their confirmation, according to the enclosure.

"As they prepare to receive their endowment and be sealed, they can qualify for and use a limited-use temple recommend for proxy baptisms and confirmations." Leaders should also encourage them to do family history and gather family names for the temple, according to the enclosure.

The First Presidency closed the letter by thanking local leaders for "helping members understand, prepare for and enjoy the blessings of eternal marriage." The policy change is one of many in recent years reflecting a growing, global Church."

Those who choose to have a civil ceremony, before their temple marriage, might want to consider incorporating elements of the following into the service. This 'Ring Ceremony' has proven to be helpful, especially when members of the wedding party are unable to attend the temple sealing for whatever reason.

The purpose of the Ring Ceremony is to joyfully acknowledge the union of those who have had, or anticipate, a temple marriage to friends and relatives who are

unable to participate in the ceremony within the House of the Lord. At the Ring Ceremony, they re-affirm their vows of everlasting love. Participants join in their love and support of the newlyweds, and bless them by their prayers. They recognize that the couple has been looking forward to their marriage for a long time, and in the very conduct of their lives, they have prepared well. Every marriage presents challenges to overcome, as two people who have grown up as individuals commence a life together, as one. As they face these exciting opportunities, they pledge to give each other the love, strength, and support that will be necessary to make their marriage succeed. Perseverance, patience, faith, and selflessness will bless them with happiness in their marriage. They will come to understand that only by sharing their lives with each other can they experience lasting fulfilment. Only by overcoming their natural inclination to dependency, and even independency, can they experience the joy of interdependency.

Their vow is a pledge of their eternal love, whereby they promise to share all that life has to offer, the good times and the bad, with patience and understanding. With unshaken faith, they have promised each other that they will grow strong together in the face of the trials and tribulations that are a part of everyday life. The pledges that they have made with each other will become the foundation for their happily married life. Together, they will embrace not only principles of love, but also of obedience, sacrifice, and consecration.

A sage once observed that "we are richer today than we were yesterday if we have laughed often, given something, forgiven even more, made a new friend, made stepping stones out of stumbling blocks; if we have thought more in terms of others than ourselves, or if we have managed to be cheerful even if we are weary." As a couple embarks upon life's journey together and remembers this advice, it will enrich their experiences together.

When they feel that marriage and family are the basic building blocks of eternal life, their faith will point them in the direction of the House of The Lord. With His blessings, they will create a union that will last forever. The vows that they pledge

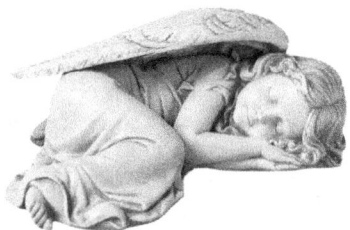

to each other are a formal and public announcement of their deeply devoted personal love for each other.

Over time, they will learn that a strong marriage is dependent upon many factors.

With shared love and respect, they will enjoy a true friendship and willingness to communicate. As they develop the qualities of acceptance, understanding, and reliance upon each other's strengths and weaknesses, they will create the foundation for a successful marriage.

Although their vows reflect their love, it is more than the words that they have spoken that will bind them together, as one. The feelings that swell within their hearts, and their shared faith, will strengthen them. They will discover, as the years go by, that their lives will draw closer together than they ever could have imagined.

Many in life pursue happiness with a passion, and yet they never find it. They do not realize that happiness is really like a lovely butterfly. If you chase after it, you will never catch it. But if you stand quietly, and contemplate the beauty of your surroundings and consider the strengths of your relationships, it will come and quietly rest on your shoulder. The couple whose union we celebrate will succeed in marriage because they have the maturity to realize that it is founded on the bedrock of their shared faith; on the eternal principles that are reflected in their character and in the quality of their lives.

Someone once said that the two most important days of your life are the day you were born and the day you find out why. These newlyweds have grown to maturity on this beautiful earth, and have now been drawn together to share their lives. They look forward to whatever the future may bring, with excitement, enthusiasm, and confidence. "May the road rise to meet them. May the wind always be at their backs. May the sun shine warmly upon their faces, and the rains fall softly on their fields. And may God hold them in the palm of His hand."

Their wedding rings, which are unbroken circles, symbolize unending and

everlasting love, and represent their devotion to each other. From this day forward, they will have many opportunities to feel the rings on their fingers and remember this special experience.

The couple that stands before you is a fresh, young reflection of the hopes and desires of each of us, as they turn to the light to face the experiences and opportunities of a lifetime. Together, they will soar to new heights. Victor Hugo counseled newlyweds everywhere, with these words of wisdom: "Be like a bird, that pausing in her flight a while on boughs too light, feels them give way beneath her, and yet sings, knowing that she hath wings."

The rational approach is doomed to failure and can never hope to plumb the depths of spiritual experience because it is grounded so firmly in the temporal world, relies so heavily upon the proofs of science, and requires the experimental confirmation of observable phenomena. Its own logic is inherently self-defeating, because it denies the existence of the only power with the capacity to convey real understanding.

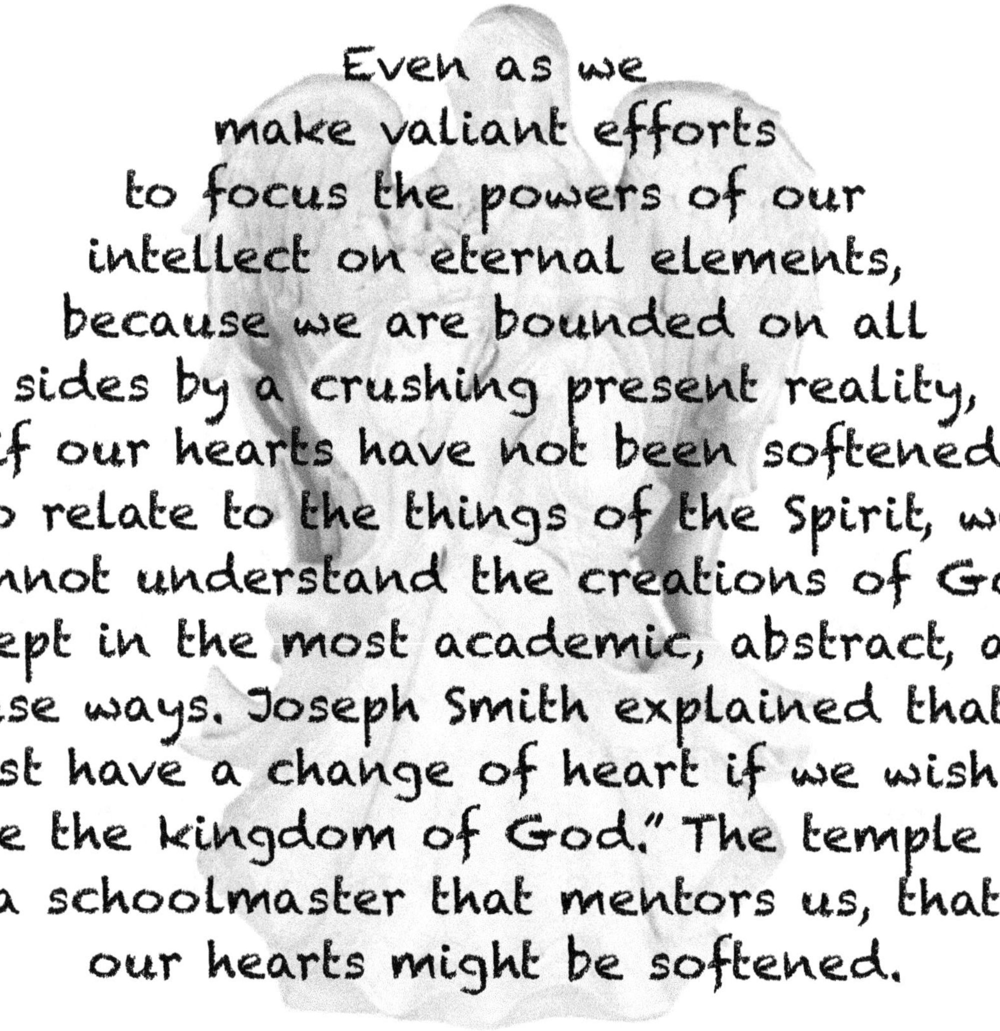

Even as we
make valiant efforts
to focus the powers of our
intellect on eternal elements,
because we are bounded on all
sides by a crushing present reality,
if our hearts have not been softened
to relate to the things of the Spirit, we
cannot understand the creations of God
except in the most academic, abstract, and
obtuse ways. Joseph Smith explained that we
must have a change of heart if we wish to
see the kingdom of God." The temple is
a schoolmaster that mentors us, that
our hearts might be softened.

Chapter Fifteen

A temple perspective on marriage and family

One of the blessings of the temple is the instruction we receive regarding the purpose of mortality; that it is to give us the opportunity to develop qualities and character traits that are consistent with God's divine nature. When the heavens opened with the Restoration of the Gospel, ordinances became available that bind us to receive its blessings by means of covenants of action between ourselves and our Heavenly Father. These bring us to a greater understanding of His nature. The marriage covenant that is found in the temple is at the zenith of these ordinances of exaltation.

The world largely regards marriage as a social custom with the participants bound by a legal contract (witness prenuptial agreements). But we know that "marriage is ordained of God unto man." (D&C 49:15). Even before they became mortal beings, Adam and Eve were joined in marriage by God. While yet in the Garden, before the Fall, Adam declared: "Therefore shall a man leave his father and his mother, and shall cleave unto his wife, and they shall be one flesh."

Marriage is the most sacred relationship that can exist between a man and a woman. It "is perhaps the most vital of all the commitments we can make, and it has the most far-reaching effects. Of all the decisions, this one must not be wrong," because our exaltation hinges upon it. (President Spencer W. Kimball). Heavenly

Father has given us the Law of Eternal Marriage so that we can become as He is. Marriage can help us to internalize His divine nature and develop His character. "In the celestial glory, there are three heavens or degrees; and in order to obtain the highest, a man must enter into this order of the priesthood (meaning the new and everlasting covenant of marriage)." (D&C 131:1-2).

We embark upon the path leading to eternal marriage by participating in an ordinance that must be performed by one who holds the sealing power of the priesthood. These keys are held by the prophet, who delegates his authority to others. The scriptures affirm that "if a man marry a wife by ... the new and everlasting covenant ... by him who is anointed ... it ... shall be of full force when they are out of the world." (D&C 132:19).

The temple is the only place where these sacred ordinances may be performed, and where the associated blessings may be sealed upon faithful couples. It is there that they kneel at a sacred altars in the presence of their family, friends, and two special witnesses. They make their marriage covenant before God, and are then pronounced husband and wife for time and all eternity. This is done by one to whom has been delegated the sealing power of the holy priesthood of God. He acts under the direction of the Lord and is empowered to promise the couple the blessings of exaltation. He explains the things they must do to receive these blessings. He reminds them that all blessings are contingent upon obedience to the laws of God. Under inspiration, he teaches the principles of The Plan of Happiness, and gives counsel that is specific to their circumstances. He promises them with a power to come into the presence of God that is only contingent upon their faithfulness. As the Savior said: "Inasmuch as my people build a house unto me in the name of the Lord, and do not suffer any unclean thing to come into it, that it be not defiled, my glory shall rest upon it. Yea, and my presence shall be there, for

I will come into it, and all the pure in heart that shall come into it shall see God." (D&C 97:15-16).

When we are married in the temple, we receive assurances that our union can last forever. We are promised that we can be with our family in eternity. After this life, we can live in the highest degree of glory in the celestial kingdom of God. We can be exalted, as God is, and receive a fulness of joy. We can be blessed to continue to nurture our family relationships in the eternities.

If we are true and faithful, the Lord has said that we will pass by angels who stand as sentinels, giving them signs and tokens, on our way to our exaltation. "If a man marry a wife by my word, which is my law, and by the new and everlasting covenant ... ye shall come forth in the first resurrection ... and shall inherit thrones, kingdoms, principalities, and powers, dominions, all heights and depths ... and shall pass by the angels" at the gates of heaven, because we are, after all, heirs of the blessings of the Abrahamic Covenant. (D&C 132:19). "Go ye, therefore, and do the works of Abraham," said the Lord. "Enter ye into my law, and ye shall be saved" with your loved ones in the Celestial Kingdom. (D&C 132:32).

Keeping that covenant puts us beyond the power of the adversary, for obedience gives us the priesthood and spiritual power necessary to overcome evil and obtain exaltation. We call this "the endowment," and so it is. The Prophet Joseph Smith said that when we receive our endowment of spiritual power, we are on the path leading to salvation, that consists of our "being placed beyond the power of our enemies, meaning the enemies of our progression, such as dishonesty, greediness, lying, immorality, and other vices." (Sermon delivered at Nauvoo temple site, 5/21/1843. Sources: Joseph Smith diary (Willard Richards), Howard and Martha Jane Knowlton Coray notebook, Franklin D. Richards "Scriptural Items" and James Burgess notebook, cf. "Teachings," p. 297-298).

Only by making covenants with God in the House of the Lord can we break the bands of death, and are we made free. "There is no other name given whereby

salvation cometh," said Benjamin; "therefore, I would that ye should take upon you the name of Christ, all you that have entered into the covenant with God." (Mosiah 5:8). Is it any wonder that the Church of Jesus Christ of Latter-day Saints builds temples, and that the Lord Himself proclaims that it "is the only true and living church upon the face of the whole earth, with which I, the Lord, am well pleased?" (D&C 1:30). No other church has the authority of the priesthood, that is necessary to bind and ratify the covenants we make with God. With this authority, couples and families can be sealed together, bound up unto eternal life, for as the Lord told Peter: "I will give unto thee the keys of the kingdom of heaven: and whatsoever thou shalt bind on earth shall be bound in heaven." (Matthew 16:19).

The marriage covenant is the highest and noblest expression of the Abrahamic Covenant, made by God so long ago with the father of the faithful. "My name is Jehovah," the Savior had explained, "and I know the end from the beginning; therefore my hand shall be over thee. And I will make of thee a great nation, and I will bless thee above measure, and make thy name great among all nations, and thou shalt be a blessing unto thy seed after thee, that in their hands they shall bear this ministry and Priesthood unto all nations; And I will bless them through thy name; for as many as receive this Gospel shall be called after thy name, and shall be accounted thy seed, and shall rise up and bless thee, as their father; And I will bless them that bless thee, and curse them that curse thee; and in thee (that is, in thy Priesthood) and in thy seed (that is, thy Priesthood), for I give unto thee a promise that this right shall continue in thee, and in thy seed after thee (that is to say, the literal seed, or the seed of the body) shall all the families of the earth be blessed, even with the blessings of the Gospel, which are the blessings of salvation, even of life eternal." (Abraham 2:8-11).

"Those portions of the Abrahamic Covenant which pertain to personal exaltation and eternal increase are renewed with each member of the House of Israel who enters the order of celestial marriage. Through that order, the participating parties become inheritors of all the blessings of Abraham, Isaac, and Jacob." (Bruce R. McConkie, "Mormon Doctrine," p. 13-14). To be a literal or adopted heir of the Abrahamic

Covenant, and to receive the ordinance of celestial marriage, is to receive the fruit of the tree of life, that is "desirable above all other fruit." (1 Nephi 8:12).

When Lehi tasted this fruit in his Vision of the Tree of Life, he described it as "the

most sweet, above all that (he) ever before tasted. Yea, and (he) beheld that the fruit thereof was white, to exceed all the whiteness that (he) had ever seen." (1 Nephi 8:11). Those who attain eternal life in the Celestial Kingdom of God enjoy that fruit which is "good and the most precious above all other fruit." (Jacob 5:61). Truly, the marriage covenant with the promise of "forever families," must be the basic building block of eternity.

When designing
The Plan, God knew
that, with only nine months
to put the final touches on our
preparation, we would transition
from the eternal world where we had
enjoyed the warmth of hearth and home
in heaven, to the bleak atmosphere of the
lone and dreary world here on earth. When
we did so, we knew that there would be an
immediate disconnect that would be both
brutal and unrelenting in its intensity.
It is that disengagement that makes
it imperative that we find our way
to the sanctuary of the House
of the Lord.

Chapter Sixteen
Temple marriage is ordained of God

*"If we work diligently in every other area of
life and neglect the family, it would be
analogous to straightening deck
chairs on the Titanic."*
(Stephen Covey).

Building upon the concept of the connections we make with each other, and with God, in chapter 13, we can see that marriage is the noblest expression of the relationship that can exist between a man and a woman. If they approach marriage believing that it is the divine model, they are more likely to start off on the right foot, working toward their shared potential. In fact, matrimony is one of the seven sacraments of the Catholic Church. This is a point upon which it is in agreement with Latter-day Saints. Both organizations believe that sacraments are necessary if we are to enjoy the grace of God that allows us to return to His presence. While marriage partners retain individual differences, their diversity can actually add to

the vitality of their union. Communication and the willingness to compromise on non-strategic issues help them to achieve success in the daunting task of creating a life together. Individual differences and even faults tend to fade in significance, if marriage partners can somehow avoid getting into the thick of thin things and refrain from arguing about matters of preference. They can agree to disagree. Just as those within organizations work to build consensus, so partners working within marriage persevere to weave threads of commonality until the tapestry is complete.

When marriage is more than a societal custom of convenience and is instead blessed with a religious foundation, there is incentive to make it work. In fact, it can become the most sacred relationship existing between man and a woman. When their vows are viewed as a covenant made with God, partners are more likely to work together to circle their wagons, to weather the storms that inevitably arise. Shared religious experiences and consistent devotions anchor their relationship on a solid footing.

Attributes of a successful marriage include morality, charity, discipline, consecration, sacrifice, and obedience. We become successful marriage partners as we share the struggle to gain self-mastery and overcome adversity, including the inclination to be disobedient to true principles. When marriage is viewed as a probationary state, a time of testing, or of putting to the proof, participants are less likely to bail out at the first sign of trouble. Marriage encourages us to endure to the end in righteousness, instead of abandoning our quest at the first sign of storm clouds on a distant horizon.

Marriage helps us to live with the consequences of our actions. In a day when the flight from responsibility is pandemic, the institution of marriage grounds us as nothing else can. Those who have worked through many trials to achieve stable marital relationships have necessarily developed successful strategies to find their way through inevitable marital minefields.

During the journey, when marriages have been blessed with children, an entirely

new dimension is introduced into the dynamic. Those who intentionally avoid the blessings and responsibilities of raising children may have progressed beyond dependency, but they become mired in the independency stage of maturation.

Without the added dimension of a family, it is more difficult to fully enjoy the freedom of interdependency that lies at the pinnacle of relationships.

When our foundations are grounded in our families, we find in our loved ones a broad base of support for our efforts to position ourselves beyond the reach of the adversary. Families provide a shield of protection from greed, selfishness, lying, and even immorality. In contrast, those who are bound by these vices do not often succeed with either marriage or family.

Looking back on over 50 years of marriage, I can see that I would not have been half the man that I am today had it not been for my wife and children. I recognize that I have a long way to go before I am the person that my dog believes me to be, but I know my marriage to the right woman has been an invaluable support. The blessing of children and grandchildren, each with a distinct personality and strengths, has added a dimension to my marriage I could not have otherwise enjoyed. Truly, no success in my life could have compensated for my failure to build a happy married and family life.

Jan has become the rudder of my ship, guiding me past unseen rocks and reefs. She is my helm, holding steady when winds of adversity blow. She is my telltale, alerting me to impending storms. She is my keel, helping me to move against the current and the wind. She is my mainsheet, holding firmly with just enough pressure to prevent me from capsizing when I am heeled over. She is my safety-line, providing security when my footing is unsure and the foaming sea is streaming across my deck. She is my compass, showing me the way, especially when the course is unclear. She is my chart, warning me of hidden dangers. She is my barometer, alerting me to impending storms. She is are my lookout, standing as my sentinel when I am distracted by trivial concerns. She holds the line that trails in my wake, offering safety should I fall overboard. She is the wind that fills my sails. We may be partners, but she is my better half."

Our feeble attempts
to describe God's reality
utilize abstractions, for thoughts
cannot be shaped, nor words formed,
nor sentences constructed that could
possibly accurately articulate His glory.
Figures of speech are employed because
we would otherwise be at a complete loss
for words when grasping for even a basic
explanation of profound metaphysical
realities. To Moses, "the presence of
the Lord appeared (as) a flame of
fire out of the midst of a bush.
And he looked, and, behold,
the bush burned with fire,
and the bush was not
consumed." (J.S.T.
Exodus 3:2).

Chapter Seventeen
In defense of the family

> We "are no more strangers and foreigners,
> but fellowcitizens with the Saints, and
> of the household of God."
> (Ephesians 2:19).

"The Family: A Proclamation to The World," is a statement by The First Presidency and Council of the Twelve Apostles of The Church of Jesus Christ of Latter-day Saints. It was introduced by President Gordon B. Hinckley as part of his message at the General Relief Society Meeting held September 23, 1995, in Salt Lake City, Utah. It reads: "We, the First Presidency and the Council of the Twelve Apostles of The Church of Jesus Christ of Latter-day Saints, solemnly proclaim that marriage between a man and a woman is ordained of God and that the family is central to the Creator's plan for the eternal destiny of His children.

All human beings – male and female – are created in the image of God. Each is a

beloved spirit son or daughter of heavenly parents, and, as such, each has a divine nature and destiny. Gender is an essential characteristic of individual premortal, mortal, and eternal identity and purpose.

In the premortal realm, spirit sons and daughters knew and worshipped God as their Eternal Father and accepted His plan by which His children could obtain a physical body and gain earthly experience to progress toward perfection and ultimately realize their divine destiny as heirs of eternal life. The divine plan of happiness enables family relationships to be perpetuated beyond the grave. Sacred ordinances and covenants available in holy temples make it possible for individuals to return to the presence of God and for families to be united eternally.

The first commandment that God gave to Adam and Eve pertained to their potential for parenthood as husband and wife. We declare that God's commandment for His children to multiply and replenish the earth remains in force. We further declare that God has commanded that the sacred powers of procreation are to be employed only between man and woman, lawfully wedded as husband and wife. We declare the means by which mortal life is created to be divinely appointed. We affirm the sanctity of life and of its importance in God's eternal plan.

Husband and wife have a solemn responsibility to love and care for each other and for their children. "Children are an heritage of the Lord." (Psalms 127:3). Parents have a sacred duty to rear their children in love and righteousness, to provide for their physical and spiritual needs, and to teach them to love and serve one another, observe the commandments of God, and be law-abiding citizens wherever they live. Husbands and wives - mothers and fathers - will be held accountable before God for the discharge of these obligations.

The family is ordained of God. Marriage between man and woman is essential to His eternal plan. Children are entitled to birth within the bonds of matrimony, and to be reared by a father and a mother who honor marital vows with complete fidelity. Happiness in family life is most likely to be achieved when founded upon

the teachings of the Lord Jesus Christ. Successful marriages and families are established and maintained on principles of faith, prayer, repentance, forgiveness, respect, love, compassion, work, and wholesome recreational activities. By divine design, fathers are to preside over their families in love and righteousness and are responsible to provide the necessities of life and protection for their families. Mothers are primarily responsible for the nurture of their children. In these sacred responsibilities, fathers and mothers are obligated to help one another as equal partners. Disability, death, or other circumstances may necessitate individual adaptation. Extended families should lend support when needed.

We warn that individuals who violate covenants of chastity, who abuse spouse or offspring, or who fail to fulfill family responsibilities will one day stand accountable before God. Further, we warn that the disintegration of the family will bring upon individuals, communities, and nations the calamities foretold by ancient and modern prophets.

We call upon responsible citizens and officers of government everywhere to promote those measures designed to maintain and strengthen the family as the fundamental unit of society."

The First Presidency and Council of the Twelve Apostles were inspired to issue this proclamation because the family is the basic building block of eternity. It is the best institution of higher education and is the best defense against an uncaring world. It has a heavenly certification, for it has received God's divine approbation. The creation of the eternal family is the magnum opus of the sealing power of the priesthood and of the ordinances of the temple, as we are linked both to our forefathers and to our descendants.

Families give us a sense of identity, and allow us to commit our lives and our fortunes to a common destiny. They mitigate the risks related to mortality. The virtues of the family indemnify us against the vicissitudes of life. Forever families are granted access to the power of God through the ordinances of the temple that

relate to the execution of The Plan of Salvation.

The ties that bind families together can be traced back to our first parents, who were the offspring of God. Each member of our family is an exact spiritual copy of our Heavenly Father, we retain His spiritual genetic code, we are carbon copies of His spiritual blueprint, and so, we become legitimate heirs, through our faithfulness, of all that He is. He has provided us with families to provide the context we need to become more like Him. Our families provide the tapestry upon which are stitched the words to the Primary song: "I am a child of God."

"I am a child of God, and He has sent me here, has given me an earthly home, with parents kind and dear. Lead me, guide me, walk beside me, help me find the way. Teach me all that I must do to live with Him someday. I am a child of God, and so my needs are great. Help me to understand His words before it grows too late. I am a child of God; rich blessings are in store, if I but learn to do His will, I'll live with Him once more." (Naomi Randall).

In nature, there are four forces that bind the universe together: the strong nuclear force, the weak nuclear force, electromagnetism, and gravity. In heaven, there are also four forces that bind eternity together: Faith, priesthood, Atonement, and the family. The family provides the mortar that holds the walls of the Celestial Kingdom in place. But it is in mortality that we get a sense of its power to anchor us to the Infinite; it blesses us with an eternal perspective. Families that are bound together by covenants made with God provide a much-needed longitudinal perspective in societies that are increasingly disposable.

The family is where we go for triage, when we have been wounded by the world. It is a safe haven where we can confidently regroup as we grasp the horns of sanctuary. In the family, we learn about the order of heaven. It is in the family that we first learn how to receive and honor the covenants we will later make with God.

The family provides a role model for us to follow. It prepares us to become parents, ourselves. God has stitched within the fleshy tables of our hearts the principles of an unwritten family constitution that is "manifestly declared to be the epistle of Christ ministered by us, written not with ink, but with the Spirit of the living God." (2 Corinthians 3:3). It is a training manual whose working model clarifies the celestial principles of service, sacrifice, fidelity, discipleship, and consecration. It instills within us the four cardinal virtues of prudence, temperance, fortitude, and justice, the three heavenly graces of faith, hope, and charity, and the four Buddhist truths of suffering, its causes, its end, and the path that leads to it. The family tutors us how to love ourselves, each other, and God. It teaches us about responsibility, accountability, and morality.

A return to the traditional values of the family may be our only hope if we are to fix the mess our society has created for itself. Far too often, the family is composed of narcissistic brats who have a room full of trophies for being participants, who never had to get up at 4 a.m. to milk the cows, who never went to Seminary, who never learned the Young Women values, who never earned a Duty to God award, who never served in the Young Women or Aaronic Priesthood, who never gave a talk in Primary or Sacrament meeting, who never went on ministering assignments with their dad, who never blessed the Sacrament, offered prayers, went on wilderness treks, or sang the hymns of Zion. Their brothers and sisters never went on missions, or returned home with honor. They never watched their fathers bless the sick, dedicate homes or graves, or write in their journals. They never were give the opportunity to follow the counsel of ecclesiastical leaders, raise their hands to God to sustain others in Church callings, and never witnessed the workings of the Spirit. They never felt its influence, followed its promptings, read their scriptures, or fasted and prayed. They never received a patriarchal blessing. They never were given the opportunity to plan, conduct, or even participate in a family home evening. They never paid tithes or offerings, or were asked to sacrifice of their means. They never saw their parents go to the temple, and never felt the spirit within the House of the Lord.

Far too often, those who could even loosely be regarded as family members are "strangers from a realm of light, who have forgotten all - the memory of their former life and the purpose of their call. And so, they must learn why they're here, and who they really are." (Doug Stewart, "Saturday's Warriors"). That is the purpose of the Gospel of Jesus Christ, of the Proclamation on The Family, and of the House of the Lord; to help us to get things right, and to make it possible, here on earth, for us to join with God in the creation of eternal families.

If we refuse
to set our lives
in order so that we
may attend the temple,
we submit to blind guides.
We deny not only God's power
to transform our lives, but also
His very grace. We turn our backs
on the habitation of the Lord, and
We dismiss the sacrifice of His Son.
We esteem as a thing of naught His
suffering, and we close our minds
to soul-expanding opportunities.
We are snared by Satan and are
bound by his strong chains, and
and all the while, we thought
it was just a flaxen cord
that was around our
necks.

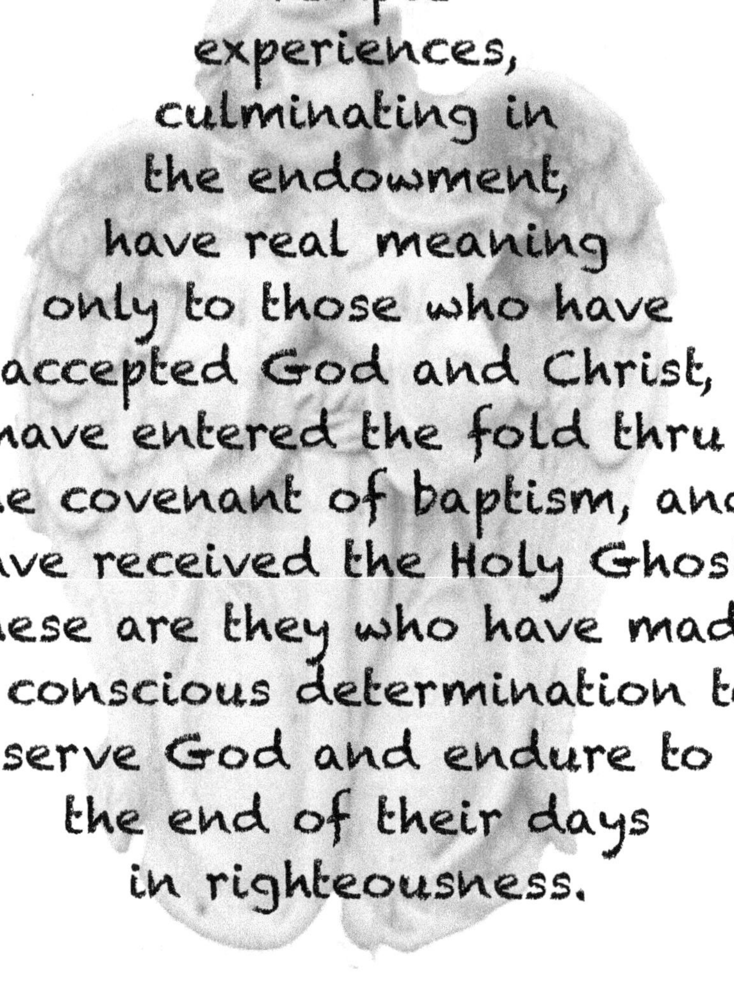

Temple
experiences,
culminating in
the endowment,
have real meaning
only to those who have
accepted God and Christ,
have entered the fold thru
the covenant of baptism, and
have received the Holy Ghost.
These are they who have made
a conscious determination to
serve God and endure to
the end of their days
in righteousness.

Chapter Eighteen
Sealed together for all eternity

Hugh Nibley said the temple is where we go to get our bearings on eternity. He also declared, on one occasion, that if he didn't learn something new every time he attended the temple, he'd stop going, and yet he continued the practice once a week, throughout his life. He went, because, as Gordon B. Hinckley declared: "The temple becomes a school of instruction in the sweet and sacred things of God. Here we have outlined The Plan of a loving Father in behalf of His sons and daughters of all generations. Here we have sketched before us the odyssey of our eternal journey from pre-mortal existence through this life to the life beyond. Great fundamental and basic truths are taught with clarity and simplicity well within the understanding of all who hear." ("Ensign, 3/1993).

Initially, we go to the temple "to receive all those ordinances in the House of the Lord, which are necessary for us, after we have departed this life, to enable us to walk back to the presence of the Father." (Brigham Young, D.B.Y., p. 416, see D&C

124:39). We call this our 'endowment.' We go, because the Lord has arranged in His Church that we learn about Him and our Father in Heaven through commandments and ordinances. We go make covenants relating to morality, charity, discipline, stewardship, sacrifice, and consecration. We go to make covenants relating to marriage that is ordained of God.

The world's definition of an endowment is to furnish an income to provide continuing support or maintenance, or to provide freely and naturally for others. But Joseph Smith had a more expansive vision of the endowment, and explained to the Saints: "For this cause I commanded Moses that he should build a tabernacle, that they should bear it with them in the wilderness, and to build a house in the land of promise, that those ordinances might be revealed which had been hid from before the world was. Therefore, verily I say unto you, that your anointings, and your washings, and your baptisms for the dead, and your solemn assemblies, and your memorials for your sacrifices by the sons of Levi, and for your oracles in your most holy places wherein you receive conversations, and your statutes and judgments, for the beginning of the revelations and foundation of Zion, and for the glory, honor, and endowment of all her municipals, are ordained by the ordinance of my holy house, which my people are always commanded to build unto my holy name." (D&C 124:38-39).

Eternal marriage is a part of that endowment of the municipals of Zion, and is essential to Heavenly Father's Plan. There are at least 14 different perspectives on The Plan, that are described in The Book of Mormon, including The Merciful Plan of the Great Creator (2 Nephi 9:6), The Plan of our God (2 Nephi 9:13), The Great and Eternal Plan of Deliverance from Death (2 Nephi 11:5), The Plan of Redemption (Alma 12:25), The Plan of Salvation (Alma 24:14), The Great Plan of the Eternal God (Alma 34:9), The Great and Eternal Plan of Redemption (Alma 34:16), The Great Plan of Redemption (Alma 34:31), The Plan of Restoration (Alma 41:1), The Great Plan of Salvation (Alma 42:5), The Great Plan of Happiness (Alma 42:8), The Plan of Mercy (Alma 42:15), The Plan of Happiness (Alma 42:16), and The Great

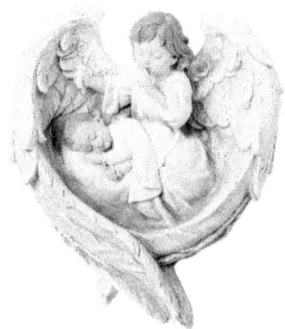

Plan of Mercy (Alma 42:31).

All of these descriptions relate to our eternal happiness within the context of marriage, which "is the object and design of our existence, and will be the end thereof, if we pursue the path that leads to it, and this path is virtue, uprightness, faithfulness, holiness, and keeping all the commandments of God." (Joseph Smith, "Teachings," p. 255). It is no coincidence that our temple covenants address each of these virtues.

We learn more about the covenant of Eternal Marriage in D&C Sections 131 & 132. Parley P. Pratt, one of the original members of the Quorum of the Twelve in this dispensation, recalled his feelings when he first heard the Prophet Joseph teach these doctrines. "I had loved before, but I knew not why. But now I love with a pureness, an intensity of elevated, exalted feeling, which lifts my soul. I felt that God was my Heavenly Father indeed; that Jesus was my Brother, and that the wife of my bosom was an immortal, eternal companion. But now, I can love with the Spirit, and also with understanding." ("Autobiography of Parley P. Pratt," p. 298).

Marriage is an essential part of God's eternal Plan because "in the celestial glory there are three heavens or degrees; And in order to obtain the highest, a man must enter into this order of the priesthood (meaning the new and everlasting covenant of marriage); And if he does not, he cannot obtain it. He may enter into the other, but that is the end of his kingdom; he cannot have an increase." (D&C 131:1-4). As Paul taught: "Neither is the man without the woman, neither the woman without the man, in the Lord." (1 Corinthians 11:11).

The Plan of Salvation cannot succeed without marriage ordained of God. Joseph B. Wirthlin said: "The sweet companionship of eternal marriage is one of the greatest blessings God has granted to His children. Certainly, the many years I have shared with my beautiful companion have brought me the deepest joys of my life. From the beginning of time, marital companionship of husband and wife has been fundamental to our Heavenly Father's great Plan of Happiness. Our lives are touched

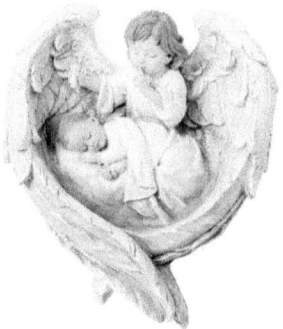

for good, and we are both edified and ennobled as we savor the sweet blessings of association with dear members of the family." (C.R., 10/1997).

Boyd K. Packer taught: "The ultimate purpose of all we teach is to unite parents and children in faith in the Lord Jesus Christ, that they might be happy at home, sealed in an eternal marriage, linked to their generations, and assured of exaltation in the presence of our Heavenly Father." ("Ensign," 5/1995). Joseph Fielding Smith said: "Marriage is the foundation for exaltation, for without it there can be no eternal progress in the kingdom of God." ("Doctrines of Salvation," 2:58).

According to the doctrine of the Church, if a husband and wife are not married in the temple, the status of their marriage when one of them dies is in grave jeopardy. "The conditions of God's law are these: All covenants, contracts, bonds, obligations, oaths, vows, performances, connections, associations, or expectations, that are not made and entered into and sealed by the Holy Spirit of promise ... are of no efficacy, virtue, or force in and after the resurrection from the dead; for all contracts that are not made unto this end have an end when men are dead." (D&C 132:7)

"Therefore, if a man marry him a wife in the world, and he marry her not by me nor by my word, and he covenant with her so long as he is in the world and she with him ... they are not bound by any law when they are out of the world. ... They cannot, therefore, inherit my glory; for my house is a house of order, saith the Lord God." (D&C 132:15 & 18).

Temple marriage and our eternal progress involve making covenants with the Lord. Promised blessings include being together "in time, and through all eternity" (D&C 132:19), being exalted in the highest degree of the celestial kingdom with Heavenly Father and Jesus Christ (see D&C 131:1-3, & 132:23-24), inheriting "thrones, kingdoms, principalities ... powers, (and) dominions," (D&C 132:19), having children in the eternities, (see D&C 1321:19, & 30-31), and "enjoying divine attributes, (and) becoming as "gods, because (we) have all power." (D&C 1322:20-21).

Temple marriage is strikingly different from its worldly counterparts. Perhaps, this is why Gordon B. Hinckley counseled: "Choose a companion of your own faith. You are much more likely to be happy. Choose a companion you can always honor, you can always respect, one who will complement you in your own life, one to whom you can give your entire heart, your entire love, your entire allegiance, and your entire loyalty." ("Ensign," 2/1999).

Richard G. Scott said: "There is more to a foundation of eternal marriage than a pretty face or an attractive figure. There is more to consider than popularity or charisma. As you seek an eternal companion, look for someone who is developing the essential attributes that bring happiness: a deep love of the Lord and of His commandments, a determination to live them, one that is kindly, understanding, forgiving of others, and willing to give of self, with the desire to have a family crowned with beautiful children and a commitment to teach them the principles of truth in the home."

He continued, "an essential priority of a prospective wife is the desire to be a wife and mother. She should be developing the sacred qualities that God has given His daughters to excel in their ordained character traits: patience, kindliness, a love of children, and a desire to care for them rather than seeking professional pursuits. She should be acquiring a good education to prepare for the demands of motherhood."

Finally, he said that "a prospective husband should honor his priesthood and use it in service to others. He should accept his role as a provider of the necessities of life, be one with the capacity to do it, while making concerted efforts to prepare himself to fulfill those responsibilities." (C.R., 4/1999).

"I was just sure the first ten years would be bliss," recalled Marjorie Hinckley. "But during our first year together I discovered ... there were a lot of adjustments. Of course, they weren't the kind of thing you ran home to mother about. But I

cried into my pillow, now and again. The problems were almost always related to learning to live on someone else's schedule and to do things someone else's way. We loved each other; there was no doubt about that. But we also had to get used to each other. I think every couple has to get used to each other." ("The Biography of Gordon B. Hinckley," p. 118). It will take love, work, and dedication to have a successful marriage, but when a man and woman are sealed in the temple, they will receive the promised blessings as they "abide in (the) covenant." (D&C 132:19).

In the temple, we interact with members of the Church who grapple with their own custom-tailored challenges, but who have somehow made the transition from hesitancy to conviction, from instability to commitment, from timidity to confidence, from indecision to resolution, from doubt to certainty, from struggle to celebration, and from vacillation to purpose. In short, they have moved beyond spiritual itinerancy to moral discipline.

When we are within
the holy precincts of the
temple, and we bring our right
arm to the square to ratify sacred
covenants with our Father in Heaven,
the Spirit quietly confirms that "happiness
is the object and design of our existence,
and will be the end thereof, if we pursue
the path that leads to it, and this path
is virtue, uprightness, faithfulness,
holiness, and keeping all the
commandments of God."
(Joseph Smith).

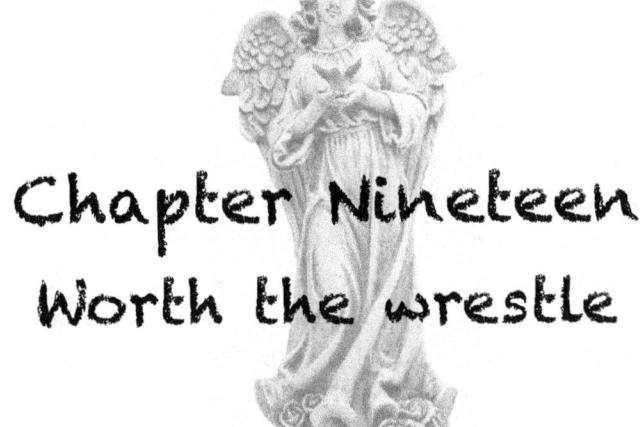

Chapter Nineteen
Worth the wrestle

"I hold forth ... to
give unto you greater riches,
even ... a land flowing with milk
and honey, upon which there
shall be no curse when
the Lord cometh."
(D&C 38:18).

A single bee can collect about 1/12 of a teaspoon of honey in its lifetime, so it would take the life's work of about 560 workers to make one pound of honey. For this, they would have to collect nectar from about two million flowers, and fly a total of about 55,000 miles.

In many ancient cultures, honey was prominently symbolic. Jeremiah characterized

ancient Israel as "a land flowing with milk and honey." (Jeremiah 32:22). In Egypt, Rameses III made an offering of 21,000 jars of honey to Hapi, the Nile god. In Greek mythology, honey was the nectar of the gods. The infant Zeus was fed honey by his nurse, Melissa, whose name is Greek for "honey bee." In Rome, Pliny the Elder called honey "the sweat of the heavens" and "the saliva of the stars."

But, today, what does the production of honey have to do with the ordinances of the temple, and particularly the sealing ordinances that culminate in the creation of forever families? If we want to succeed in this work that more than any other produces "soul sweat" and generates "the saliva of the stars," we are going to have to perform around 6 diaper changes per day for three years, or somewhere in the neighborhood of 6,570 changes for each child. We will need to prepare around 20,000 meals, 3 times a day, every day of the year for 18 years or so. We are going to get our kids ready for church around 1,000 times, on 52 Sundays a year for 18 years. We will help each of them get to Seminary over 700 times, or 180 mornings a year for 4 years. The only way to come to grips with this, in our minds, is to think of it as theatrical encore, conceived by a loving God with an immense sense of humor.

For active Church members, these exercises may seem normal, but many of our routines have undergone dramatic changes in the past few years. A generation ago, we all sat down in our family rooms in front of the television, to watch episodes of "Father Knows Best," "The Waltons," and "The Life of Reilly." Now, our unsupervised kids watch "The Simpsons," "The Bachelorette," "Jackass," "Celebrity Wife Swap," "Naked Survival," and "The Real Housewives of (Fill in the Blank)." It is even worse, with the almost universal dissemination of personal electronic devices.

What's taking a beating here is the traditional family. Once, the Church was pilloried for its unconventional view of the family. Now, it is ridiculed for its traditional view of the family. It may be that our easy days are over.

The recurring cycle seems to be a period of righteousness that begets prosperity, followed by apostasy that leads inevitably to destruction. When we "sow the wind, (we) shall reap the whirlwind." (Hosea 8:7). Long ago, Alexis de Tocqueville is reported to have written: "I sought for the greatness and genius of America in her commodious harbors and her ample rivers, and it was not there; in her fertile fields and boundless prairies, and it was not there; in her rich mines and her vast world commerce, and it was not there. Not until I went to the churches of America and heard her pulpits aflame with righteousness did I understand the secret of her genius and her power. America is great because she is good, and if America ever ceases to be good, America will cease to be great." Could it be that our worship of gods of wood and stone has something to do with silicon chips and microprocessors?

"A microprocessor is a computer processor that saves the functions of a central processing unit on a single integrated circuit, or sometimes up to 8 integrated circuits. The microprocessor is a multipurpose, clock-driven, register-based, digital integrated circuit, that accepts binary data as input, processing it according to instructions stored in its memory, and provides binary results as output." ("Wikipedia"). Personally, I can smell trouble in the air when I read sentences like this, understanding the individual words, but not the complete sentences. Even in the Twenty-first century, I am like the engineer at the Advanced Computing Systems Division of I.B.M., who in 1968 wrote a short memo about the recent invention of the microchip: "But what is it good for?" We might ask ourselves the same question, today.

Civilizations rise and fall for complex reasons, but there may be one underlying cause of societal implosion. Satan has focused significant energies and invested immense resources on technology in particular, to destroy traditional family values. He goes about it by working under the radar. He creates economic burdens to get mothers out of the home and into the workplace. He employs political pressures, under the guise of "equality" and "equal opportunity." Within the ivory towers of academia, he tutors the rising generation with carefully groomed mentors who

are rebels without a cause and rail against the establishment and every proven principle. He infiltrates government, and suppresses the will of the silent majority by legitimizing the wild, rabid, and morally indefensible demands of the vocal minority. He snuffs out freedom of expression within democracy, and with gold and silver buys up armies and navies, and false priests who oppress.

He uses pride and covetousness, to make us want to keep up with our neighbors. He uses prejudice and intolerance to suppress the expression of any opinion that challenges his twisted viewpoint, to which he has given the oxymoronic name "politically correct." He manipulates the media with the pervasive influence of robotic talking heads who lack any real evidence of higher-level brain function. He panders to the lowest common denominator, and rewards mediocrity and laziness. He launches hostile takeovers within the executive, legislative, and judicial branches of government, to validate affirmative action and Title-9, access to abortion, and gay, lesbian, bisexual and transgender favors that infringe on the rights of the moral majority. He uses medicine to make contraceptives easily available to minors, and to make the latest laboratory innovation available over-the-counter in drug stores.

He takes legitimate venues of inquiry, like philosophy, and distorts and perverts them by grooming articulate spokespersons with golden tongues to advocate his cause. Across the broad spectrum of business, he influences the hearts of conspiring men and women with evils and designs that threaten our economic and moral equilibrium. He poisons our innate yearning for genuine heroes by substituting those who should be our role models with one-dimensional celebrities whose manufactured credentials are only skin deep, and who use their unmerited fame and fortune to make intellectually unqualified and morally unsupportable endorsements.

He rails against the pattern of heaven itself, which is the vehicle through which eternal principles are communicated and transmitted, and the setting in which

God's mission statement is accomplished. He mounts offensives against everything that is intrinsically virtuous, lovely, of good report, and praiseworthy. He belittles the institutions that are the adhesive that holds our society together, and that are key to our understanding of where we came from, why we are here, and where we are going. He initiates repetitive offensives on the traditional concept of marriage between a man and a woman as a covenant that is representative of the order of God and that has divine implications.

He launches cyberattacks on everything that is decent about our culture, and hides them behind catch phrases and charismatic monikers. When his schemes are exposed, he uses malware in all of its insidious forms, such as computer viruses, worms, Trojan horses, ransomware, spyware, adware, and scareware, to continue the conflict on fields that are increasingly difficult for those who play by the rules to defend.

He knows that our firewalls are formidable, but he preys upon our distractions, indifference, laziness, impatience, intemperance, and procrastination. In all these ways, and more, in everything that he touches, he contaminates the very things that bind families together for time and eternity.

Because of the powerful opposing influence of the anti-malware software that is represented by the Light of Christ and the Holy Ghost, Satan knows that, at face value, immorality, dishonesty, covetousness, and lasciviousness, will be a hard sell. But he has discovered that "vice is a monster of so frightful mien, as to be hated, needs but to be seen. Yet seen too oft, familiar with her face, we first endure, then pity, then embrace." (Alexander Pope). He is determined to persevere, and is counting on the protestations of those with a weak will, who claim that, in spite of a cascading avalanche of lasciviousness, all is well in Zion. (Se 2 Nephi 28:21).

A study conducted by the Organization for Economic Cooperation and Development found that 26% of American children are raised by a single parent, a number high above the 15% average seen in the other 26 countries surveyed. Among African-Americans, the rate nearly tripled, with 72% of black children relying on a single

parent. The research also found that 53% of births to American women younger than 30 are outside marriage.

We have sown the wind, with free sex, abortion on demand, and easy access to divorce, and now we are reaping the whirlwind, with the destruction of the family and a self-serving and yet harmful redefinition of marriage. Lot pleaded with God to spare Sodom and Gomorrah, with what he initially thought would be a reasonable request: "Peradventure there be fifty righteous within the city," he begged, "wilt thou also destroy and not spare the place for the fifty righteous that are therein?" (Genesis 18:24). Then, the pragmatist that he was, he revised his expectations, and asked that the city be spared for 45, and then 40, then 30, then 20, and finally 10 righteous souls. To which, the Lord said: "I will not destroy it for ten's sake." (Genesis 18:29-32).

Sadly, there were not ten righteous individuals to be found, and so the Lord had compassion for Lot, and told him: "Escape for thy life; look not behind thee, neither stay thou in all the plain; escape to the mountain, lest thou be consumed." (Genesis 19:17). "Then the Lord rained upon Sodom and upon Gomorrah brimstone and fire from the Lord out of heaven; And he overthrew those cities, and all the plain, and all the inhabitants of the cities, and that which grew upon the ground." (Genesis 19:24-25).

Our salvation lies in remaining true to our temple covenants. If we do so, there will be no empty chairs around the table when we gather as families in the eternities. When we return home from our mortal mission, we will fondly remember the people we met, and those we helped. We will recall how we have grown both physically and spiritually. We will find mother there, waiting to embrace us, as she stands beside father, who will be bursting with pride. We will brush away tears of happiness on our cheeks. Father will strike hands with us, and then hug us tenderly. Mother will put her arm around our waist, and escort us to the familiar surroundings of the room that has been prepared for our homecoming. The atmosphere will be pungent with a heavenly aether that is punctuated by melodious whispers in our native tongue.

Every detail will be just as we had imagined it would be, including the reassuring radiant heat of a celestial fire kindled beforehand by Father. We will know that this is just where we belong, at home once again, with our heavenly parents.

In anticipation of that reunion, our families can be our greatest source of joy, as well as of protection, both in time and in the eternities. In moments of deep reflection, we "think of stepping on shore, and finding it heaven! We visualize taking hold of a hand, and finding it God's hand. We envision breathing a new air, and finding it celestial air. We imagine feeling invigorated, and finding it immortality. We dream of passing from storm and tempest to an unbroken calm, and of waking up, and finding it home." (Anonymous).

Longfellow may have been thinking of the blessings of family, of hearth and home, as well as of their contrasts, when he wrote: "Breathes there the man, with soul so dead, who never to himself hath said, 'This is my own, my native clan!' Whose heart hath ne'er within him burned, as home his footsteps he hath turned from wandering on a foreign strand! If such there breathe, go, mark him well. For him no minstrel raptures swell. High though his titles, proud his name, boundless his wealth as wish can claim; despite those titles, power, and pelf, the wretch, concentered all in self, living, shall forfeit fair renown, and, doubly dying, shall go down to the vile dust, from whence he sprung, unwept, unhonoured, and unsung." ("The Lay of the Last Minstrel").

The temple stands as God's testament that the dire situation described by Longfellow, or even those less dramatic circumstances in which we find ourselves, need not be so. A popular commercial for a motel chain reassures us: "We'll leave the light on for you." The temple stands a celestial homing beacon that will never fail, for it is illuminated by the inexhaustible power of God. It is a constant reminder that our struggles to create "forever families" are worth the wrestle.

Profound obedience
and recurring repentance
release us from the bondage of
sin, and qualify us by worthiness to
enjoy the blessings of the temple. The
Atonement of Jesus Christ, which is the
centerpiece of the instruction that we
receive in the endowment, allows us
to overcome our limitations while
unleashing the powers of heaven
in our behalf. It shatters the
bands of death, and throws
open the gates of the
Celestial Kingdom
itself.

Chapter Twenty
Eternal progression in a dynamic universe

*"All men's souls are immortal, but
the souls of the righteous are
immortal and divine."
(Socrates).*

Abinadi declared that "the time shall come when all shall see the salvation of the Lord; when every nation, kindred, tongue, and people shall see eye to eye and shall confess before God that his judgments are just." (Alma 16:1). This shall take place as a result of the universality of the resurrection just before, during, and at the end of the Millennium. In the meantime, the ordinance of the endowment provides repetitive dress-rehearsals in anticipation of that coming day.

Salvation is a gift of God given to all mankind. For "the way is prepared from the fall of man, and salvation is free." (2 Nephi 2:4). We are redeemed from the Fall

and overcome physical death because of the resurrection of Christ. "O how great the plan of our God!" exclaimed Jacob. For all are "incorruptible, and immortal, and they are living souls." (2 Nephi 9:14). In this sense, God denies "none that come unto him, black and white; bond and free, male and female; and he remembereth the heathen; and all are alike unto God, both Jew and Gentile." (2 Nephi 26:33).

Exaltation, however, is a gift of God that is reserved for the obedient. "He that overcometh shall inherit all things, and I will be his God, and he shall be my son," the Lord told John. (Revelation 21:7). "We are the children of God," wrote Paul to the Romans. "And if children, then ... heirs of God, and joint-heirs with Christ." (Romans 8:16-17). As such, we will "receive a crown of glory that fadeth not away." (1 Peter 5:4). Its quality is of a different nature than salvation. Exaltation represents eternal life in the Celestial Kingdom of God; it is a gift given to those who have conformed their nature to that of their Father in Heaven. They have taken to heart the admonition to be perfect, even as our Father Who is in heaven is perfect. (See Matthew 5:48). They have taken advantage of the ordinances of the House of the Lord to become holy and without spot.

For many, redemption will occur only when the demands of Justice have finally executed the required consequences for the violation of eternal law, after which they will be released from bondage in the Spirit Prison of the Unjust. (See 1 Peter 3:18, & D&C 76:73). Or, it may occur at some point in the eternities when formerly disobedient children of God have improved their nature to the point that a fullness of joy is justified.

This may be an element of the doctrine of Christ that is simply unclear. To his son, Alma once declared: "Now these mysteries are not yet fully made known unto me; therefore I shall forbear." (Alma 37:11). He felt that it was better to keep his opinion to himself, rather than to speculate without the foundation of revelation. Sometimes, it is better to remain silent and be thought a fool, than to speak, and remove all doubt. Still, a measured appraisal of the avenues open to the post-

mortal children of our Heavenly Father seems indicated, in light of the latitude on the subject that is afforded by the scriptures and is encouraged by the Spirit of truth. (See Moroni 10:5).

Joseph Fielding Smith, Jr. agreed with Abinadi that "the time will come when every knee will bow and every tongue confess that Jesus is the Christ," and yet he felt that "the vast majority of mankind will go into the Telestial Kingdom eternally." ("Doctrines of Salvation," 2:30-31). He could be right. It may be that the time when we may elect to live a celestial law has passed when we leave mortality. If that is the case, when some of God's children are judged, they may very well be assigned to a lesser kingdom of glory. According to this scenario, those spirits could thereafter progress only within the limitations of whichever kingdom they were in. Their progression would not be to the extent that it would ever lead them to live a celestial law. To put it another way, they would lose their ability to exercise their capacity to become as God is because they had neglected to take advantage of the opportunity of a lifetime during the lifetime of the opportunity.

It does seem that if we wish to obtain exaltation and eternal life in the Celestial Kingdom, we must do more than simply acknowledge that Jesus Christ is Lord. The ordinances of the temple make this abundantly clear. The critical point of conversion, beyond which lie the encircling flames of fire in the Celestial Kingdom of God, rests in making a conscious decision to accept not only Jesus Christ, but also obedience to the principles of His Gospel, and these include the pronounced blessings of the initiatory ordinance, as well as the covenants made with God before holy altars in the temple.

A simple yet uncommitted recognition of Jesus will not qualify us for the Celestial Kingdom. Christians of convenience lack the fire that is ignited by the demands of discipleship. Many honorable people who accept Jesus will still go to the Terrestrial Kingdom. According to the scriptures, these are they who "received not the Gospel, neither the testimony of Jesus, neither the prophets, neither the everlasting covenant. Last of all, these are all they who will not be gathered with the Saints, to

be caught up unto the Church of the Firstborn, and received into the cloud." (D&C 76:101-102).

A fundamental teaching in the temple endowment is that only those who passionately embrace the Gospel with its ordinances and covenants, and who then make every effort to partake of the divine nature, may go to the highest degree of glory and live in the presence of God Himself. "These are they who are priests and kings, who have received of his fullness, and of his glory; and are priests of the Most High, after the order of Melchizedek, which was after the order of Enoch, which was after the order of the Only Begotten Son. Wherefore, as it is written, they are (as the) gods, even the sons of God." (D&C 76:56-58, see John 10:34).

This distinction becomes vitally important to those billions of souls whose improvement would seemingly come to a halt at the Last Judgment because of unwise decisions they had made in mortality. However, our faith in the divine Plan of our Father is confirmed in the temple, where we learn that its implementation was designed to bring His children back into His presence, but only after they had achieved spiritual maturity and had learned to rely upon the Atonement of His Son. His work and glory is a given; it is to bring to pass not only our immortality, but also our eternal life in the Celestial Kingdom. (See Moses 1:39). We take Him at His word when He declared through the mouth of His prophet: "For I am the Lord your God, and will save all those of your brethren who have been pure in heart." (D&C 124:54).

In fact, The Plan was so magnificent and so all-encompassing in its scope, that when the "foundation of the earth" was laid, "the morning stars sang together, and all the sons of God shouted for joy." (Job 38:7-8, underlining mine). The principle of equality that is taught in the temple makes it almost inconceivable that a Plan of such transcendent perfection could have been intentionally created to save in the Celestial Kingdom only a small percentage of those who shouted for joy at the Council. To believe such is to dismiss God's mission statement, cited above.

In General Conference assembled, Dallin Oaks taught: "What we do know about the

spirit world is that the Father's and the Son's work of salvation continues there. Our Savior initiated the work of declaring liberty to the captives (see 1 Peter 3:18-19 & 4:6, & D&C 138:6-11, 18-21, & 28-37), and that work continues, as worthy and qualified messengers continue to preach the Gospel, including repentance, to those who still need its cleansing effect. (See D&C 138:57). The object of all of that is described in the official doctrine of the Church, given in modern revelation. "The dead who repent will be redeemed, through obedience to the ordinances of the house of God," and after they have paid the penalty of their transgressions, and are washed clean, shall receive a reward according to their works, for they are heirs of salvation" (D&C 138:58-59).

The duty of each of us is to teach the doctrine of the restored gospel, keep the commandments, love and help one another, and do the work of salvation in the holy temples. I testify of the truth of what I have said here. ... This is all made possible because of the Atonement of Jesus Christ. As we know from modern revelation, He "glorifies the Father, and saves all the works of his hands." (D&C 76:43)." (C.R., 10/2019).

The question thus becomes: "Are our actions during mortality so significant that they will determine our status forever?" Before the Fall, Adam lived in the Garden of Eden in a morally static, vegetative state. It seems Satanic to argue that, for all practical purposes, most of his posterity will do so again, in a telestial existence stretching on endlessly throughout all eternity, in mindless monotony. After all, it was the devil, and not our Elder Brother Jesus Christ, who sought "that all men might be miserable like unto himself." (2 Nephi 2:27). None of us would choose to believe that The Plan stacks the deck in favor of Satan, and that he is to be declared the ultimate numerical winner of the ideological conflict that gripped heaven so long ago? Opposition in all things is necessary for The Plan to function properly, but nowhere in scripture is it suggested that the negative element of opposition will prevail, condemning billions of God's children to a lesser degree of glory in eternity. If such were the case, would not the work and glory of God be largely nullified?

With this in mind, it might be more palatable to consider the revolutionary possibility that we may add to our glory to such a degree that we can eternally progress not only within a kingdom, but also from one degree of glory to another. In essence, when we have outgrown the apartment that once satisfied our needs, it may be possible to move on to a domicile that more adequately suits our then current circumstances. The definitive answer to this question remains unsettled in the Church, and the position of the First Presidency is one of neutrality. "The Church has never announced a definite doctrine upon this point. Some of the Brethren have held the view that it (is) possible in the course of progression to advance from one glory to another, involving the principle of eternal progression; others of the Brethren have taken an opposite view." (Joseph Anderson, Secretary to The First Presidency, Letter to Ward Magleby, 3/5/1952).

This statement by Joseph Anderson recognizes that there are faithful members of the Church who believe that it may still be possible to progress, after the Final Judgment, from one degree of glory to another. But, one might ask, does not D&C 76:112 teach that progression between degrees of glory is impossible? "And they (referring to those who inherit telestial glory) shall be servants of the Most High; but where God and Christ dwell they cannot come, worlds without end."

A careful study of this verse reveals that it is not talking about progression from one degree to another. It only states that individuals with telestial characteristics cannot come where God and Christ dwell. This passage refers to qualities of general classes of people rather than to those of individuals, and does not say what will happen to those who are able to change their nature. In other words, those with the described characteristics obviously cannot dwell where Christ is. But what happens if they are able to make behavioral changes, and if they can change their nature so that as they mature their character more comprehensively reflects that of their Father? Perhaps, then, they will be invited to sup with Him at His hearth and home. Does not the story of the Prodigal Son supports this thesis? (See Luke 15:11-32).

Those who inherit telestial glory are described as heirs of salvation through the

ministration of angels, and who shall be servants of the Most High. (D&C 76:88 & 112). But, as cited above, the Lord revealed to Moses that His whole focus of attention, His very work and glory expressed in His mission statement, is to bring about both our immortality and our eternal life. (Moses 1:28-29).

Misunderstanding has also arisen from a casual reading of D&C 76:73-74: "These are they who are of the terrestrial ... Behold, these are they who died without law; and also they who are the spirits of men kept in prison, whom the Son visited, and preached the gospel unto them, that they might be judged according to men in the flesh; Who received not the testimony of Jesus in the flesh, but afterwards received it."

Some misinterpret these verses, erroneously concluding that those who accept the Gospel after departing this life will be eligible to inherit only a terrestrial degree of glory. If that were true, then much of the work done in the temple would be ineffectual in accomplishing the end for which it has been designed. The whole point of vicarious work, whether it is performed in the temple, or whether it is through the infinite and eternal Atonement of Christ, is to do for others what they cannot do for themselves, worlds without end. (See Ephesians 3:14-21).

A difficulty arises out of failure to recognize the aforementioned distinction between the acceptance of Jesus Christ and acceptance of His Gospel with its ordinances and covenants that are administered by the priesthood and that lead to the sealing ordinances of the temple. These are covenants of salvation, sanctification, and justification, that lead to the covenants of exaltation. Those "who shall come forth in the resurrection of the just (are) they who" accept the Fullness of The Gospel, who "received the testimony of Jesus, and believed on his name and were baptized ... that by keeping the commandments they might be washed and cleansed from all their sins, and receive the Holy Spirit by the laying on of the hands of him who is ordained and sealed unto this power; And those who overcome by faith, and are sealed by the Holy Spirit of promise ... are they who are the church of the Firstborn." (D&C 76:51-54).

The crux of the matter comes down to whether or not we accept the premise that

hell is a reformatory designed to improve the quality of our moral nature. Is hell a penitentiary where faith can still convict us of our sins? Has hell been designed to help disobedient spirits recognize that Christ is the Mediator of the Covenant through His infinite and eternal Atonement? D&C 76 teaches that the Gospel was taught to the spirits kept in that prison. If, while there, they exercise their agency and accept only Christ, and not the fullness of His Gospel, then it is logical that they would inherit the Terrestrial Kingdom.

However, because of the infinite reach of the Atonement, was it not mercifully foreordained that the prisoners thronging the pit should in due time be visited, (see Isaiah 24:21-22), and be offered a means of amelioration? (see Isaiah 42:7). Even David rapturously declared: "Thou wilt not leave my soul in hell." (Psalms 16:10). James E. Talmage acknowledged that it is true that "the scriptures speak of endless punishment, and depict everlasting burnings, eternal damnation, and the sufferings incident to unquenchable fire, as features of the Judgment reserved for the wicked. But," he reasoned, "none of these awful possibilities are anywhere in scripture declared to be the unending fate of the individual sinner."

Elder Talmage went on to say: "Blessing or punishment ordained of God is eternal, for He is eternal, and eternal are all His ways. His is a system of endless and eternal punishment, for it will always exist as the place or condition provided for the rebellious and disobedient, but the penalty will terminate when through repentance the necessary reform has been effected and the uttermost farthing paid.

Even to hell there is an exit as well as an entrance; and when the sentence has been served, commuted perhaps by repentance and its attendant works, the prison doors shall open and the penitent captive be afforded opportunity to comply with the law which he aforetime violated. But the prison remains, and the eternal decree prescribing punishment for the offender stands unrepealed. So it is even with the penal institutions established by man." ("The Vitality of Mormonism," p. 264-265).

J. Reuben Clark, Jr. similarly reasoned: "I am not a strict constructionist, believing

that we seal our eternal progress by what we do here. It is my belief that God will save all His children that He can; and while, if we live unrighteously here, we shall not go to the other side in the same status, so to speak, as those who live righteously; nevertheless, the unrighteous will have their chance, and in the eons of the eternities that are to follow, they, too, may climb to the destinies to which they who are righteous and serve God, have climbed." ("Church News," 3/23/1960).

Perhaps God will leave his unrighteous and disobedient children in the Spirit Prison of The Unjust only long enough for them to recognize the error of their ways, and to motivate them to make behavioral changes that are consistent with the teachings of the Gospel of Jesus Christ. With a full recognition of their violation of law, such individuals might then be required to pay directly for the sins committed in mortality that had fallen outside the merciful sphere of influence of the Atonement of the Savior. Such a punishment would be eternally and endlessly in harmony with the Law of Justice.

Heavenly Father urges us to frequently attend the House of the Lord, that we might accept in a covenant of exaltation His Firstborn Son and Gospel, and that we might avoid the "weeping and gnashing of teeth" that accompany the recognition that our "days of probation are past; (when we) have procrastinated the day of (our) salvation until it is everlastingly too late, and (our) destruction is made sure." (J.S.M. 1:54, & Helaman 13:38).

The temple stands as a bastion of spiritual security, and obedience to the commandments is the only requirement for entry. If we seek "all the days of (our) lives for that which (we) cannot obtain, and ... have sought for happiness in doing iniquity, which thing is contrary to the nature of that righteousness which is in our great and Eternal Head," we must face inevitable consequences. (Helaman 13:38). It is only then, in the most difficult circumstances imaginable, when the uttermost farthing must be paid to satisfy the demands of Justice, that the necessary reform may take place.

How much better it would have been to have listened to the prophets. "And in the days of your poverty ye shall cry unto the Lord; and in vain shall ye cry, for your desolation is already come upon you, and your destruction is made sure; and then shall ye weep and howl in that day, saith the Lord of Hosts. And then shall ye lament, and say: O that I had repented, and had not killed the prophets, and stoned them, and cast them out. Yea, in that day ye shall say: ... O that we had repented in the day that the word of the Lord came unto us." (Helaman 13:32-36).

Such a scenario is in harmony with Brigham Young's belief that "all organized existence is in progress either to an endless advancement in eternal perfections, or back to dissolution. There is no period in all the eternities," he believed, "wherein organized existence will become stationary, that it cannot advance in knowledge, wisdom, power, and glory." (J.D., 1:349). It was for this very reason that the Lord instructed His servants to "establish themselves, and prepare every needful thing, and establish a house, even a house of prayer, a house of fasting, a house of faith, a house of learning, a house of glory, (and) a house of God."
(D&C 109:8).

Joseph Smith once declared to an assembly of the Saints: "I could explain a hundred-fold more than I ever have of the glories of the kingdoms manifested to me in vision, were I permitted, and were the people prepared to receive them." (H.C., 5:402) After all is said and done, when all the leaders of the Church have been quoted and the scriptures cited, the fact remains that we have not been given the revelations that answer the questions relating to progression between kingdoms of glory. When we attend the temple as patrons, however, and perform vicarious work for the dead; when the veil seems almost transparent, and we sense inaudible whispers of thanksgiving from the other side, the Spirit speaks peace to our souls, and intuitively, we want to believe that, "with God, all things are possible." (Matthew 19:26).

In
the life of
every individual
whose behavior is not
in harmony with The Plan,
there will come a time when
a readjustment must obliterate
a façade of hypocrisy. As painful
as the process of reformation may
be, it is necessary to allow for the
cultivation of the more nurturing
lifestyle that is made possible
only when we embrace the
special promises we are
invited to make
with God.

The priesthood
energizes the grace
of God by administering
the ordinances of salvation,
sanctification, justification, and
exaltation, that allow us to receive
the blessings of the Gospel by binding
us to Him through covenants of action.
The temple endowment, in particular,
helps us to enjoy a wider perspective
of our place in the cosmos, as well
as a greater understanding of
The Plan of Salvation, and
of His divine nature.

Chapter Twenty One
In the temple, we are as one

Who in the Church, or which office, do you think is the most important? The Apostle Paul compared members of the Church to the parts of the body. "For the body is not one member, but many ... And the eye cannot say unto the hand, I have no need of thee: nor again the head to the feet, I have no need of you." (1 Corinthians 12:14-21). Just as the eye, the hand, the head, and the feet are important in their unique functions, so are all members of the Church important with their different skills and talents, and nowhere in the Church is this equality better demonstrated than in the temple. With the possible exception of workers who have been set apart to perform ordinances for the patrons, all who worship in the House of the Lord do so as equals.

In the temple, there is no contention, because of the love of God which dwells in the hearts of its patrons. There is no envy, or strife, or tumult, or whoredoms, or lying, or murder, or any manner of lasciviousness, "and surely there could not be

a happier people among all the people who had been created by the hand of God." There are no robbers, nor murderers, neither are there any class distinctions such as "Lamanites, nor any manner of -ites;" but they are "in one, the children of Christ, and heirs to the kingdom of God." And how blessed are they! (4 Nephi 15-18).

In the Apostolic Church, its congregations grew rapidly, which was cause for great rejoicing, but it also created some challenges. With the increasing burdens of the work of the ministry, the Apostles needed the help of others in their efforts to build and strengthen the kingdom. So they called seven men of honest report, full of the Holy Ghost and wisdom, who were appointed, or set apart, to focus on the day-to-day administrative responsibilities of the Church. "And in those days, when the number of the disciples was multiplied, there arose a murmuring of the Grecians against the Hebrews, because their widows were neglected in the daily ministration. Then the twelve called the multitude of the disciples unto them, and said, It is not reason that we should leave the word of God, and serve tables … And (so) they chose Stephen, a man full of faith and of the Holy Ghost, and Philip, and Prochorus, and Nicanor, and Timon, and Parmenas, and Nicolas a proselyte of Antioch: (seven in all) Whom they set before the apostles: and when they had prayed, they laid their hands on them" and set them apart. As a consequence, "the word of God increased; and the number of the disciples multiplied in Jerusalem greatly; and a great company of the priests were obedient to the faith." (Acts 6:1-7).

Then, as now, when different needs among members were recognized and handled appropriately, the Church was strengthened and enriched. Today, we find that Zion comes in many different colors. It speaks Aymara, Dutch, Fijian, French, Mandarin, Russian, Slovene, Tongan, Zulu, and dozens of other languages. It lives in 3,341 stakes (as of March 2017), in practically every country in the world, from Argentina to Zimbabwe. It has over 16 million members (as of March 2017) whose skin is red, yellow, brown, black, or white. Zion wears a sarong, a grass skirt, a blue collar, a tupeno, a ta'ovala, a kilt, and a business suit. It lives in igloos, huts, fales, and high-rises. Most importantly, it shares a common testimony that Jesus is the Christ, and that His love, indeed, makes the world go around. Today, it is more important than ever to remember that there is no United States of America in heaven. The

great equalizer in the sight of God is the obedience of His children to His will, so they may all be at-one with Christ. Nowhere is this practiced more faithfully and energetically, than in the temple.

How can we have such diverse needs, living in dramatically different cultures as we do, and still be unified? How can Saints from all over the world come to the temples, all 167 of them, found in over 40 countries, as of 2019, and have strikingly similar experiences? Coast redwoods are among the largest living things. The tallest trees reach heights of over 360 feet, weigh hundreds of tons, and have been living for well over 2,000 years. But, curiously, while most other trees of massive size have deep roots to support their great weight, the root system of the redwood is very shallow. The key to its survival is the intertwining of the roots of one tree with those of several of its neighbors. Redwoods live in groves; they cannot stand alone. Interdependence is critical to the stability and longevity of each individual tree.

In a similar fashion, the structure and organization of temples help in many ways to unify the Saints. The roots of one temple are intertwined with those of all of the others, increasing the stability of the dwelling place of God, be they in Argentina, Brazil, Cambodia, Denmark, England, Finland, Germany, Hungary, India, Japan, Kenya, Mexico, Nicaragua, Okinawa, Peru, Russia, Spain, Thailand, Uruguay, Venezuela, or Zimbabwe, to name a few locations.

Temples are a lot like snowflakes, one of nature's most fragile creations and at the other extreme from coast redwoods. Although delicate in structure, look at what they can do when they stick together. As in the case of redwoods and snowflakes, so it is with the temples of the Lord, which "hath need of every member," that the whole may be kept in perfect working order, and so that all who go to worship there may expand their capabilities to the level of their potential. (D&C 84:110).

As He did during the Apostolic ministry, the Lord has inspired latter-day Church leaders to make organizational changes as the Church grows, to help meet the

needs of individual members in wards, branches, stakes, and missions throughout the world. Temples now serve the needs of the members on 6 continents and upon the isles of the sea. Their ordinances create a unifying backdrop to the worldwide tapestry that is being woven by the 65,000 (2018) Christian soldiers in the Army of God who seek out and find the elect, and draw them into the fold.

New converts and well-established Church members alike find their way to the temple, where their actions give a latter-day voice to Paul, who declared to the Romans: "We, being many, are one body in Christ." (Romans 12:5). The ripple effect of such spiritual unification is confirmed by powerful evidences. For example, the streamlining of the presentation of the temple endowment has made it easier for patrons throughout the world to enjoy similar spiritual experiences. In spite of the translation of the endowment into many languages, there is remarkably little disagreement as to its meaning. It is a Gospel "given," similar to the Standard Works, inasmuch as it is part of the foundation for the actions of the Lord's worldwide priesthood government. Like the scriptures, into the endowment is written every member's personal Handbook of Instructions, and yet it remains remarkably free of private interpretation. Its meaning is discerned by the Spirit that is universally accessible to those who have been blessed with the Gift of the Holy Ghost.

I witnessed this unity when I attended the Munich Area Conference in 1973. (This was the second Area Conference to be held. The first had been a year earlier, in Mexico City.) As the closing hymn was sung, I made my way to a central station within the Olympic Sports Arena to return my audio headsets. As I passed by the Saints who had gathered from all over Europe, I could hear them singing "The Spirit of God" in their native languages. On the stage, the Mormon Tabernacle Choir led the congregation, singing each of the four verses in a different language. It was quite moving, because the words in English became unimportant. Instead, we were collectively carried away by the Spirit to a higher plane where the common bonds of shared experience made us as one. We spoke and understood the same universal language.

In Church organization and government, and particularly in the temple, ecclesiastical leaders enjoy similar harmony in spite of individually different cultural, social, political, and economic circumstances. The ordinances of the Gospel, from baptism to the endowment in the temple, are understood and administered by those whose Latter-day Saint heritage overshadows any perceived or superficial differences. For example, the January 2019 updates to the audio-visual presentation of the endowment help it to flow more poetically on a world-wide stage.

The Church is growing rapidly in the Last Days. As it does so, we may be privileged to serve in individual capacities within the kingdom. Even as we recognize and appreciate our unique qualities, talents, and experiences, the temple helps us to be bound together in ways that bridge any cultural chasms that might otherwise separate us. If it were not for the temple, our ministering efforts might very well fall short of our capability and Heavenly Father's expectations.

With this understanding, we can squarely face our most stubborn challenges. We can be unified, even as we celebrate our diversity and our different needs. When we join the Church, we quickly move from dependence, through independence, to interdependence. We enjoy conformity without giving up our individuality. Our membership prepares us to go into all the world to spread the Lord's message, and to invite "all to come unto him and partake of his goodness; and he denieth none that come unto him, black and white, bond and free, male and female; and he remembereth the heathen; and all are alike unto God, both Jew and Gentile." (2 Nephi 26:33). The temple can be the pinnacle of our worship, as it blesses us with the capacity to be far greater than the sum of our individual parts.

Families that have
been organized in the
temple are as role models for
us to follow. They prepare us to
become the parents we want to be.
They are the corporeal embodiment of
training manuals whose working models
teach us about the celestial principles of
service, sacrifice and consecration. They
teach us about the four cardinal virtues
of prudence, temperance, fortitude, and
justice, and about the three heavenly
graces of faith, hope, and charity.
They teach us how we can learn
to love ourselves and each
other, and to be moral,
accountable, and
responsible

Chapter Twenty Two
The unknown possibilities of existence

"The Comforter, which is the Holy Ghost,
whom the Father will send in my name,
he shall teach you all things."
(John 14:26).

Q: "You just don't get it, do you Jean Luc? The trial never ends. We wanted to see if you had the ability to expand your mind and your horizons. And for one brief moment you did. For that one fraction of a second, you were open to options you had never considered. That is the exploration that awaits you. Not mapping stars and studying nebula, but charting the unknown possibilities of existence." ("Star Trek, The Next Generation," Episode 185).

The temple endowment enables us to do just as Q said; to chart the unknown possibilities of existence. We come to the temple "like gentle rain through darkened

skies, with glory trailing from our feet as we go, and endless promise in our eyes. We are strangers from a realm of light, who have forgotten all - the memory of our former life and the purpose of our call. And so, we must learn why we're here, and who we really are." (Adapted from "Saturday's Warrior," lyrics by Doug Stewart).

We come to the temple hoping to receive answers to life's greatest questions, that are simple in their expression, but profound in their implications: "Where did we come from?" "Why are we here?" and "Where are we going?" There are about 3,300 questions that are posed in the Bible, and many expand upon these three. They include: "Adam, where art thou?" (Genesis 3:9). "Where is he that is born king of the Jews?" (Matthew 3:2). "Which is the greatest commandment in the law?" (Matthew 22:36). "Who is my neighbor?" (Luke 10:29). "Am I my brother's keeper?" (Genesis 4:9). "If a man die, shall he live again? (Job 14:14). "If God be for us, who can be against us?" (Romans 8:31). "What must I do to be saved?" (Acts 16:30). "Where wast thou when I laid the foundations of the earth? (Job 38:4). "Whom say ye that I am?" (Mark 8:29). "For what shall it profit a man if he shall gain the whole world, and lose his own soul?" (Mark 8:36).

The answers to these questions require that we embark upon a personal journey in the temple that is similar to the on-going mission of the Starship Enterprise: "To explore strange new worlds, to seek out new life and new civilizations, to boldly go where no-one has gone before." Our experiences in the temple remind us of the observation of Dag Hammarskjöld: "The longest journey is the journey inward, for he who has chosen his destiny has started upon a quest for the source of his being." For each of us, our experiences in the temple are our own personalized and individualized "Genesis Project," where, while our "being" may be taken for granted, our "becoming" expands to emotionally, intellectually, and spiritually infinite proportion.

When we attend the temple with the objective of charting the unknown possibilities of existence, we sweep aside the self-limiting belief that "the sky is the limit." We substitute, and act upon, the supposition that "heaven is the limit." We begin to appreciate the contribution of Joseph Smith, namely, his sharing of the "knowledge

of what is to come after death. He did much to clarify our understanding of heaven and to make it seem worth working for." ("My Religion & Me" Course Manual).

When, in the temple, as we open our minds to options we have never before considered, we envision a special place called Kolob, signifying the first creation, nearest to the celestial, or the residence of God. Of our revelatory relationship to that realm, William W. Phelps wrote: "No man has found pure space, nor seen the outside curtains, where nothing has a place." In the matrix within which he imagined Kolob, there was no end to matter, space, spirit, or race; virtue, might, wisdom, or light; union, youth, priesthood, or truth; glory, love, or being. (See: William W. Phelps, "If You Could Hie to Kolob"). These are the tell-tale signtures on the chart that is unfurled in the temple endowment, upon which are revealed the bounds and conditions of the unknown possibilities of existence.

A point of reference like Kolob grounds us to metaphysical markers, even if they remain elusive to the world. As we chart the unknown possibilities of existence, we struggle to wrap our minds around an expansion of telestial knowledge that doubles every 12 months, but with resignation we realize that there is no way to keep up. If we do not stay focused on Kolob, we risk succumbing to the pessimistic observation that not only has knowledge outpaced truth, but that truth has a hard time even holding its own. Knowing that Kolob exists gives us a measure of hope that we will be able to separate knowledge from wisdom, and then make correct choices based on the intelligent application of the former in order to release the power of the latter.

Accepting the gauntlet of the temple endowment, to expand our minds and our horizons as we consider the unknown possibilities of existence, forces us to ask ourselves if we have embraced the moral element of responsibility to goes hand in hand with knowledge? Do we have the spiritual and intellectual maturity to handle knowledge with accountability? When we dare to grapple with these interrogatives, we come to an epiphany, even as we determine to do our best to be righteous stewards. Our covenant of consecration that is made before holy altars in the

temple provides the rebar that is needed to strengthen our resolve. It was with this in mind, that Joshua was able to confidently ask Israel: "Choose you this day whom ye will serve ... but as for me and my house, we will serve the Lord." (Joshua 24:15). It is in the temple that we realize that we have been given the privilege to be bathed in an innervating vitality even as we are empowered by an otherworldly serenity. As Bagheera, the powerfully built black panther confided to Mowgli the man-cub, in Rudyard Kipling's "The Jungle Book:" "I had never seen the jungle. They fed me behind bars from an iron pan until one night I felt that I was Bagheera the Panther, and no man's plaything, and I broke the lock with one blow of my paw, and I came away."

Interstellar voyagers in the temple embrace the task that lies ahead, knowing that their undertaking is consistent with God's mission statement to bring to pass their immortality and eternal life. (See Moses 1:39). These enlightened explorers use the 3.3 pounds of grey matter with which they have been endowed (consisting of around 100 billion cells with 100 thousand billion neural connections) to good advantage. Such a breathtaking network blesses them with enough resources and to spare, as they expand their minds and their horizons. God has clearly provided sufficient capacity to allow them to do so. He has created the means for them to confidently step off divine the moral obligations that press upon us here and now.

We realize that intellect will not save us, because what is at stake is feeling and not knowledge. As we undertake the long journey of self-discovery, our hearts and our nature are changed, the scales fall from our eyes, and the path before us is illuminated, so that we may see with the eye of faith into the cosmos. God stands ready to bestow upon us His eternal perspective, and only waits upon our initiative before He acts in our behalf, to open up the expansion of our view into the unknown possibilities of existence.

In the aforementioned Star Trek episode, Captain Jean Luc Picard asked: "Q, What is it you're trying to tell me? To which, Q tantalizingly replied: "You'll find out."

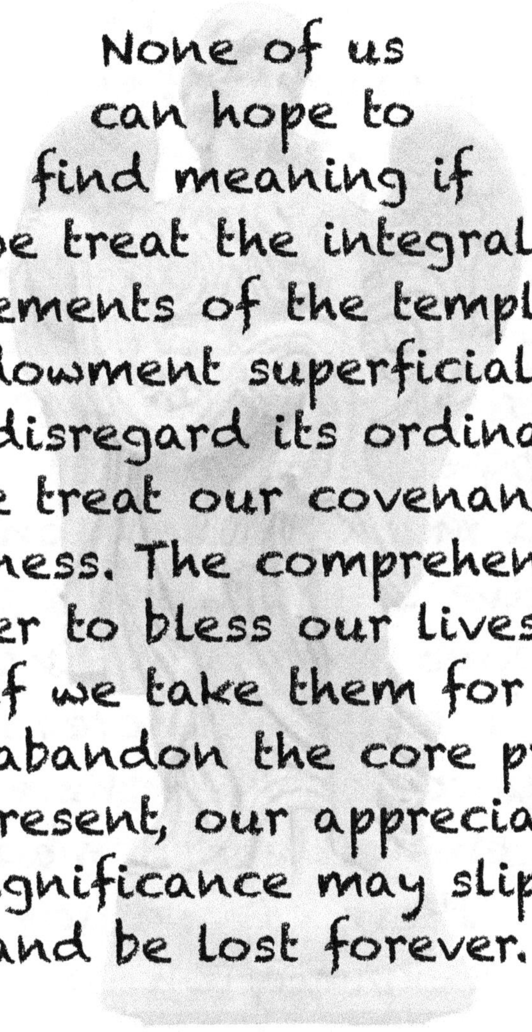

None of us
can hope to
find meaning if
we treat the integral
elements of the temple
endowment superficially,
if we disregard its ordinances,
or if we treat our covenants with
recklessness. The comprehension of
their power to bless our lives must be
earned. If we take them for granted
or if we abandon the core principles
they represent, our appreciation of
their significance may slip away
and be lost forever.

Our forever families
that have been sealed in the
temple provide the mortar that
holds the parapets of the Celestial
Kingdom together. Family grounds us
to mortality, but also anchors us to the
Infinite, by blessing us with a perspective
that is eternal. Families that are bound
together by covenants made with God
provide a much needed longitudinal
perspective in those societies where
just about everything, including
relationships, is increasingly
disposable. When there has
been no deposit made,
there can be no
expectation of
a return.

Chapter Twenty Three
Beyond the power of the adversary

> "I had rather be a doorkeeper in the
> house of my God, than to dwell
> in the tents of wickedness."
> (Psalms 84:10).

Many of us have served in teaching capacities or in administrative positions that are oriented toward redemptive practices that encourage and provide support to members of the Church who are struggling with the trials and temptations of life. Our efforts can be emotionally exhausting, and the realization of satisfactory solutions on behalf of our brothers and sisters can be elusive.

In the temple, however, we interact with members of the Church who grapple with these same challenges, but who have somehow made the transition from hesitancy to conviction, from instability to commitment, from timidity to confidence, from indecision to resolution, from doubt to certainty, from struggle to celebration,

from vacillation to purpose, and from spiritual itinerancy to moral discipline.

Temple patrons take their ministering responsibilities to a new level. They redefine dedication, and exercise their duties in ways that are truly selfless. The Gospel has transformed their lives. They are as the people of Zarahemla, who declared to King Benjamin: "The Spirit of the Lord Omnipotent ... has wrought a mighty change in us, or in our hearts, that we have no more disposition to do evil, but to do good continually." (Mosiah 5:2).

King Benjamin could have been speaking of temple patrons and the ordinances of exaltation, when he declared of the people of Zarahemla: "Because of the covenant which (you) have made, (you) shall be called the children of Christ, his sons, and his daughters; for behold, this day he hath spiritually begotten (you); for (you) say that (your) hearts are changed through faith on his name; therefore, (you) are born of him and have become his sons and his daughters." (Mosiah 5:7).

Nothing that takes place in the temple directly benefits its patrons who have already received their endowment and have participated in the ordinances that seal them to their families. Their service is wholly, completely, and unequivocally in behalf of those who have passed beyond the veil, and it is through their efforts that those who might have otherwise been forgotten are clothed in the robes of the priesthood, and in a holy remembrance to pass through the veil into the presence of the Lord. With an anointing, they are endowed with the power to come forth in the morning of the first resurrection, as kings and priests, and queens and priestesses, conditional only upon their worthiness, to rule and reign in the House of Israel forever. The ordinances of the temple celebrate lives in a commemoration that would have otherwise remained everlastingly incomplete. These ordinances impart dignity, nobility, and worth to Heavenly Father's children, and insure that their memory will be memorialized. They will not be neglected in time, nor will they be forgotten in eternity. These ordinances reassure us that when the process of securing the eternal legacy of our Heavenly Father's children has been completed, there will be no gaps

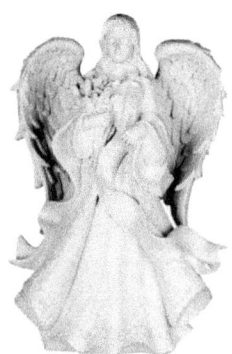

in our family history, that no names will be missing from the book of life that is being carefully compiled by the angels in heaven, and that there will be no empty seats around the table when we gather to celebrate eternal life at the banquet of consequences. It is because of the temple that we may take God at His word, when

He says that it is His work and glory to bring to pass our immortality and eternal life. (See Moses 1:39).

This may be why Alma's descriptions of The Plan of Salvation were so expansive. Like so many of us, he had seen life from both sides of the tracks, and was effusive in his desire to share his joy with others. He envisioned the Merciful Plan as our Great Creator's vehicle to generate the celestial sparks that would initiate the combustion of the Atonement, to power the engine that saves our souls. (See 2 Nephi 9:6). The Plan of our God testifies that He is the Author of our eternal life and the facilitator of our exaltation. (See 2 Nephi 9:13). The Great and Eternal Plan of Deliverance from Death speaks to the doctrine that when the time comes to lay our mortal bodies by, our spirits will be propelled upward toward uncharted opportunity. It testifies that when Adam was sent into the Garden of Eden, it was with the understanding that he would violate or transgress God's law in order to bring to pass not only our mortality, but also our immortality and our eternal life. (See 2 Nephi 11:5). Through the Atonement, the Plan of Salvation would become a Plan of Redemption, a Plan of Mercy, and a Plan of Happiness, paving the way for the resurrection of our otherwise imperfect mortal bodies to eternal lives of glory that would be inseparably joined to our spirits. (See Alma 24:14). It would allow God to be both just and merciful at the same time. We see this in the symbolism of the cherubim and a flaming sword, that guarded the way to the Tree of Life. (See Moses 4:31).

Those who attend the temple have found meaning in their lives because they do not treat its ordinances superficially or carelessly. They have earned a conscious appreciation of the promised blessings of the Lord's House. They realize that if they were to take them for granted or if they were to abandon the core principles they represent, their power to bless their lives would slip away and be lost forever.

Because The Plan guarantees free will, we are given wide latitude to use our agency inappropriately to make poor choices. The endowment provides us with currency sufficient for our needs, and illustrates what would happen if we were to substitute the legal tender of the Atonement with wads of counterfeit cash with which only late payments could be made, with interest tacked on for bad behavior. If we were to attempt to subvert The Plan by turning our backs on the blessings that could have been ours through obedience to the ordinances of the temple, our futile and destabilizing efforts to obtain and retain opportunities that we did not merit, and blessings that we did not deserve, would reward us with a pyrrhic victory, at best.

If we do not conduct our lives in harmony with The Plan, there will come a time when a requisite readjustment will tear down our façades of corruption and hypocrisy. As painful as that process sounds, it will be necessary if we have not aforetime cultivated a special relationship with God. To have the assurance that we can become holy and without spot through the Savior's Atonement is one of the greatest blessings enjoyed by those who frequent the temple; its ordinances become the threads in a coat of many colors that they wear as their holy vestments.

Even if we fail to measure up to our covenants, and the law of compensation demands that we suffer the consequences, the endowment reassures us that Jesus Christ stands ready to intervene in our behalf to restore our purity, as He promised to do at the Council. Those who faithfully attend the temple have applied the principles of Repentance to unlock the power of the Atonement. They have Recognized their mistakes, have experienced Remorse for having made them, have attempted to make Restitution if their behavior has wronged others, have learned from their mistakes and have Reformed their ways, and have Resolved to Refrain from Repeating them. The Atonement Reorients them to the path of progress, with a complete Resolution of what would have otherwise been incapacitating shortcomings.

When we have been Reinvigorated by Repentance, we will Receive a holy anointing

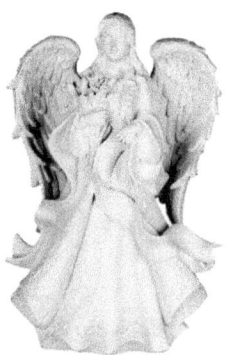

in the temple, never to "Rest until the last enemy is conquered, death destroyed, and truth reigns triumphant." (Parley P. Pratt, "Deseret News," 4/30/1853). Our joy will be full because of our confidence in the capacity of our temple covenants to Redeem us from our sins, and propel us in the direction of our celestial destiny.

When we reach out to heaven as we bring our right arm to the square in supplication to God, He symbolically takes our outstretched hand, and draws us up, our of harms' way, into His bosom. We are infused by His power. The Spirit quietly whispers that the adversary no longer has control over us.

We are endowed by divine design with happiness if we follow the path that guides us to the endowment in the temple. That path is defined by the cobblestones of virtue, honesty, morality, decency, uprightness, faithfulness, holiness, gratitude, reverence, devotion, charity, benevolence, forbearance, empathy, compassion, purity, and obedience.

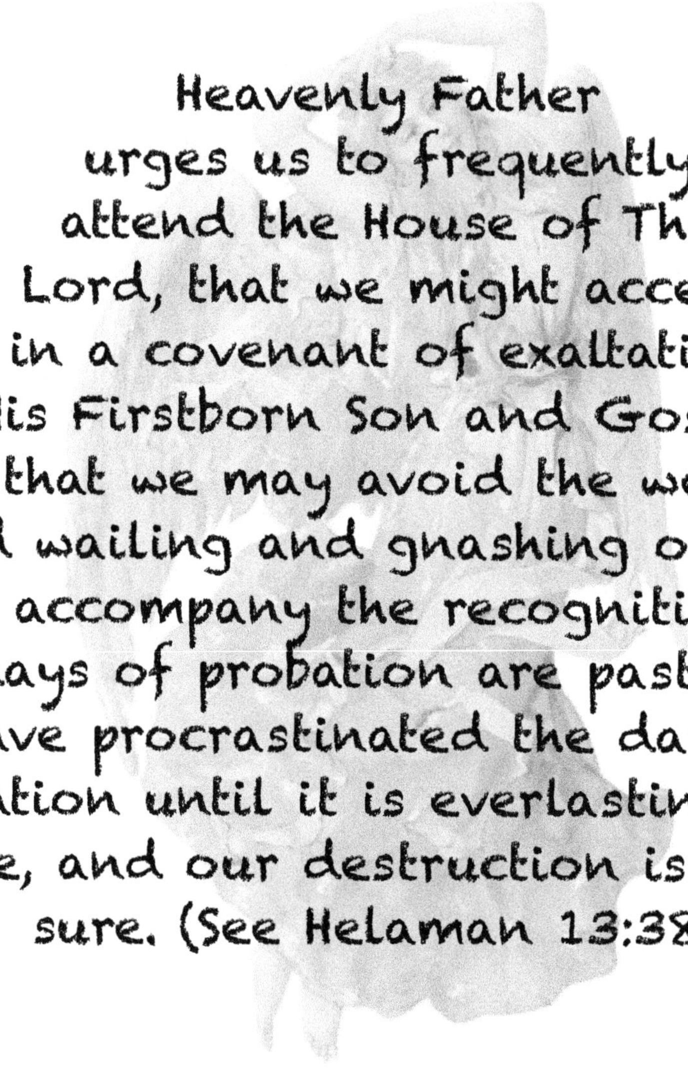

Heavenly Father
urges us to frequently
attend the House of The
Lord, that we might accept
in a covenant of exaltation
His Firstborn Son and Gospel,
so that we may avoid the weeping
and wailing and gnashing of teeth
that accompany the recognition that
our days of probation are past because
we have procrastinated the day of our
salvation until it is everlastingly too
late, and our destruction is made
sure. (See Helaman 13:38).

Epilogue
The edge of forever

"Worlds without number
have I created."
(Moses 1:33).

Jesus Christ is the Architect of the cosmos, including the "Pillars of Creation," elephant trunks of interstellar gas and dust in the Eagle Nebula, 7,000 light years from Earth. In an 1857 sermon entitled "The Condescension of Christ," London pastor Charles Spurgeon used the phrase to describe both the physical world and the force that binds it all together, stemming from the Divine. "Now wonder, ye angels," Spurgeon wrote of the birth of Christ, "the Infinite has become an infant; He, upon whose shoulders the universe doth hang, nurses at his mother's breast; He who created all things, and bears up the pillars of creation."

The Pillars of Creation were first photographed by the Hubble Space Telescope in 1995. They are 5 light years wide and 10 light years tall. New stars are constantly feeding off the pillars. They provide some needed perspective relating to how we fit into the Cosmos. Perhaps the mind-boggling information in this chapter will

provide some food for thought, as we ponder the ordinance of the endowment in the temple.

Astronomers have conjectured that, in a typical galaxy, there may be one hundred billion stars. They also estimate that there are one hundred billion galaxies. This means that, in round numbers, there are ten billion trillion total stars in the observable universe. (10,000,000,000,000,000,000,000 stars).

If only one in a thousand of those stars has a planetary solar system, that is still ten million trillion stars with a solar system. (10,000,000,000,000,000,000 stars).

If only one in a thousand of those stars that have planetary solar systems has planets within the habitable zone (that are capable of supporting life), that is still ten million billion stars. (10,000,000,000,000,000 stars).

If only one in a thousand of those stars that have planetary solar systems has planets within the habitable zone that are not only capable of supporting life, but that actually do support life, that is still ten trillion stars. (10,000,000,000,000 stars).

If only one in a thousand of those stars that have planetary solar systems with planets within the habitable zone that are not only capable of supporting life, but that actually do support life, and that life is as we know it, that is still ten billion stars with civilizations similar to our own. (10,000,000,000 stars).

Looking at it another way, if only one in one thousand billion stars in our known universe supports a planet just like Earth, with families and babies who need diaper changes, and soccer teams, and parades, hot dogs with mustard and relish, and rush hour traffic jams, that is still ten thousand million, or ten billion "earths" just like ours, in every conceivable way.

Oh, and if you try to count those ten thousand million "earths" at the rate of one

per second, twenty four hours a day, three hundred and sixty five days a year, it will take just under thee hundred and seventeen years to accomplish the task, at the rate of just over three and a half million "earths' per year. So, if you want to begin to comprehend the creations of God, you'd better drop everything, and begin right now.

Think of these incomprehensible numbers the next time you're calmly sitting in an endowment session, and you quietly take your pulse. If your heart is beating sixty times a minute, that's eighty six thousand times a day, or thirty one and a half million times a year. The proverbial drop in the bucket when compared to ten thousand million.

Repentance
detoxifies us
from the cares
of the world and
homogenization of
our standards, even
as we are subjected to
the vicissitudes of life.
It allows us to return to
the hallowed halls of the
temple, to be re-vitalized,
as we are re-introduced to
God's Magical Kingdom
where dreams really
do come true.

Afterword

"Organize yourselves;
prepare every needful thing;
and establish a house, even a house
of prayer, a house of fasting, a house of
faith, a house of learning, a house of
glory, a house of order, a house
of God." (D&C 88:119).

I
love
to see
the temple.
I'm going there
someday to feel
the Holy Spirit,
to listen and
to pray.

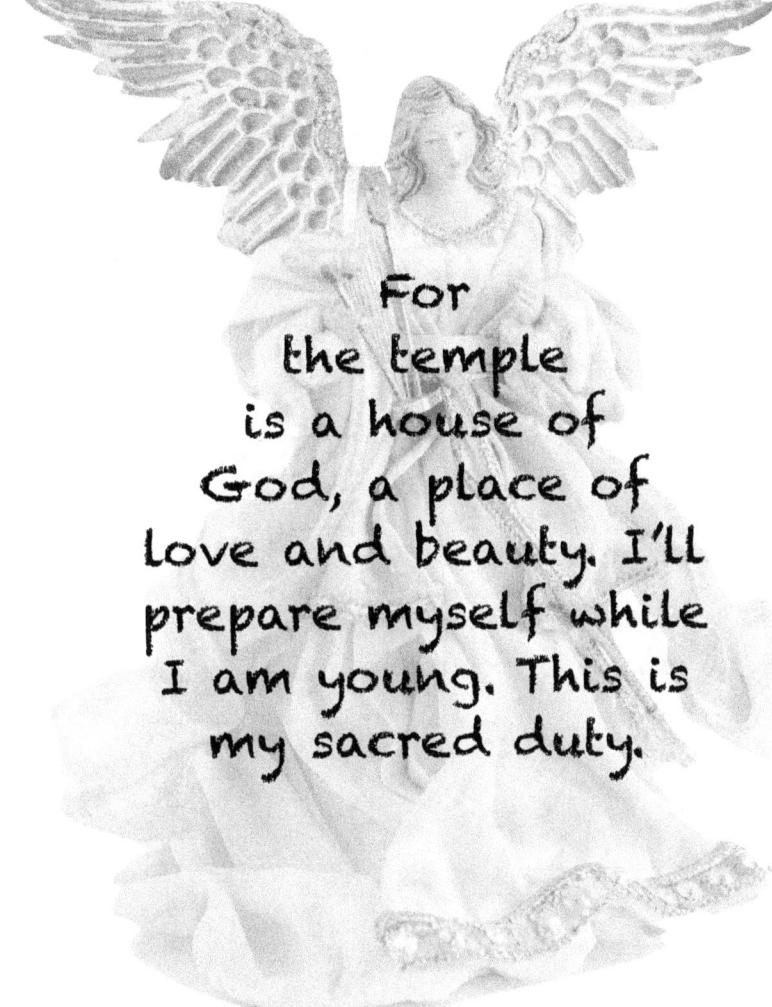

For the temple is a house of God, a place of love and beauty. I'll prepare myself while I am young. This is my sacred duty.

I love to see the temple. I'll go inside some day. I'll covenant with my Father; I'll promise to obey.

For
the temple
is a holy place
where we are sealed
together. As a child of
God, I've learned this
truth: a family is
forever.

(Janice Kapp Perry).

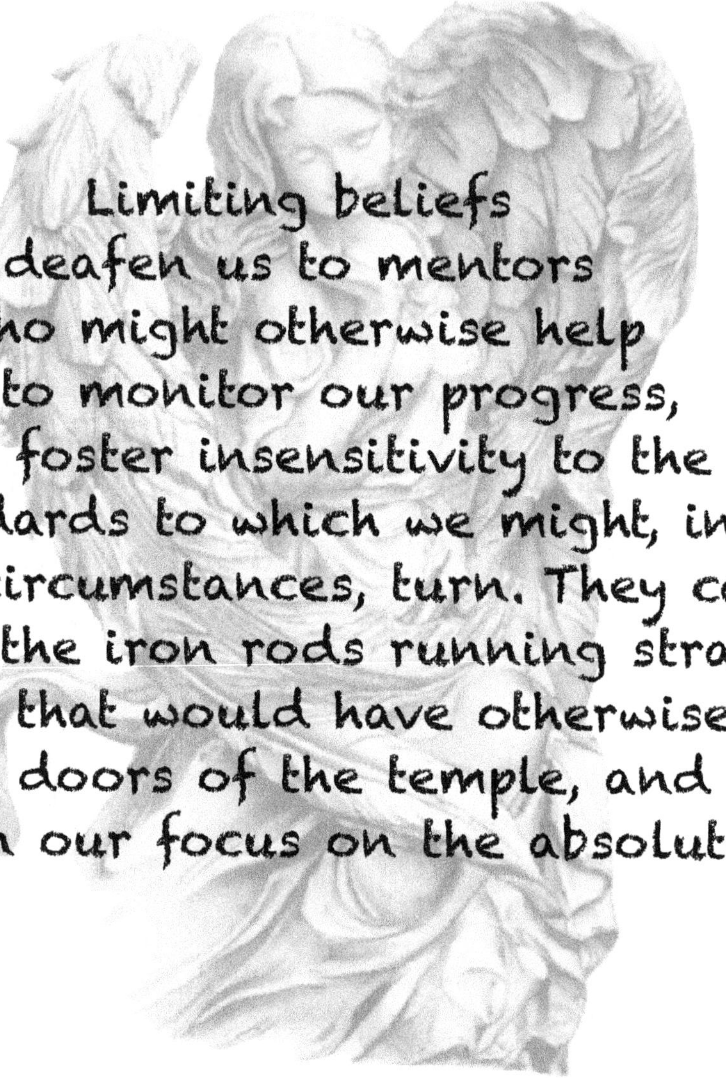

Limiting beliefs
deafen us to mentors
who might otherwise help
us to monitor our progress,
and foster insensitivity to the
standards to which we might, in
other circumstances, turn. They can
corrode the iron rods running straight
and true that would have otherwise led
us to the doors of the temple, and they
weaken our focus on the absolutes

About The Author

Phil Hudson and his wife Jan have 7 children and over 25 grandchildren. They enjoy spending time with their family at their cabin nestled in the Selkirk Mountains, on the shore of Priest Lake, the crown jewel of North Idaho. Phil had a successful dental practice in Spokane, Washington for 43 years, before retiring in 2015. He has an eclectic mix of hobbies, and enjoys the out of doors. He always finds time, however, to record his thoughts on his laptop, and understands Isaac Asimov's response when he was asked: If you knew that you had only 10 minutes left to live, what would you do?" He answered: "I'd type faster."

Phil received the inspiration to write this book while he and Jan were serving as missionaries for The Church of Jesus Christ of Latter-day Saints, in the Kingdom of Tonga. While there, they celebrated their 50th wedding anniversary.

Of all the holy sanctuaries that have been created by God to be as safe havens from the follies of the world, it is the temple that stands out as the least understood. It reminds us that the natural man does not receive the things of the Spirit of God, for they are foolishness unto him. He cannot know them, for they are discerned spiritually.

By The Author

Essays

    Volume One: Spray From The Ocean Of Thought
    Volume Two: Ripples On A Pond
    Volume Three: Serendipitous Meanderings
    Volume Four: Presents Of Mind
    Volume Five: Mental Floss
    Volume Six: Fitness Training For The Mind And Spirit

First Principles and Ordinances Series

    Faith - Our Hearts Are Changed
    Repentance - A Broken Heart and a Contrite Spirit
    Baptism - One Hundred And One Reasons Why We Are Baptized
    The Holy Ghost - That We Might Have His Spirit To Be With Us
    The Sacrament - This Do In Remembrance Of Me

Book of Mormon Commentary

    Volume One: Born In The Wilderness
    Volume Two: Voices From The Dust
    Volume Three: Journey To Cumorah

Doctrine & Covenants Commentary

    Volume One - Sections 1 - 34
    Volume Two - Sections 35 - 57

Minute Musings: Spontaneous Combustions of Thought

    Volume One
    Volume Two
    Volume Three

Calendars:

    In His Own Words: Discovering William Tyndale
    As I Think About The Savior
    Scriptural Symbols

Children's Books

    Muddy, Muddy
    The Thirteen Articles of Faith
    Happy Birthday

Doctrinal Themes

    The House of the Lord
        Poetry in the Hebraic Style

A Thought For Each Day of the Year

    Faith
    Repentance
    Baptism
    The Holy Ghost
    The Sacrament
    The House of the Lord
    The Plan of Salvation
    The Atonement
    Revelation
    The Sabbath
    Life's Greatest Questions

Professional Publications

    Diode Laser Soft Tissue Surgery Volume One
    Diode Laser Soft Tissue Surgery Volume Two
    Diode Laser Soft Tissue Surgery Volume Three

These, and other titles, are available from online retailers.

New converts
and well-established
members alike find their
way to the temple, where they
echo Paul, who declared to the
Romans: "We, being many, are one
body in Christ." (Romans 12:5). The
spiritual unification of the Saints
has been repetitively confirmed
in the universally recognizable
ripple effects that range from
simple Sabbath day services
to more formal worship
in the House of the
Lord.

Quid magis possum dicere?

www.ingramcontent.com/pod-product-compliance
Lightning Source LLC
Chambersburg PA
CBHW060507240426
43661CB00007B/943